German Idealism Today

German Idealism Today

Edited by
Markus Gabriel and Anders Moe Rasmussen

DE GRUYTER

ISBN 978-3-11-065343-4
e-ISBN (PDF) 978-3-11-049861-5
e-ISBN (EPUB) 978-3-11-049751-9

Library of Congress Cataloging-in-Publication Data
A CIP catalog record for this book has been applied for at the Library of Congress.

Bibliographic information published by the Deutsche Nationalbibliothek
The Deutsche Nationalbibliothek lists this publication in the Deutsche Nationalbibliografie; detailed bibliographic data are available on the Internet at http://dnb.dnb.de.

© 2019 Walter de Gruyter GmbH, Berlin/Boston
This volume is text- and page-identical with the hardback published in 2017.
Printing and binding: CPI books GmbH, Leck

♾ Printed on acid-free paper
Printed in Germany

www.degruyter.com

Table of Contents

Preface —— VII

I Themes from Kant

Katerina Deligiorgi
Interest and Agency —— 3

Sebastian Gardner
Kant's Practical Postulates and the Development of German Idealism —— 27

Günter Zöller
Homo homini civis. The Modernity of Classical German Political Philosophy —— 73

II Themes from Hegel

Markus Gabriel
A Very Heterodox Reading of the Lord-Servant-Allegory in Hegel's *Phenomenology of Spirit* —— 95

Stephen Houlgate
Right and Trust in Hegel's Philosophy of Right —— 121

Robert Pippin
Hegel on the Varieties of Social Subjectivity —— 135

Sebastian Rödl
The Science of Logic as the Self-Constitution of the Power of Knowledge —— 151

Jens Rometsch
Why there is no "recognition-theory" in Hegel's "struggle of recognition": Towards an epistemological reading of the Lord-Servant-relationship —— 159

III Themes from the Post-Hegelian Tradition

Catherine Malabou
"Idealism": a new name for metaphysics Hegel and Heidegger on *a priori* synthesis —— 189

Anders Moe Rasmussen
Self and Nihilism. Kierkegaard on Inwardness, Self and Negativity —— 203

Camilla Serck-Hanssen
Rediscovering the *Critique of Pure Reason* as a Propaedeutic to Metaphysics: What Heidegger Saw and McDowell Missed —— 215

Index —— 231

Preface

Topics from so-called German Idealism continue to play a central role in contemporary philosophy. Somewhat surprisingly, one of the reasons for the recent trend to read the proposals by philosophers from that tradition as potentially serious contributions to contemporary debates is the ambitious scope of their projects. It is fair to say that the fundamental ambition of German Idealism (including Kant) is an overall theory of human rationality and its place in nature. How is it possible to make sense of our first-person, engaged point of view in light of the anonymizing pressure modern philosophy ascribes to the ever-increasing influence of natural-scientific discoveries on our self-image as *animalia rationalia?* German Idealism is a response to the naturalistic challenge that takes naturalism very seriously. All thinkers of that tradition offer different diagnoses of naturalism and different strategies of restricting its potentially damaging effect on the human being, for they all agree that the human being constitutively acts in light of a conception of what the human being is. Depending on the conception of ourselves and our place in nature, the space of possible actions accordingly varies, which is why it is important in their view to figure out which elements in our conceptual repertoire are actually grounded in anonymous, purely natural forces, and which are not.

In light of Kant's major contributions to the project of giving an adequate account of the relation of finite human thought to nature which provide him with a picture of the position of human agency with respect to the natural (sensible) world, it became clear to his successors that only a complete reconstruction of the logical space of concepts designed to make sense of ourselves is capable of addressing the issue head-on. Where in their eyes Kant ultimately failed to give a complete account of ourselves as minded natural agents due to his particular brand of theoretical agnosticism concerning things in themselves, they adjust their metaphysics so as to respect the overall requirement that nature must not be thought of as alien to human thought. However, for them the reason why nature is intelligible should not be located in our modes of gaining access to nature in itself, as if it lied on the other side of a dividing line between the realm of concepts and a purely causal domain of material-energetic structure formation. Nature can neither be conceived of as a transcendent other to reason nor as produced by reason in a pre-critical sense of a first-order event in reality. Reason is not immanent to reality in the same way in which natural forces are thought of as operating so as to give rise to new structures.

The metaphysical ambitions of German Idealism can play a role in contemporary philosophy again in virtue of the overall return of metaphysics and ontology as central topics of philosophical concern. The climate in contemporary philosophy across the former divide between continental and analytical philosophy has drastically changed in that most philosophers would nowadays be hesitant to describe our time as "post-metaphysical". Post-metaphysical thinking, it turns out, has been a rather short episode in the history of philosophy. To be sure, many of the post-metaphysical proposals (including such diverse figures as Carnap, Heidegger, Habermas, Derrida and many post-war analytical philosophers) of the post-war period were designed to give a certain primacy to agency over the spectatorial view from nowhere often associated with metaphysics. In that respect, post-metaphysical thinking was able to inherit certain themes from the Kantian tradition; in particular, its focus on normativity. However, it is not hard to put pressure on the notion that recourse to normativity theory alone will safeguard the space of reasons from an unfriendly naturalistic take-over. A clear-cut example of how this can be done can be found in Daniel Dennett's work, which subscribes to the traditional conception of ourselves as intentional beings guided by norms, but accounts for this fact from the intentional stance. To the extent to which it is possible to sever the intentional stance from a strong anti-naturalistic metaphysical commitment, post-metaphysical normativity theory is an easy target for a sophisticated Dennettian naturalist.[1] It is not sufficient to refrain from metaphysical thinking in order to combat naturalism.

In part, this also explains the ontological turn discussed under the headings of "speculative" and "New Realism" in contemporary philosophy.[2] Metaphysics, ontology, and epistemology easily become the bulwark against the overextension of methods and results from the natural sciences into the domain of human agency. Without ambition in theoretical philosophy, it is hard to work out the right place for human agency in the larger framework that matters for its reality. This is why Kant and his Post-Kantian successors did not simply dismiss metaphysics, but rather wanted to put it on firmer grounds so as to accommodate the reality of human thought and agency in the broadest domain conceivable from the human standpoint.

The contributions to this volume all deal with the exciting interface of theoretical and practical philosophy in the tradition of German Idealism. In this context, some contributions focus on the metaphysical and logical underpinning of the large-scale pictures of human agency and mindedness we inherited from

---

[1] See Dennett's most recent large-scale *summa anti-theologica:* Dennett (2017): *From Bacteria to Bach and Back.* New York: W. W. Norton & Company, Inc.
[2] For representative collections of papers on the resurgence of realism, see Bryant, Levi/Srnicek, Nick/Harman Graham (eds.) (2011): *The Speculative Turn.* Melbourne: re.press and Gabriel, Markus (ed.) (2014): *Der Neue Realismus.* Berlin: Suhrkamp.

the tradition under discussion here. For it is clearly impossible to isolate the prominent practical strands in German Idealism from their specific metaphysical backgrounds. All German Idealists agree with Kant that we need a revisionary meta-metaphysics and accordingly a new conception of metaphysics itself if we want to live up to the complexity of the problem of finding the right place for our form of life and thought about what there is. We cannot sidestep the issue of metaphysics and epistemology driving the debates in the Kantian and Post-Kantian era in order to content ourselves with bits and pieces from the social or political philosophies to be found in German Idealism.

The essays collected here represent the state of the art in the kind of German Idealism scholarship which seeks to make a contribution to contemporary problems on the basis of rational reconstructions of unsurpassed insights passed on to us by the "mighty dead," as Brandom calls them. What matters for the voices collected in this volume is what is alive in the tradition of German Idealism and what ought to be made more fruitful with respect to current philosophical challenges.

In our view, the most pressing issue for systematic, philosophical scholarship in our time is the reconciliation of the theoretical and practical aspects of the Kantian and Post-Kantian ambition. The recent widespread return to metaphysics in both continental and analytic circles makes it clear that we cannot leave nature to science and study norms of thought or action in philosophy regardless of any conception of the physical universe. As soon as we confront the issue of how to integrate our account of ourselves as knowers and agents of a specific kind with what we know about nature, it should transpire that not all conceptions of nature are compatible with our self-description as autonomous agents. Yet, this does not mean that nature itself exerts pressure on our freedom! The point is precisely to separate the first-order question concerning the "furniture of natural reality" from the question of how said nature can make an appearance in the realm of truth-apt thought. *The way nature is thought of is not merely an extension of nature into the realm of thought.* At least, this is one of the fundamental tenets of German Idealism and a common thread running through all their major systems.

Ever since Kant, the primary reason for relying on versions of this somewhat anti-naturalistic insight derives from the point of view of the engaged intellect: as thinkers and knowers we are always engaged in practical projects, including the project of coming to know something about the furniture of natural reality. From this basic insight, all German Idealists draw the lesson that our account of nature has to be compatible with our account of ourselves as minded agents. Yet, the status of the minded agent is actually threatened by various conceptual forces. If we do not manage to work out a philosophy of nature compatible with our manifest image of the human being, then it seems as if we will be forced to radically revise that image. But there are limits to the degree to which this can be done, as we are in no position to completely eradicate elements of subjectivity (of the first-person point of view) from our conception of nature. If we eliminated subjectivity altogether, we would be left with no grasp whatsoever of how we could have achieved such an extraordinary feat of self-effacement. Another problem posed by Kant and his successors is what I have called the "hard problem of free will".[3] The problem is familiar in many guises. Roughly, it says reasons for action go out at some point or other without there ever being a fundamental level of choices for which we can claim responsibility in the sense that we caused the choices to happen. The minimal structure of action and action explanation, according to which any action has an end in view without which it would not be intelligible as an action to the agent and her interpreter, suggests that the agent has to choose her end in advance of the action and its realization. However, she cannot be credited with having to choose to choose her end in advance along the same lines, as this immediately triggers a vicious infinite regress. Given this problem, it seemed to many – most notably to Schopenhauer – that there is an inherent limit to freedom itself: free actions are only possible on the basis of a set of choices for which no one is responsible. But this implies that there are actions, namely choices, for which no one is responsible. They merely happen to an agent. However, if the basic framework governing our actions simply happened to us, this would threaten our sense of responsibility for all other actions. This is why it is necessary to work out an account of the structure of human action that allows us to come to terms with the hard problem of free will and tell us something about how our actual freedom cannot be reduced to the carrying out of natural forces.

This volume documents some of the crucial contemporary arguments and readings of figures from German Idealism. It is designed to be a collection of contributions to the question of the lasting significance of German Idealism. This is why all essays go beyond mere historical scholarship in order to rethink and rewrite the philosophical topics from the past in various contemporary keys.

Most papers in this volume were originally presented at the conference "German Idealism Today", which took place at Aarhus University on October 31-November 2, 2011. The conference was organized by the "Nordic Network for German Idealism" and sponsored by the "Nordic Research Foundation". The printing of the volume is sponsored by "Aarhus University Research Founda-

---

3 See Gabriel, Markus (2017): *I Am Not a Brain. Philosophy of Mind for the 21st Century.* Cambridge: Polity Press.

tion". We would like to thank these institutions together with the "International Center for Philosophy" of the University of Bonn for their kind support of our project. Particular thanks to Dr. Jens Rometsch and Marin Geier for helping us to put the volume together. Thanks also to Stuart Pethick for copy editing the first draft of the manuscript.

I **Themes from Kant**

Katerina Deligiorgi
Interest and Agency

Undeterred by Kant's cautionary advice, contemporary defenders of free will advance substantive metaphysical theses in support of their views.[1] This is perhaps unsurprising given the mixed reception of Kant's solution of the conflict between freedom and natural necessity, which is supposed to vindicate reason's withdrawal from speculation.[2] Kant argues that neither libertarians nor determinists can win, because they deal with concepts of unrestricted scope, and proposes instead to regiment the reference conditions of each concept and to specify the domain, 'world', proper to each. However, the precise character of this solution, its conceptual and metaphysical commitments, continues to be a matter of controversy among Kant scholars.[3] In particular, there is ever-renewed concern about the incipient dualism of the position. Although I will be examining some of this material, my primary aim in this paper is not to make a contribution to the interpretative debate about the antinomy. Rather, I want to draw on two lessons from Kant's treatment of the antinomy to argue for the importance of a certain way of putting the problem of human freedom.[4]

---

[1] There is a position of 'mysterianism' about free will, extensively defended by Peter van Inwagen, that reaches Kant's negative results but through a very different path; see (van Inwagen 2000). More typical and representative views include (Kane 1999), (O'Connor 2000), (Clarke 2003), (Lowe 2008) and (Steward 2012).
[2] References to the immediate reception of Kant's theory of freedom are given in footnotes. In the twentieth century, an early generation of interpreters influential in the Anglophone reception of Kant's thought considered the solution a failure or in need of radical re-thinking; see (Strawson 1966), (Bennett 1974 and 1984) and (Walker 1978). Their criticisms are summarised in (Allison 1990, p. 1–7), who together with (Korsgaard 1989) is one of the original champions of the two-standpoint view discussed below in section 1.2.
[3] The root of the controversy is disagreement about the nature and commitments of transcendental idealism, which is reflected in disagreement about the correct characterisation and best defence of Kant's position on freedom. Recent compatibilist defences include (Hudson 1994) and (Rosefeldt 2012). (Wood 1984), associated with a compatibilist reading of Kant, defends the compatibility of compatibilism and incompatibilism, a characterisation also adopted by (Allison 1990, p. 249). On the incompatibilist side, see (Watkins 2005) and (Allais 2015). (Watkins 2005) offers an agent-causal account inspired by Tim O'Connor, though he also endorses the compatibility of compatibilism and incompatibilism, see (Watkins 2005, p. 333). (Hanna 2006, p. 419) proposes 'post-compatibilism', but see (Ameriks 2012, p. 87–99).
[4] I use 'human' here to suggest a contrast not with divine freedom, but rather with conceptions of freedom that seek to arrogate god-like powers to human beings and which are justly criticised in the literature; see Strawson 1994.

The first lesson is that to think well about freedom, we ought to consider why freedom matters and to whom. A more Kantian way of putting this is that we have an interest in freedom, which we cannot renounce.[5] This inability is not a matter of brute compulsion; our interest in freedom is rational. Kant then explains the rationality of our interest in freedom by drawing a connection between normativity and freedom: freedom matters because it secures guidance by strong normative standards, and it matters to us, because we are beings who are responsive to such standards as 'a measure and a goal' for our strivings (*KrV* A 548, B 576).[6] The main task of section 1 is to examine the philosophical motivation for the connection Kant draws between freedom and normativity. Because a certain conception of authoritative norms is essential to this task, I also examine in that context the extent to which influential deflationary interpretations of the antinomy can sustain a conception of norms with the requisite authority to provide for our rational interest in freedom.

Section 2 takes its cue from the second lesson of the antinomy, namely that the philosophical discussion about the nature and reality of freedom cannot be conducted fruitfully without careful regimentation of our use of the term. Whatever else follows from it, given particular interpretations of Kant's broader philosophical commitments, this is also a point about good practice, which comes down to making sure that we relate the sense of freedom to its reference conditions, and to do this we need to establish our epistemic rights over the putatively referring domain. In practice, this means that we can start with the resources of empirical self-knowledge, seek to answer the question whether there is any sense in which human actions can be said to be free, then move on from there, through a form of regressive argument, to the more abstract conception of agency that supports the demanding and controversial sense of freedom as spontaneity.

Well apart from the specific substantive theses concerning normativity and agency I shall defend in the process of applying these Kantian lessons to the problem of freedom, I want to recommend this approach for allowing conceptual

---

[5] Kant variably describes this interest as a need of reason, a cognitive need, or a human interest; see *KrV* A x; A 314, B 370; A 464, B 492; A 475, B 503. I take interest of reason to be unproblematically rendered as rational interest. This interest is to be distinguished from the interest human beings take in moral laws (see G 4:460). The point I am focusing on here is somewhat obscured by received tradition, which encourages the view that the dialectic deals with the problems created when metaphysics overreaches; the *locus classicus* is (Strawson 1966) but its influence is widespread as illustrated by (Callender 2011).

[6] By 'strong' I mean precisely not the normativity exemplified by rules of etiquette discussed in (Foot 1978), which (Copp 2007, p. 257–258) calls 'generic' to distinguish it from 'authoritative' normativity, which is closer to the ought in Kant's sense of 'categorical'. I explain this further below in 1.1; for extended discussion see (Deligiorgi 2012, chap. 4).

connections to emerge across fields of enquiry which, in contemporary philosophy, are usually kept apart. In the concluding section of the paper, I return to this topic and outline the basic features and prospective advantages of the moderate methodological holism I attribute to Kant.

1 Interest

The idea that human beings have an interest in freedom and that this has to do with the value we place on it is not original to Kant. Contemporary defences of free will also begin with an acknowledgement that it matters to show that we are free, and it matters because freedom preserves a good that is of central value to our moral lives, namely the applicability of robust conceptions of moral responsibility, which in turn enables ordinary practices of holding each other responsible.[7] This good can be secured, so the familiar libertarian argument goes, only if it is possible to locate genuine authorship within the agent.[8] In essence then, free will is a location problem created by the need to secure what is sometimes called 'ultimate' responsibility for our actions. It is appreciation of this location problem that has motivated theories that posit a distinctive sort of agent-causal power which is irreducible to any other sort of causal power. [9] The idea of a noumenal self is regularly taken to be a version of this view.[10] This is not the interpretation I defend here, mainly because I do not think that this would solve the problem that interests Kant.[11] Especially in the first *Critique*, Kant presents reason as confronting a different location problem: the location of norms. Briefly, reason has an interest in freedom because reason is concerned with strong au-

---

[7] See (Kane 1996); (Clarke 2003).
[8] The libertarianism in question is what (Coffman 2010, p. 157) calls 'main brand', which endorses incompatibilism and the principle of alternative possibilities; see (Clarke 2005, p. 408) and (Mele 2005, p.116).
[9] See (Chisholm 1976) for a clear and economic presentation for the case in favour. See (Strawson 1994) for a refutation that draws the implications for moral responsibility.
[10] See Watkins (2005, pp. 408–419).
[11] This is not to deny that Kant is concerned with moral imputability, e.g. *KrV* A 555, B583, *KpV* 5:98–100, or *Vigilantius* 29:1018–19. It is simply to deny that this is the main motive for the argument, or more weakly, that there is another location problem that is crucial to Kant's normative commitments and which needs to be taken seriously. In parallel, as we shall see in section 2.3., he does use a causal vocabulary to describe what looks like agential powers of origination. Again, there is no point denying this. I see my task as showing how the shift in perspective I propose here, both about interest and in the next section about spontaneity, makes sense of the text and coheres with Kant's metaphysical, epistemic, and moral commitments.

thoritative norms, for which an external perspective on normative practices is required and which only freedom, in the transcendental sense, can provide. In the following section, I examine the arguments adduced in support of this relation between norms and freedom, before I turn to consider an influential deflationary interpretation of the antinomy and examine how it deals with this relation.

1.1 One version of the location problem is given in a compact sub-section on the 'Resolution of the cosmological idea of the totality of the derivation of occurrences in the world from their causes':

[T]he latter [practical freedom] presupposes that although something has not happened, it nevertheless **ought** to have happened, and its cause in appearance was thus not so determining that there is not a causality in our power of choice such that, independently of those natural causes and even opposed to their power and influence, it might produce something determined in the temporal order in accord with empirical laws, and hence begin a series of occurrences **entirely from itself** (*KrV* A 534, B562).

The passage is complicated, because Kant runs together a number of things. First he draws a contrast between different causal powers, the human power of choice and the power of natural causes. This contrast raises deep issues that are central to the analysis of human agency in the following section. Secondly he suggests that there are different laws relevant to the different powers, determining their manifestations. It is in this context that the rational interest in freedom is expressed as concerning the location of the 'ought'.

Kant states that it must be possible for the occurrences that are actions to embody – and be intelligible in terms of – an idea of what ought to have happened, even when that 'something' has not happened. There are two ways of interpreting this claim.

On the first interpretation, the claim is about unrealised possibilities. Support for this reading comes with the clarification that 'this "ought" expresses a *possible* action' (*KrV* A 548, B576 emphasis added). On this reading 'ought' is equivalent to 'can' – as ordinarily understood – and not the moralised 'can' in *KpV* 5:104. The claim then would be about the nature of freedom, understood as a two-way power, to do or to leave undone. This sense of freedom, which Kant, as we shall see, endorses at the empirical and psychological level, confronts us with a theoretical problem of accounting for what we mean by options. This is a theoretical modal problem about the very nature of possibility, on which Kant does not elaborate.[12]

---

[12] I believe that Kant's theory of modality, presented in the first *Critique* much earlier in the

Grounds for not resting content with this interpretation come from the further specification of 'ought' as expressing 'a species of necessity' which does not occur in nature, the 'ought, if one has the course of nature before one's eyes, has no significance whatever' (*KrV* A 547, B575). This ought is clearly normative. As such, it is a matter of practical cognition (*KrV* A 633, B 661). Such cognition is defined in contrast to any possible empirical cognition of nature. The content and modal profile of the ought is provided by reason itself: reason gives 'laws which are imperatives, i.e., **objective laws of freedom**, and that say **what ought to happen** ...and that are thereby distinguished from **laws of nature**, which deal only with **what does happen**' (*KrV* A802, B830). Although this is the conceptual space that the moral law occupies, as the one authoritative and therefore categorical imperative, it is not invoked here and there is no immediate need to invoke it.[13] That is, we do not need to concern ourselves with substantive normative matters, in order to understand the rational interest in freedom.

This is why: the basic thought is that there are some concepts with the following characteristic, they are concepts that have a claim to our attention and this claim to our attention is not explicable or accountable by pointing to any empirical facts. 'Have a claim' captures the idea that these concepts appear to us in the form of an imperative or a law. 'Explicable or accountable by pointing to any empirical facts' is a way of avoiding talk of derivation of the 'ought' from the 'is', since this is not Kant's point here. The implied contrast, rather, is between two sorts of 'ought', one that is explicable or accountable by pointing at facts about physical bodies in space, or human beings in societies and so on, and one that has no such relation to these facts. Aside from this very general characterisation, we are not told anything about the content of this 'ought'.[14] That there is no substantive normative theory defended at this stage is philosophically significant, and not just a matter of intellectual history. It is significant because Kant appears to think that the conditions for norms that are non-arbitrary ('objective') and rationally commanding ('reason ...gives laws') – what I have been calling strong authoritative norms – *can* be given without ref-

---

context of the discussion of judgements, can provide us with an account of possibility that allows for robust alternatives. Very interesting in this context is Baldwin 2002.
13 Looking back at the Dialectic from the vantage point of the second *Critique of Practical Reason*, Kant sums the matter in slightly different modal terms: 'Then [i.e. in the first *Critique*] the only point at issue was whether this *can* be changed into *is*' (KpV 5:104–5)
14 In addition, Kant simply presupposes that such 'ought' exists; he does not countenance scepticism about it. I argue below that an argument about the need for such an ought, though not for its reality, can be reconstructed from the material given in the Dialectic.

erence to a substantive normative system.¹⁵ With these clarifications in place, the claim that captures the interest of reason in freedom can be put as follows: strong authoritative norms require or presuppose transcendental freedom (*KrV* A 534, B 562). Transcendental freedom, in this context, has the negative sense of offering us a perspective on human doing that is external to any stretch of human experience – this externality can be further underlined by the use of the term 'world'. What are we to make of the relation between freedom and 'ought' that explains this interest of reason?

At first glance there is a threat of circularity: a sort of 'ought' is introduced to the discussion that is explicable without regard to natural facts, and then an external perspective to natural facts is invoked to secure this 'ought'. Here is one way to avoid this incipient circularity. The contrast that gives the 'ought' that interests Kant is a contrast he refines later in terms of hypothetical and categorical imperatives. This refinement is important because it helps us get a grip on the right sort of strength and objectivity. Hypothetical imperatives can be felt very strongly, and they may also be non-arbitrary in the sense that they may be supported by excellent reasons. They are still not strong authoritative norms in the sense that is captured by 'categorical'. Hypothetical imperatives are rules for which the antecedent may or may not hold; the antecedent, in other words, is deniable. Categorical imperatives possess no deniable antecedent. Hence they apply unconditionally. The formal characteristic of categorical imperatives, the absence of a deniable antecedent, does not require reference to natural facts and so averts the immediate danger of circularity. On the other hand, it underlines, for lack of a better word, the nature-transcendent character of the norms under discussion, which prompts the question about whether such norms exist.

Kant clearly believes there are such norms and indeed that they are essential to making sense of our ethical commitments. In the first *Critique*, he claims that the 'ought' just described is not just intelligible but eminently rational (*KrV* A 547, B 575; also A 802, B 830) and that we, qua rational beings, are responsive to the 'ought' for setting a measure and goal to our strivings (*KrV* A 548, B 576). These statements need not be taken on faith. The Dialectic, which is the broader context of this discussion, has as its general topic the search of reason for the unconditioned. So an argument could be made that the claim about the existence of strong authoritative norms is the product of rational reflective evaluations of

---

15 The significance of this point becomes clearer if we contrast Kant's optimism about the possibility of giving a general account of strong and authoritative norms with contemporary philosophers who, troubled by the ontological status of such norms, opt for an internal standpoint from within some substantive normative system, see (Scanlon 1998). I also pick up these points below in the discussion of Allison.

the problem of regress of evaluative criteria. Kant does not offer this argument, but it would not be hard to reconstruct it. In the evaluative dialectic, any answer that aims to explain why some thing or some course of action is good is met with a further question about what explains the goodness of the *explanans*. If every answer we give is conditional on some other good, then its goodness can come into question and so on. Rational reflection on this problem leads us to an unconditioned norm that expresses a good without qualification.[16] Such an unconditioned norm is located outside all conditioned series, and this is just the perspective of transcendental freedom. So reason has an interest in freedom because it has a stake in such normative standards, which represent reason's 'own order' (A 548, B 576). Put differently: strong authoritative norms are irreducible to hypothetical norms, and this irreducibility requires a commitment to an external perspective, such as the transcendental perspective of freedom.

There are various ways of avoiding Kant's conclusion, of course. One is by adopting an error-theoretical or a fictionalist position, both of which basically deny that the sort of 'ought' Kant is describing here exists, but concede that we may act as if such 'ought' did exist. These options absolve us of a commitment to transcendental freedom. At the same time, they do not directly challenge the way Kant spells out the interest of reason; rather, they represent ways of reducing the metaphysical burden and thereby the interest of reason to human interests. The danger in tying the account of freedom to our interest in this way is that all we are left is a reductive *argumentum κατ' άνθρωπον*.[17] A more ambitious and radical option is to offer a naturalist theory of norms. Normative naturalism, in its various guises, is usually – though not always – a rival to Kantian normativism, and in both its most prominent forms, reductive and neo-Aristotelean, it does not sustain an interest in transcendental freedom. Since my aim here is to explain the motivation for Kant's holistic approach to the problem of freedom, engaging with various naturalisms exceeds the scope of the paper. Nonetheless, one important attempt to integrate Kantianism with naturalism is highly relevant to the paper's concerns. I turn to it presently.

1.2 The interest of reason in freedom presented above goes against the grain of the currently influential defences of Kant's conception of freedom that either seek to integrate it within an acceptably naturalistic framework or fully natural-

---

[16] The expression good without qualification is one that Kant uses in the *Groundwork*, and it is significant that the latter starts with it since it is not just a ground-clearing work, but also a grounding work. I argue for this more extensively in chap 2 in (Deligiorgi 2012).

[17] It is the reduction to interests that is the problem, not the form of the argument itself, which Kant himself endorses; see the 'Real Progress' essay, 20:306.

ise it. These defences are formulated in response to perceived problems with Kant's resolution of the antinomy of freedom and natural necessity.

In the antinomy, Kant states that reason finds itself in contradiction with itself on the topic of the relation between freedom and nature. To see the problem, nature must be conceptualised as the realm of efficient causality, and freedom as a rival type of causal force. So understood, nature and freedom form a disjunct. If we accept the former, we need to deny the latter. In other words, nature leaves no room for freedom. Interventions by a causally efficient force that is not conceptualisable in terms of natural causality simply do not make sense. As the proponent of thoroughgoing causal determinism argues in the antithesis, once you allow such extra-worldly interventions you loose all grip on lawfulness in nature (*KrV* A 451, B 479). Importantly, this problem does not just arise within the pre-critical context that shapes the assumptions of the champion of determinism in the antinomy. It also arises given the basic assumptions of critical theoretical philosophy, centrally that nature is a causally closed system; as a unifying concept of the manifold, causality is a condition for sense-making in the first place.

Kant's official strategy for dealing with the antinomy is *divide et impera*: determinism obtains within certain limits, freedom without these limits; in other words, natural causality and freedom are each the case in their appropriate domains. As a result, actions are explicable by reference to sensible conditions of experience and knowable as products of antecedent causes, and they are also intelligible through pure reason as products of freedom. As I said in the introduction, however, the precise commitments of this solution of the antinomy remain disputed and controversial. If the solution depends on ontological dualism, then it faces a difficult problem, namely to explain how the two worlds, the one in which determinism is true and the other in which it is not, relate to one another. As a result, ontological dualism is by and large rejected by sympathetic commentators. So, the question is how to apply the *divide et impera* strategy on a monistic ontology. Given the way Kant puts things in the antinomy, the options are either to argue that nature, as the realm of efficient causality, is in fact continuous with freedom, e.g. by showing emergent natural structures that are not subject to efficient causality, or to argue that efficient causality is not an obstacle to freedom, because we can look at things from a different perspective/aspect/point of view, or under a different description.[18] I am interested here in the latter family of views because they are directly responding to the antinomy and the prob-

---

[18] Wood is one well-known representative of this. But the current popularity of neo-Aristotelean interpretations partly though not wholly inspired by Korsgaard's recent work are also relevant here.

lem of ontological dualism. Aspect dualism is not immediately better off than ontological dualism, since it still has the problem of reconciling two mutually contradictory claims made by the inhabitant of our world, the only world available, who affirms both that she is free and that she is not free. The two-aspect solution is to specify the conditions under which each assertion is made. The popularity of this family of views, despite encounters with trenchant criticism, consists in its promise to capture what Kant himself thought to be a genuinely new take on the old problem of freedom.[19] In what follows, I will look at Henry Allison's version, partly because it remains the most detailed and influential one, and partly because of its sensitivity to the issue of authoritative norms.

Allison's interpretation depends on two important distinctions. First is his distinction between ontological and epistemic conditions. Ontological conditions are necessary for something to be; in traditional theistic arguments, for example, God is the ontological condition for the world. 'Epistemic' conditions are a Kantian innovation on Allison's reading; they explain how something becomes an object of cognition for us. Causality is such an epistemic condition. Once this is accepted, a 'conceptual space' opens up 'for the non-empirical thought (though not knowledge) of objects, including rational agents' (Allison 1990, p. 44). In other words, we can think of objects and of rational agents without reference to conditions that allow us to know them.

Second is the distinction between the theoretical and the practical standpoint. The theoretical standpoint is subject to scepticism about freedom; consciousness of freedom may well be thought to be illusory, e.g. I can doubt my belief that I am free. The practical standpoint is the standpoint of agents. Although it is possible to argue that from the first person perspective of deliberating and choosing what to do, agents presuppose that they are free, this is not the option taken by Allison, who argues that only if we choose to do the right thing as reason prescribes do we adopt the practical standpoint (Allison 1990, p. 247). The practical standpoint then is the standpoint of moral agency. Allison is keen to show that moral agency is not something extraordinary and otherworldly, but rather that it is continuous with rational agency broadly understood, that is, 'our capacity to deliberate, choose, adopt maxims, and the like' (Allison 1995, p. 25). At the same time, it is only an explicitly moral conception of the practical stand-

---

19 Two-aspects views include those that embrace Davidson's anomalous monism; (Meerbote 1984), (Hudson 2005); (Allison 1990); (Korsgaard 1989 and 1996); (Hill 1989); (Bok 1998); (Nelkin 2000). An alternative to both two worlds and two aspects views is the view of atemporal causality that does not disturb natural laws, but which is not provable and therefore dogmatic; see (Ameriks 1982 and 2008). For rejections of different versions of the two-aspects interpretation, see (Irwin 1984) and (van Cleeve 1999).

point that can secure the argument about transcendental freedom, because only the moral practical standpoint presupposes that one acts under the idea of freedom. Note that Allison insists that transcendental freedom is not the real ground for our actions, so it should not be seen as explanatory for our capacity for rational agency; rather, he says, it is 'the defining feature' of our conception of ourselves as rational agents (ibid.). Of course, freedom as 'defining feature' is not analytically true of 'rational agency', but instead forms part of a synthetic conception of rational agency which comes to view when we assume the practical standpoint.[20]

Accepting the argument so far, the question can still arise as to whether we can do without the sort of demanding exercises in rational agency required for morality; if we can, then the argument will be irrelevant. Allison suggests that we simply cannot sacrifice our view of ourselves as moral agents (Allison 1990, p. 247). Allison is not engaged in constructive metaphysics, so what supports the synthetic conception of our rational agency is actual normative practices. To take an interest in morality, in the sense of recognizing it as a source of reasons to do and to avoid doing, is an important, possibly essential, feature of human life. This type of argument is familiar from Peter Strawson's defence of freedom as a presupposition for human reactive attitudes in his 'Freedom and Resentment'. In the conclusion of that essay, he writes that 'in the absence of *any* forms of these [human reactive] attitudes it is doubtful whether we should have anything that *we* could find intelligible as a system of human relationships, as human society' (Strawson 1962, p. 25). Allison, like Strawson, seeks to approach and resolve metaphysical questions from within known facts about human relationships and society. From within the horizon formed by practices of excusing and condemning behaviour, in Strawson, or of figuring out what is right, in Allison, freedom is safe because it is presupposed in such practices and their demise is unthinkable.

Because Allison's argument is very close to the one I presented in the previous section, it is essential to show where the difference between the two accounts lies. The basic difference is that on Allison's account, it is the demand for normative justification addressed to and met by the rational agent that motivates the argument.[21] As rational beings we are responsive to requests for jus-

---

20 (Allison 1995, p. 16) draws on a disanalogy between the self-certifying character of the spontaneity of the understanding and practical spontaneity where reflection can yield a conditional result only, if I take myself to be a rational agent, I must regard myself as free.

21 (Allison 1990 and 2011) presents the argument in terms of various formulations of the so-called 'Reciprocity Thesis' that transcendental freedom and an unconditioned practical law stand in reciprocal relation.

tifying the things we do. Justification for doing the morally right thing requires transcendental freedom because anything else falls short. This is why from the practical, i.e. moral, standpoint entertaining doubts about freedom borders on the paradoxical. It is a practical version of the Moorean paradox: '*P*, but I do not believe that *P*'. Allison's Kantian version would be something like 'I am under the moral law and so free but I do not believe that I am free'. As we said before, it is not just any norms that secure freedom, but the moral law ('the ultimate rational norm' Allison 1990, p. 248; see too Allison 2011, p. 274). Notice, however, that the matter of the authority of the moral law is supposed to be dissolved in the substantive discussion about whether in acting on this or that maxim, the agent acts morally, i.e. has the law as her reason. But what does this mean? It is not a demand for introspection, because this is not a discussion about motivation. Rather it is about whether the agent's prospective maxim is a good reason for action, that is, good for the agent to take it up as her maxim. In other words, the normativity of the standard (the law) she invokes in deliberating, choosing, and adopting maxims is analysable in terms of substantive discussions about competing reasons favouring this or that course of action – her reasons for acting in effect. Though the continuity Allison establishes with ordinary normative reasoning behaviour might be thought an advantage, the obvious question is whether the account has the resources to support the standard it invokes. Ordinary normative reasoning can sustain conclusions about what is best to do given such and such reasons, so the justification task confronted by Allison's rational agents is carried out in a way that does not allow for the recognition of the unconditionality of the norm, unless there is some missing step, say, rational intuition, which Allison explicitly denies. The rational agent is now vulnerable to doubts of the practical sort because she may well ask herself what it is that she is doing while she is acting morally, and whether her actions exhibit transcendental freedom or upbringing.

The options are: either to abandon the modest methodology, and engage in constructive metaphysics in an effort to support the belief that human beings are free; or to abandon incompatibilism and give up on transcendental freedom, perhaps by embracing the possibilities of upbringing. In what follows I present Kant as giving us a further option: a discussion of human agency that sustains the interest in freedom without being reducible to such interest.

2 Agency

'Agency' is shorthand for the powers and abilities Kant attributes to human beings when it comes to considering actions. Immediately striking is Kant's use of a causal vocabulary to describe the exercise of these different powers and his insistence that such exercise is free. To tease apart the different layers of the account, I start with a fairly uncontroversial, psychological and empirical sense of freedom, before moving to more general, controversial and demanding theses about the relation between causality and freedom.

2.1 A basic sense of 'free' with a long philosophical history and prominent in contemporary theories of personal autonomy concerns the idea of self-control. This basic sense ties to everyday experiences that confirm its soundness: each time we overcome a fear or yield to a temptation, we experience ourselves as exercising control or failing to do so. In theories of personal autonomy, control is judged by reference to 'decisive best judgments' (Mele 1995, p. 7) and to the range of 'agentic skills' that secure control (Meyers 2004, p. 69).[22] Although not devoting nearly as much attention to it as contemporary authors, Kant does have a use for this sense, acknowledged in the first *Critique* as 'psychological' and 'for the most part empirical' (*KrV* A 448, B 476) and discussed in the moral and anthropological writings as attainment of 'governance' (*MS* 6:407) or 'composure' (*Anth* 7:252). It is important to recognise this empirical sense for a number of reasons. First and more generally, because it is the one most people can readily relate to and it would be a failing simply to ignore it. Second, in the context of Kant interpretation, because it helps qualify the traditional view that from the perspective of empirical psychology actions are not free. Third, and for current purposes, identifying what is 'for the most part' empirical and its shortcomings explains the motivation for moving to the enquiry onto what is not empirical.[23]

---

22 The literature on epistemic and psychological skills for autonomous agents is vast. (Mele 1995) and (Meyers 2004) are indicative of the range of views on offer. Mele explicitly ties his account to the long tradition I mention here (1995, pp. 3–6). From the perspective of the free will debate, the question is whether such accounts need to be supplemented by the elusive 'ultimate' control, the sort that does not admit of deterministic backtracking; see (Kane 1999). I discuss Kant's version of this issue below.
23 See (McCarty 2009) for a recent version of the claim that empirical psychology equals determinism. Unlike his empiricist predecessors, and successors, Kant shows little interest in external constraints of the sort that still figure prominently in current discussions, see (Mele 1995, chap 1). By contrast he is concerned with internal impediments to agential control and their overcoming. Kant does have a use of control (*Gewalt*) in passages such as (*KpV* 5: 94) where he gives his own version of a consequence argument, and (*KpV* 5: 101) where the challenge to human freedom comes from an almighty being. Kant speaks of failure of control as an illness (*Anth* 7: 251) and attainment of composure (*Anth* 7: 252) as desirable; see too the discussion of moderation and tranquility (*MS* 6: 409) and especially of ascetics (*MS* 6: 412). Kant is interested in that sense of free, which he sometimes calls 'psychological' (*KrV* A 448, B 476), because it secures as a corollary freedom as a two-way power 'to do or to refrain from doing' (*MS* 6: 213). Securing

Minimally, to act is to make a difference in the world: when we act, we bring about something in the world that 'does not exist but which can become real by means of our conduct' (*G* 4:437). Obviously Kant is mainly interested in the sort of difference we make. Still before we look into evaluating an action, we have to account for it as what *has* become real by means of our conduct, in short, as 'occurrence' (*KrV* A 543, B 571). When it comes to explaining actions we explain them like any other occurrence, by reference to causes. When, for example, we want to find out why someone told a malicious lie, 'one proceeds as with any investigation in the series of determining causes for a given natural effect' (*KrV* A 554, B 582). The causes can be traced back to the person's character, upbringing, bad company and the like. We cite all these facts as causal for the behaviour and therefore explanatory. Such deterministic explanations are available to us when we consider the action as *observers* (see *KrV* A 550, B 578).

Observation, however, also affords us a more intimate view of ourselves that takes into account feelings, desires, inclinations and the like. Actions are the product of a power: the *Begehrungsvermögen* or *facultas appetitiva*. This is the 'power to be, by means of one's representations, the cause of the objects of these representations' (*MS* 6:211, translation modified).[24] The 'cause of the objects' is further analysed into 'impelling causes' (*Mrongovius* 29: 895, *Dohna* 28:677, *Vigilantius* 29:1014), which are distinguished into 'intellectual' causes, which Kant also calls 'motives', and 'sensible' or 'sensitive', which he also calls 'stimuli'.[25] This more intimate perspective on human psychology allows for 'free' to have application, in a negative sense, just in case the action is not the product of reflexes or unchecked inclinations, instincts, feelings or desires; in short, sensible causes.

If we ask why this negative sense of 'free' matters, there is an obvious answer to be found in Kant's moral philosophy: freedom from sensible causes is

---

the application of reflection matters in light of the normative interest we have in freedom and more generally to respond to explanations of actions that merely cite differential response to environmental factors or conditioned association. It is an important part of the Kantian argument presented here that securing reflection is not a straightforwardly empirical task.

24 The faculty of desire, from now on 'desire' in the singular to distinguish it from desires, is mainly discussed, in the published works, in the *Critique of Practical Reason* (*KpV* 5: 21), the *Metaphysics of Morals* (*MS* 6: 211–213), the *Critique of the Power of Judgement* (*KU* 5: 178–179 and 178n), and *Anthropology from a Pragmatic Point of View* (*Anth* 7: 251–282) and, among the lecture notes, in the *Lectures on Metaphysics*, dating from the mid-seventies to mid-nineties L_1 28: 253–254; L_2 28: 577; *Dhona* 28: 676; *Mrongovius*: 893–894; *Vigilantius* 29: 1012–1013.

25 The distinction, if not the precise terminology, is familiar from the moral writings especially, which feature desires, feelings and sensuous impulses (*Antriebe*) e.g. in G 4: 434 though see too A 534, B 562.

freedom from pathological causes (*G* 4:397–99, *MS* 6:378), which opens the way for determination by potentially free-making motives, in particular the free-making motive in the singular, which is the moral law (*G* 4:427). Let's call this the moralist shortcut. As we shall see, moralist shortcuts will be available at several stages of this regressive argument, and as a general strategy I shall seek to avoid them because they effectively allow the interest in freedom to overtake the argument about its nature and reality. More specifically, at this juncture, the effect of morally interpreting the positive sense of 'free' will be to make 'unfree' equivalent to immoral; if unfree is immoral, free immoral actions are not possible.[26] This is an avoidable problem.

An alternative positive sense is given if an action is the product of control exercised over the various psychological prompts to action Kant collectively calls sensible causes. Obviously, there is scope for filling in the psychological elements that constitute and improve the exercise of control, but the bare idea of a check on prompts to action suffices to justify its importance: control is desirable because it allows the agent to 'rise to *reflection*' (*Anth* 7:251) and in so doing affords the agent freedom as a two-way power, to do or to leave undone (*KpV* 5:100; also *G* 4:455, *MS* 6:213, *Vigilantius* 29:1014).

However we refine our explanation by citing psychological causes, we still concern ourselves with the contrast between some antecedents, control, which we count as freedom-conferring, and some others, unchecked sensible causes. Since we are within the sphere of efficient causality, there is no reason to limit ourselves with the proximate causes and not to ask what antecedents are causal for the presence of control. In short, we have no *principled* way of blocking deterministic backtracking.

Deterministic backtracking is one of the reasons that motivates Kant's criticism of those who call an action 'free' just in case it is 'caused from within, by representations produced by our own powers, whereby desires are evoked on occasion of circumstances and hence actions are produced at our own discretion' (*KpV* 5:96). Kant's point is that the empiricist model cannot deliver on the promise that action is produced at our own discretion, because it does not touch the worry that the agent is simply acting out instructions of tradition, upbringing or

---

26 It is precisely this problem that motivated Reinhold's proposal that freedom should be considered as fundamental self-activity of the will permitting a choice for either good or bad (see (Reinhold 2008) and see too (Watkins 2005, pp. 408–419). Effectively Reinhold argues for the metaphysical basicness of a two-way power, which Kant rejects under the label *libertas indifferentiae* (*MM* 6: 226–227). For Kant having such a two-way power is important (as in the pre-modern tradition of thought about *arbitrium*, see Aquinas) but it is not basic. Rather, it is a corollary of empirical psychological freedom.

nature.[27] And a parallel worry can arise about empirical freedom, that is, actions caused through the exercise of reflective control over sensible causes. Composure is not a good in itself: 'the calmest reflection' can accompany passions, which 'can co-exist with rationalizing' (*Anth* 7:266). At issue are the reflective standards the agent brings to bear on the various contents she is trying to control, which can be woefully short of liberating (perhaps an example would be the maxim 'do whatever pleases the master').

There are a number of ways of addressing the worry. One is to take the moralist path again: since we look for genuinely liberating maxims, the obvious thing to do is to turn to the moral test for maxims that can ensure moral freedom. I do not dispute that for Kant genuine control is moral control. The problem with a substantive answer at *this* juncture is that control becomes something we stand to exercise very rarely. This problem also arises with contemporary non-moral substantive accounts of autonomy that make it a fine but rare achievement. In addition a particularly Kantian scepticism can arise when we seek to self-evaluate morally psychology about the genuineness of the empirically accessible contents that are causes for action.

Another option is to attack deterministic backtracking directly by asserting noumenal freedom (as Kant does in *KpV* 5:102–3). This is where some of the standard problems with two worlds begin to emerge. But there is a further conceptual problem, which was immediately picked up by Kant's contemporaries. The assertion of noumenal freedom is an assertion of a global fact, that is, it concerns all actions. This is what it takes to counter another global fact that all appearances are subject to deterministic efficient causality. So actions are free full stop. But in this picture there is no space for a differential sense of freedom, which is necessary both if we are interested in control and to distinguish between moral and immoral actions. This is nothing to do with dualism, rather it has to do with the explanatory power of global facts: they explain everything.[28]

These problems force us to examine the conditions that permit agents to control causes; such an account would need to be sufficiently general so as not to tie control to very demanding conditions, but not so general that it back-

---

27 Empiricist and rationalist compatibilists are targeted here for espousing this psychological and comparative sense of freedom (*KpV* 5: 97–102). The problem is familiar in the contemporary literature on compatibilist free will, see (Kapitan 2000) and on personal autonomy, see (Noggle 2008) for useful discussion and references.
28 This problem was posed sharply in (Ulrich 1788). For this reason, I think a more cautious interpretation of the noumenal self is a privative one that identifies the limits of what can be said on the topic of authorship as ultimate causal control.

fires. Such an examination is not an empirical inquiry into the specific circumstances that facilitate or impede control, but about its very possibility.[29]

2.2 To establish the possibility of control, we do not seek the true conditional that spells out the circumstances for (proximally) controlled manifestations of the power of desire – for sure, control is sometimes possible in light of such and such conditions, and not possible at other times when such conditions fail to obtain. We seek rather to establish a permanent or necessary possibility. Necessity is not an empirical matter, hence the need for regressive questioning of the conditions for control. Kant provides these conditions by introducing the human power of choice.

For 'power of choice' Kant uses *arbitrium*, literally 'judgment', and of course also *Willkür*.[30] *Willkür* is mainly a foil concept for moral willing, *Wille*, whereas *arbitrium* has a dialectically different role, which is to distinguish human from animal *arbitria* and to make the point that human choice is a choice that is free irrespective of how individuals respond to particular prompts to action:

> For a power of choice is **sensible**, insofar as it is **pathologically affected** (through moving-causes of sensibility); it is called an **animal** power of choice (*arbitrium brutum*) if it can be **pathologically necessitated.** The human power of choice is indeed an *arbitrium sensitivum*, yet not *brutum* but *liberum*, because sensibility does not render its action necessary, but in the human being there is a faculty of determining oneself from oneself, independently of necessitation by sensible causes (*KrV* A 534/B562).

> That which can be determined only by inclination (sensible impulse, *stimulus*) would be animal choice (*arbitrium brutum*). Human choice, however, is a capacity for choice that can indeed be *affected* but not *determined* by impulses. (*MM* 6:213)

---

[29] The requisite generality is a feature of transcendental psychology, understood in the sense employed by (Rickert 1909) and occasionally revived in (Sullivan 1989, p. 79–80), (Allison 1990, pp. 54–56) and, more recently, (Wuerth 2014). Kant himself has no settled way of referring to these general features of free agency. He avoids and disparages the term 'transcendental psychology' (*Reflexion* 5553, 18: 228) because he associates it with 'rational' psychology, which is not the topic here. At the same time, he does not expect important structural distinctions to be a matter of empirical psychology (see for example *KU* 5: 258, also the *Prolegomena* 4, p. 304 and *KrV* A 848–849, B876–877).

[30] Allison translates *arbitrium* as 'will' (1990, p. 55–56). Kant himself translates *arbitrium* as *Willkür* (e.g. *Mrongovius* 29: 896). Ameriks makes use of this terminological equivalence when he contrasts human *Willkür* with that of brutes (2012, p. 13, p. 185). *Willkür* is translated variously as 'will' and as 'power of choice', although I think the latter is preferable both for *arbitrium* and for *Willkür*.

In these passages Kant is describing a choice that is 'free' just in case it is a type that is independent from necessitation (or determination) by sensible impulses.

There are two contrast classes for human choice. One is animal choice, which is not just affected but necessitated by impulses; I'll return to this shortly. The other is godlike choice, which does not require any sensible input and can create *ex nihilo*. Kant places human choice between these two, calling it free but sensible. In so doing, he stakes a claim against his rationalist predecessors, especially Baumgarten, who argued that sensitive choice cannot be free.[31] For Kant, what affects choice is also what makes it possible: we choose on the basis of things we believe, desire or feel. Any of these things can be causes for actions, as per the account given previously. The only new element is choice, and what Kant is emphasising is that choice is exercised on contentful mental items, that is, facts about the agent's various intentional states, about what she thinks, believes, desires, hopes, fears, etc.[32] These facts give us the antecedent states that are causal for actions, and explain the claim that human choice is affected. Human choice is also free because these antecedents are not sufficient for its determination. This negative claim sounds like a familiar indeterministic thesis, defended by contemporary libertarians, but that is not quite what is at issue here: the substance of the claim is about the nature of choice; in particular, the constitution of the intentionality of choice such that the kind of agential control described previously is possible.[33]

We said earlier that actions are occurrences, and indeed they are. However, they have a distinctive causal profile that they do not share with natural occurrences and which permits teleological concepts to apply to them. Actions are

---

[31] In the German rationalist tradition, discussed in (Sgarbi 2013), *arbitrium*, 'choice', can be either sensitive *or* free; see (Baumgarten 2013: 254–256, esp. 255). Sometimes Kant uses 'pure' in the sense of godlike (*KrV* A 534, B562, *Vigilantius* 29: 1015–1016,), sometimes in a positive sense as determination by the moral law (*Dohna* 28: 677), and sometimes to mean both (*MS* 6: 213).
[32] In the contemporary literature, there is much discussion about whether it is the fact or the psychological attitude of the agent that is explanatory of the action. For present purposes it suffices to allow that facts about intentional states are causal.
[33] For example, Kant says that actions that arise from one's choice are 'actions intentionally performed' (*KpV* 5: 100). In a typically dense passage in the *Metaphysics of Morals*, Kant joins desire, choice and reason to argue for the determinability of desire by reason and the determinability of choice by pure reason, where the two are not identical. So the question is how choice can, as (Ameriks 2012, p.185) put it, have 'primary orientation toward the intellect' without being already morally determined. Though some Kantians (see esp. (Allison 1990, p. 38)) have been tempted to locate freedom in ability to deliberate – a form of deliberative libertarianism as (Clark 2000) describes it – as I argue here I do not think this to be a stable position. For the kind of indeterministic argument I mention here, see (Kane 1996 and 1999).

characteristically and essentially end-directed: 'Every action ... has its end' (*MS* 6:385). The notion of an end connects to choice: 'an *end* [*Zweck*] is an object of the choice [*Willkür*] (of a rational being), through the representation of which choice is determined to an action to bring this object about' (*MM* 6:381; see too *MM* 6:384).

To understand how efficient and final ends fit in the account, let's use the earlier example of the malicious lie. The liar has an end she wants to achieve through her lying. The end is, let's say, 'to spread confusion in society'. The end is not a fact; it is a representation of an object that is not yet real as something *to be* achieved. The end makes sense in light of the facts about what she believes, for instance, 'that confusion is entertaining and that lying maliciously is the best means for spreading confusion'. These facts are eventually causal for her lying. They exist alongside many other facts, the nonactional intentional states of the agent. The claim then is that in order for some of those states to lead to action, an end is necessary, and this is the representation that determines choice. Therefore, choice is not a link in a causal chain, made up of facts about the agent's intentional states.

What then is choice? Kant discusses it usually in contrastive terms (human v animal). He does however also give the following helpful clue: choice is 'consciousness' of our ability to bring something about (*MS* 6:213). This is helpful because it sets choice in parallel with the 'I think' as playing a similarly unifying function: choice is the power to attend to and be moved by those facts among the many that are true about an agent's intentional states in light of some end that appears worthwhile to the agent. Unless there is such a 'unifying' process of choice in light of some end, these facts cannot move the agent to act; they have to be lit by the representation of the end as wanted or worth pursuing. While it is true to say that such a representation cannot be the efficient cause, nothing in the model blocks the possibility that some facts about the nonactional intentional states of the agent are causal for some end which appears worth pursuing. More simply: choice is not free if we are programmed to pursue some pre-given ends. So, the final question is: in virtue of what is choice free?

2.3 The last question is about grounds. It leads us straight into metaphysical territory. Kant claims that the matter of grounds is beyond our comprehension; 'no one can grasp the origination [*entstehen*] of a free action, since it is the beginning of all origination' (4180, 17:446) and 'the first ground of origination is not graspable' (6446, 18:720).[34] At the same time, Kant insists that we can *think*

---

[34] The point about freedom is a particular case of a more general confession of ignorance of

this more fundamental sense of freedom, which 'contains nothing borrowed from experience' (*KrV* A 533/B 561). When we consider any action that realizes some end empirically, we ascribe it to some agent as its proximate source, both spatially and temporally. If the thought of freedom as first ground is to contain nothing borrowed from experience, 'beginning' cannot be understood temporally nor 'origination' spatially. In addition, excluding temporal properties from our thought means that we cannot think of the performance of an action in terms of efficient causality. This leaves us with little more than the term 'spontaneity'.

Kant takes up the notion from the Leibnizian tradition.[35] For Leibniz, spontaneity is essential for securing freedom. At the same time, within Leibnizian metaphysics spontaneity is a correlate of pre-established harmony. Pre-established harmony is the negation of interaction of substances. The doctrine fits well then with the idea of spontaneity, namely, that the principle of the action lies *within* the agent. Kant rejects the theory of pre-established harmony (in the Amphiboly and Paralogism in the first *Critique*; see too 'On a discovery' 8:250). In addition, he is scathing about what he calls 'comparative freedom', which states that it is sufficient to secure freedom if actions are 'caused from within' (*KpV* 5:96). At the same time, Kant continues to have a use for 'spontaneity' to describe the beginning of a state from itself (*KrV* A 533, B561). I suggest we understand spontaneity, in this practical context, as a relation agents have to ends. So spontaneity is now the very antithesis of pre-established harmony: it states simply that ends are *set* by agents.[36] Interpreting spontaneity teleologically, as a direct rebuttal of Leibnizian teleology, conforms with the instruction to understand beginning and origination without borrowing from experience and allows us to side-step the topic of efficient causality by focusing narrowly on ends (rather than on effects). [37] Importantly, this conception of spontaneity counteracts the worry that we are programmed to pursue pre-given ends.

The question now is whether we have good reason to believe that we have a power of spontaneity as here described, which underwrites the freedom of

---

ultimate grounds. The two *Reflections* show consistency over pre-critical and critical period, but see too *KrV* A 546/B 574, *G* 4: 459, *KpV* 5: 49, *MS* 6: 226, 22, p. 53.

35 See (Sgarbi 2009).

36 The contrast would be ends set by an all-powerful supra-individual agent, the theistic God or nature in some neo-Darwinian accounts.

37 The difference between ends and effects is captured in 'Matter causes [*wirkt*]. Will acts [*Willkür handelt*]' (*OP* 21: 226) from the *Opus Postumum*. My interpretation of spontaneity goes against the widely accepted view that spontaneity is a force apart. I think that Kant uses 'spontaneity' to engage with the tradition while moving beyond *both* the Aristotelian and Humean conceptions of force or energy.

choice, and which enables specific instances of control. We can think of this regress as reaching down to the conceptual conditions that enable us to make certain judgements, for example, that such and such action is free, or that human choice is free. To have a use for the predicate 'free' in the first judgment, we need to be in position to assert the second and so on. But we can also think of it more simply – and more ambitiously – as a regressive examination of what it takes to be free. Either way, we reach the ground of freedom that can be thought of and described as spontaneity but not known, let alone proven. This lack of proof means that our claim to this concept is not theoretically secure. Kant argues, however, that it is both cognizable *and* enforceable 'as soon as it comes to doing our duty' (*Dohna* 28:677). This is because only as addressees of the moral law and so as standing 'independent of the whole of nature' (ibid.) do we commit ourselves to the idea that we *can* deliberate about ends. And here we reach the point at which the previous discussion about interest and the discussion about agency meet, namely in the notion of morally guided evaluative control (*Wille*). In the last section, I spell out the relation a bit more and how it is a fruitful approach to the topic of freedom.

3 Conclusion

I said at the start that Kant's way of posing the problem of human freedom allows for the emergence of conceptual connections between two large fields of enquiry into the nature of normativity and the nature of freedom that are usually kept apart – to say nothing of sub-fields into epistemology, metaphysics, and psychology of normativity and freedom. The original connection comes down to a simple question: why does freedom matter? Or, in more Kantian terms, what is it to have a rational interest in freedom?

The answer is given in terms of the idea of a rational interest. Central to this is an answer about the importance of a type of norm that is unconditional, and capable of bringing to a halt the evaluative dialectic about the goodness of some thing or some course of action. Such a norm must be external to all series of conditional goods: a location given as 'transcendental freedom'. We thus arrive at a type of normative externalism and anti-naturalism which explains the interest in transcendental freedom. At the same time, Kant is highly sensitive to ordinary understandings of human actions. This side of the enquiry is rooted in empirical psychology and a long tradition of thought about agential control over actions which conceptualises freedom as a two-way power. However, these connections with tradition and empirical psychology are incorporated in a theory that carefully delimits their range. Admitting that the predicate 'free' is applicable to actions just in case they display the requisite degree of executive control highlights the problems involved in establishing what the requisite degree of control is, and opens the way for deeper questions about the model of mind that underpins agential control. The enquiry that considers what must be the case for certain experiences of being in charge of our own affairs to be true, and which I called transcendental psychology, brings into view a different application of the predicate 'free' as characterising human choice. Choice is free because it consists in deliberation about ends in light of reasons and the formation of the intention to act in the pursuit of some end in light of the said reasons. At this stage, a metaphysical question emerges with some urgency: in virtue of what is choice free? With the answer to that question, spontaneity, given here as the power human beings have to set ends, we reach the farthest limit of our epistemic powers. Note that we reach this stage through a regressive argument which is not designed to offer the binding conclusions that deductive arguments, for example, are supposed to offer. To clinch the argument, Kant shifts the discussion to the idea of morally guided evaluative control. And because morally guided evaluative control is guidance by authoritative normative standards, the discussion about agency finally re-connects with the earlier discussion about the rational interest in freedom.

The advantage of treating the discussion of rational interest and of free agency together is that it brings to the foreground their complementarity. The end-setting claim about human agency is a non-normative fact about the sort of being we are talking about, more precisely the sort of powers such a being possesses. The claim about strong authoritative normative standards, namely that at the end of normative enquiry there is a norm which is unconditioned, i.e. has no deniable antecedent, is a normative fact, and a fact of reason no less. The connection Kant seeks to establish between normativity and teleology carves out a very distinct position in a domain of enquiry currently dominated by various neo-Aristotelean naturalisms. But when I said at the outset that this is a distinctively Kantian way of thinking about freedom, I did not just mean the content, but also the procedure. Kant invites us to think about freedom in a way that manages to respect distinct areas of enquiry while also showing the way they interconnect. Although, of course, morality is central to his concerns, moral theory is not the sole load-bearing component of his theory of freedom. And it is part of his negative argument that metaphysics cannot do the job alone either. Kant's procedure is a kind of modest methodological holism: it is modest because it insists on proper boundaries for component enquiries, it is holistic because the theory of freedom is not reducible to any of the component enquiries, and it is methodological because it describes a way of going about the problem of freedom by identifying and calibrating the component parts proper to the topic. I believe this way of going about it is promising because it not only sets out to discover how things are, but also how we stand before them.

Bibliography

Allison, Henry (1990): *Kant's Theory of Freedom*. Cambridge: Cambridge University Press.
Allison, Henry (1995): "Spontaneity and Autonomy in Kant's Conception of the Self". In: Karl Ameriks/Dieter Sturma (Eds.): *The Modern Subject*. Albany: SUNY Press.
Allison, Henry (2011): *Commentary on the Groundwork to the Metaphysics of Morals*. New York: Oxford University Press.
Ameriks, Karl (2012): *Kant's Elliptical Path*. Oxford: Oxford University Press.
Baumgarten, Alexander (2013): *Metaphysics*. C. D. Fugate and J. Hymers trans. & ed. London: Bloomsbury.
Callender, Craig (2011): "Philosophy of Science and Metaphysics." In: Steven French/Juha Staatsi (Eds.): *The Continuum Companion to the Philosophy of Science*. London/New York: Continuum, pp. 33–54.
Chisholm, R. 1976. 'The Agent as Cause.' M. Brand and D. Walton eds., *Action Theory*, Dordrecht: Reidel, 199–212.
Clarke, Randolph (2000): "Modest Libertarianism." In: *Philosophical Perspectives* 14, pp. 21–46.
Clarke, Randolph (2003): *Libertarian Accounts of Free Will*. Oxford: Oxford University Press.
Clarke, Randolph (2005): "Agent Causation and the Problem of Luck." In: *Pacific Philosophical Quarterly* 86, pp. 408–421.
Coffman, E. J. (2010): "How (not) to Attack the Luck Argument." In: *Philosophical Explorations* 13. No. 2, pp. 157–166.
Copp, David (2007): *Morality in a Natural World. Selected Essays in Metaethics*. Cambridge: Cambridge University Press.
Deligiorgi, Katerina (2012): *The Scope of Autonomy. Kant and the Morality of Freedom*. Oxford: Oxford University Press.
Foot, Philippa (1978): *Virtues and Vices and Other Essays in Moral Philosophy*. Oxford: Blackwell.
Hanna, Robert (2006): *Kant, Science, and Human Nature*. Oxford: Oxford University Press.
Hudson, Hud (1994): *Kant's Compatibilism*. Ithaca: Cornell University Press.
Irwin, Terence (1984): "Morality and Personality in Kant and Green." In: A. W. Wood (Ed.): *Self and Nature in Kant's Philosophy*. Ithaca, London: Cornell University Press, pp. 31–56.
Kane, Robert (1996): *The Significance of Free Will*. Oxford: Oxford University Press.
Korsgaard, Christine (1989): "Morality as Freedom". In Yirmiyahú Yovel (Ed.): *Kant's Practical Philosophy Reconsidered*. Boston: Kluwer, pp. 23–48.
Lowe, E. J. (2008): *Personal Agency: The Metaphysics of Mind and Action*. Oxford: Oxford University Press.
McCarty, Richard (2009): *Kant's Theory of Action*. Oxford: Oxford University Press.
Mele, Alfred R. (1995): *Autonomous Agents. From Self-Control to Autonomy*. New York: Oxford University Press.

Meyers, Diana T. (2004): *Being Yourself. Essays on Identity, Action, and Social Life.* Oxford: Rowman and Littlefield.
Neta, Ram (2004): "The Normative Significance of Brute Facts". In: *Legal Theory* 10, pp. 199–214.
O'Connor, Timothy (2000): *Persons and Causes: The Metaphysics of Free Will.* New York: Oxford University Press.
Pereboom, Derk (2006): "Kant on Transcendental Freedom". In: *Philosophy and Phenomenological Research* LXXIII. No. 3, pp. 537–567.
Pink, Thomas (2011): "Thomas Hobbes and the Ethics of Freedom". In: *Inquiry* 5:54, pp. 541–63.
Reath, Andrews (1989): "Kant's Theory of Moral Sensibility: Respect for the Moral Law and the Influence of Inclination". In: *Kant-Studien* 80, pp. 284–302.
Reinhold, Karl Leonhard (2008): *Briefe über die kantische Philosophie,* Bd.2. Ed. By M. Bondeli. Schwabe Verlag: Basel.
Rickert, Heinrich (1909): "Zwei Wege der Erkenntnistheorie; Transcendentalpsychologie und Transcentdentallogik". *Kant-Studien* 14:1–3, pp. 169–228.
Rosefeldt, Tobias (2012): "Kants Kompatibilismus". In: Mario Brandhorst/Andree Hahmann/Bernd Ludwig (Eds.): *Sind wir Bürger zweier Welten? Freiheit und moralische Verantwortung im transzendentalen Idealismus,* Hamburg: Meiner, pp. 77–109.
Sgarbi, Marco (2012): *Kant on Spontaneity.* London: Acumen.
Sgarbi, Marco (2009): "Kant's Concept of Spontaneity within the Tradition of Aristotelian Ethics". *Studia Kantiana* 8, pp. 121–139.
Steward, Helen (2012): *A Metaphysics of Freedom.* Oxford: Oxford University Press.
Strawson, Galen (1994): "The Impossibility of Moral Responsibility." *Philosophical Studies: An International Journal for Philosophy in the Analytic Tradition* 75. No. 1/2, 5–24.
Strawson, Peter F. (1966): *The Bounds of Sense.* London: Methuen.
Strawson, Peter F. (1962): "Freedom and Resentment." In: *Proceedings of the British Academy.* XLVIII, pp. 1–25.
Sullivan, Roger J. (1989): *Immanuel Kant's Moral Theory.* Cambridge: Cambridge University Press.
Ulrich, J.A.H. (1788): *Eleutheriologie, oder über Freyheit und Nothwendigkeit.* Jena:Cröker. Stable URL provided by the Bayerische StaatsBibliotek digital http://www.mdz-nbn-resolving.de/urn/resolver.pl?urn=urn:nbn:de:bvb:12-bsb10044652-6
van Cleeve, James (1999): *Problems from Kant.* New York: Oxford University Press.
van Inwagen, Peter (2000): "Free Will Remains a Mystery". In: *Philosophical Perspectives* 14, pp. 1–19.
Walker, Ralph C. S. (1978): *Kant.* Boston: Routledge & Kegan Paul.
Watkins, Eric (2005): *Kant and the Metaphysics of Causality.* Cambridge: Cambridge University Press.
Wood, Allen W. (1984): "Kant's Compatibilism". In: Allen W. Wood (Ed.): *Self and Nature in Kant's Philosophy.* Ithaca: Cornell University Press.
Wuerth, Julian (2014): *Kant on Mind, Action, and Ethics.* Oxford University Press.

Sebastian Gardner
Kant's Practical Postulates and the Development of German Idealism

Abstract. Kant's moral theology was a subject of intense debate in the early reception of Kant's philosophy. At the same time, Kant's notion of practical postulation held considerable interest for Fichte, Schelling, and Hegel. What I seek to show is the systematic connection of these two facts: examination of the ways in which Kant's postulates of pure practical reason exposed the Kantian system to criticism sheds light, I argue, on some of the fundamental moves made by the German Idealists in their transformation of Kant's philosophy.

It is a familiar idea that, in order to understand German Idealism, we need to go back to Kant and see how there might be found *in* him the grounds and means for going *beyond* him, and there are no shortage of points in Kant from which the German Idealist development may be projected: Kant's theories of the self and of human freedom, the subjectivism of transcendental idealism and its questionable solution to the problem of skepticism, and the problematic bifurcation of freedom and nature, to name but a few. What I seek to do here is add another element to the narrative, which it seems to me has not received due emphasis, namely the central role played by the practical postulates of Kant's moral theology.

The moral theology and Kant's conception of practical postulation held considerable interest for Fichte, Schelling, and Hegel. Writings which stand out as testifying to the German Idealists' concern with this part of Kant's system, and displaying a wide range of attitudes towards it, include the following, in chronological order: Fichte's *Kritik Aller Offenbarung* (1792); Schelling's writings in his earliest Fichtean period, in particular the *Philosophische Briefe über Dogmatismus und Kritizismus* (1795) and *Abhandlungen zur Erläuterung des Idealismus der Wissenschaftslehre* (1797–98); Hegel's Jugendschriften (from 1793 to 1799); Fichte's divine governance essay (1798) and *Die Bestimmung des Menschen* (1800); and Hegel's *Glauben und Wissen* (1802), along with the discussion of the moral world-view in the *Phenomenology* (1807). And for good measure, there is the striking assertion in the Oldest System-Programme fragment (1796/97[?]):

> Since the whole of metaphysics will in the future fall under *moral [theory]* – of which Kant, with his two practical postulates, has given an *example*, but not exhausted anything – this

ethics will be nothing other than a complete system of all ideas [Ideen], or, what comes to the same, of all practical postulates. (Unkown 1995, 199)

I am not of course going to attempt to go over all of this territory, or even very much of it. In particular, I will say little about Hegel. What I want to explore, with reference to Fichte and Schelling, is the idea of a logical continuity from Kant's conception of practical postulation to the formation of post-Kantian idealism. The notion I wish to make plausible is that the references to Kant's practical postulates scattered across German Idealist texts reflect a systematic connection, can be described in a unified way, and which casts light on both the reasons *why* a transition was made from Kantianism to the post-Kantian idealisms, and also the *means* by which it was effected.[1]

This is therefore something more than a simple claim of historical influence, but it is obviously not to say that the moral theology and practical postulates hold a golden key to the German Idealist development, and I am not going to enter any claim about their relative weight in comparison with other motivating sources internal to Kant's system. In fact, what I hope will come clear is that that would be the wrong way of viewing the role played by the postulates, which has to do not so much with substantive first-order issues – the self, freedom, skepticism, etc. – but rather, at a metaphilosophical level, with how those issues are *taken up*.

That there should have been much engagement with Kant's moral theology on the part of the German Idealists, and that any of it should be positive, as it is in the System-Programme, is in a way somewhat surprising. The moral theology is the most philosophically conservative part of Kant's system, the point where Critical philosophy supplies the "practico-dogmatic metaphysics" which rejoins and redeems the Leibnizian-Wolffian philosophy, and the theism for which it provides does not form part of the motivating agenda of the Wissenschaftslehre, and is explicitly rejected by Schelling in his early days.[2] Indeed, parting company with theism – and rejecting the idea that reconstruction of religious orthodoxy is any criterion of philosophical success – seems to be one of the features which distinguishes the German Idealist development from the early Kant reception of Reinhold *et al.*, and which in the eyes of many helps to give it a congenially late modern character.

---

[1] Writers who single out and ascribe importance to the connection include (Düsing 1999), (Franks 2005, Ch. 6), (di Giovanni 2005), (Jaeschke 1990, Ch. 1), and (Timm 1974).
[2] Most explicitly in Schelling's letter to Hegel, 4 February 1795; in (Frank/ Kurz 1975, pp. 125–128).

Furthermore, it is not easy to see how the standing of Kant's moral theology in the early to mid 1790s – on the one hand subject to fierce and effective philosophical criticism, and on the other endorsed and appropriated by religious conservatives[3] – could have led a progressive Kantian to consider it a promising part of the Critical system to fix their attention on. But what I will also try to show is that the difficulties of the moral theology are part of the systematic connection; the problems of Kant's moral theology help to define the philosophical solutions of German Idealism.[4]

My discussion falls into four parts. In the first I look at the use made of the concept of a postulate in Fichte and Schelling, and in the second at the problems of Kant's moral theology. The third part spells out their systematic connection. The fourth part reviews contrasting treatments of the same Kantian material in Beck, Fries, and Novalis.

1 The postulates in German Idealism

1.1 Fichte

Fichte's use of the concept of a postulate or postulation runs from the beginning to the end of his philosophical development. After beginning to rethink Kant's moral theology in the *Kritik aller Offenbarung*, where Fichte claims that transcendental idealism itself – the doctrine that things are appearances not things in themselves – is "just as much a postulate of practical reason as a theorem of theoretical reason" (Fichte 1978, p. 25 [FW: V, 36]),[5] the concept recurs in early writ-

---

[3] Kant's moral theology had been annexed to the Lutheran orthodoxy by senior figures at the Tübingen Stift. The central figure in the so-called 'Älteren Tübinger Schule' of biblically grounded rational supernaturalism, Christian Storr, published in 1794 his *Bemerkungen über Kants philosophische Religionslehre*, which took up Kant's religion book and Fichte's *Kritik aller Offenbarung*, seeking to recruit Kantian philosophy to the cause of Church doctrine by showing that there is no real conflict between it and Scripture, and even that there are positive Kantian grounds for ecclesiastical doctrines (such as the Trinity) which Kant himself had not underwritten. Schelling and Hegel had intensive exposure to Storr's views from the day of their arrival.
[4] What I wish to show, then, is that the significance of the postulates exceeds, and is not just a matter of their close association with, the unificatory project of the third *Critique* and the doctrine of the primacy of the practical of the second: they are concerned with what *results* from Kant's attempt to unify Freedom and Nature on a practical basis.
[5] In addition Fichte classifies as a postulate the bare possibility that the moral law should be related to the world of sense (Fichte 1978, p. 27 [FW: V, 38]). This assertion of a fundamental unity of Freedom and Nature is a much broader version of Kant's notion of practical reason's

ings from the period when Fichte was preparing the Wissenschaftslehre, the "Eigene Meditationen" and "Praktische Philosophie", where the primary proposition that I am aware of my *Ich* is referred to as a postulate or "Heischesatz" ((Fichte 1971a, [FW/GA: II, III, 26–28, 49–50, 100]), and (Fichte 1971b, [FW/GA: II, III, 265])),[6] said to express the very intuition which it demands;[7] and as late as 1812 Fichte talks of the "Postulat" of the "appearance of the absolute as such", the postulate of its projection of a "Bild" and representative of its own being.[8]

Standardly Fichte uses the concept of a postulate in foundational contexts which have to do with the unification of the theoretical and the practical, and hence with the basis of ontological talk, and at points where none of the other and more familiar concepts in Fichte's lexicon could express adequately the distinctive status of the claim that he wants to make.[9] Three texts in particular reveal this.

---

requirement of the necessary unity of happiness and moral worth: Fichte treats that narrower notion, of the congruence of the fortunes of moral being with their behaviour, as deducible from the broader. Fichte's conception of the necessity of a fundamental unification of realms goes back to his early reflections on Kant's third *Critique*, his *Versuch eines erklärenden Auszug aus Kants Kritik der Urteilskraft*, where he says that the 'Vereinigungspunct' of Freedom and Nature must be 'weder theoretisch noch practisch' (Fichte 1962, [FW/GA: II, I, 329–330]). Fichte is also much less insistent than Kant on the need for the theological postulates to enable effective moral motivation (consequently Fichte denies religion even *subjective* universal validity: (Fichte 1978, p. 42 [FW: V, 56–57]). The overall tendency of the *Kritik aller Offenbarung* is thus to absorb Kant's antinomy of practical reason into the much more general and fundamental problem, acknowledged by Kant in the Introduction to the third *Critique*, of the 'Kluft' between Freedom and Nature (Kant 2000, [AA 5:175–176]). It is to be noted that, at this point, Fichte is not aiming to modify the concept of a practical postulate, Kant's definition of which he simply restates: a postulate is a theorem immediately connected with reason's requirement of practical law, which is 'not *commanded* by the law', yet 'must necessarily be assumed if reason is to be legislative', and which we call a '*belief*' (Fichte 1978, p. 31 [FW: V, 41]).

6 Two interconnected reasons are given: that intuition is required, and that each can become aware only of his own *Ich*. One formulation of the primary proposition entertained by Fichte is imperatival: 'Schaue Dein Ich an.' The second proposition, concerning the necessity of consciousness of *Nicht-Ich*, is also called a postulate. In (Fichte 1971b, [FW/GA: II, III, 190–191]), Fichte talks of an *Erfahrung* of our original striving as *postulirt* – 'das Postuliren der Erfahrung … es *soll* empfunden werden können' – and of our having come to 'all possible practical postulates'.

7 'Die Anschauung, welche in diesem Satze gefordert wird, ist durch ihn selbst ausgedrückt', (Fichte 1971a, [FW/GA: II, III, 50]).

8 '… aus dem Postulate der Erscheinung des Absoluten als solchen', (Fichte 1971, [FW: X, 352]).

9 Fichte's usage is not entirely consistent; in some contexts he uses the term as a mere synonym for positing (Fichte 1982, pp. 196 and 260 [FW: I, 218 and 296]).

(1) In the 1794 *Grundlage* Fichte refers to a postulate not formulated by Kant but which, he supposes, underlies Kant's moral theory (Fichte 1982, pp. 230n2 and 232 [FW: I, 260n and 263]).[10] This is the "absolute postulate of conformity with the pure self", the demand "that everything should conform to the self". Fichte suggests that the categorical imperative *is*, or may be considered "as", just this postulate. Whatever the justice of this construal of Kant, the important point is what seems to be Fichte's further claim, that what the imperative requires, for its intelligibility, is a *theoretical* grounding. It requires the notion that "the self is itself absolute": "Only *because* and *insofar as* the self is itself absolute [Nur *weil*, und *inwiefern* das Ich selbst absolut ist], does it have the right to postulate absolutely." (Fichte 1982, p. 230n2 [FW: I, 260n]). Fichte says that Kant could never "have arrived at the categorical imperative' without 'presupposing an absolute being of the self [absoluten Seyns des Ich]".[11]

This immediately raises the question: Is Fichte thinking of the absolute self, with its absolute being, as a *metaphysical* ground? Or is it a mere ideational correlate, the theoretical echo as it were, of a practical norm? The first is suggested by Fichte's claim that the absolute being of the self is the "ground of the authority [Grund der Befugniss]" of the absolute postulate,[12] and the second by the fact that his broader intention is, we know, to in some way ground theoretical on practical reason.

The passages later in the *Grundlage* where Fichte tells us what it means for the self to have absolute being favour the second interpretation, but fail to fully

---

10 The theism of Kant's moral theology, more or less conserved in the *Kritik aller Offenbarung*, has by this point disappeared. Fichte's theological views are not on open display in the *Grundlage* but can be gleaned from the contemporaneous 'Praktische Philosophie' (Fichte 1971b, [FW/GA: II, III, 238]): belief in the existence of God derives from the subject's original striving, which 'geht darauf hinaus, Gott zu werden'; in the *Trieb* to *discover* God shines the law, 'werde selbst Gott'. Fichte describes this result of his investigation as a 'guter Fund'. This is not in fact the position that Fichte defends publically in his later essay on divine governance (Fichte 1994), but it is very close to the recognizably Fichtean analysis that Friedrich Karl Forberg articulated (Forberg 1912), precipitating the *Atheismusstreit*.
11 In one place Fichte contrasts the Wissenschaftslehre, which distinguishes 'absolute being' from 'real existence' and takes the former as a ground for the latter, with Stoicism, which does not distinguish them (Fichte 1982, p. 245 note 4 [FW: I, 278n]).
12 The point is this: Fichte has claimed that the moral imperative of the moral law presupposes an assertoric, non-imperatival ground, so it cannot be Fichte's view that we grasp *what it is* for the self to be absolute merely by assenting to certain norms; the absoluteness of the self is what is supposed to *ground* (rationalize our assent to) those norms. This reading is suggested, moreover, by remarks in 'Praktische Philosophie' (Fichte 1971b, [FW/GA: II, III, 238]) to the effect that the unconditioned is not realized in theoretical reason (for which it is merely regulative), but that pure reason, in the pure *Ich*, *realizes* absolute unity (though only *for* the pure *Ich*).

clarify the situation (Fichte 1982, pp. 238–239, 244–245 [FW: I, 270–271, 277–278]). Fichte says that the self *is* infinite, "but merely in respect to its striving": it merely *strives to be* infinite (Fichte 1982, p. 238 [FW: I, 270]). Again, he says that the self *demands* that it encompass all reality, that this demand rests on the *idea* of the absolutely posited infinite self, and that the meaning of the principle, *the self posits itself absolutely*, becomes clear when we appreciate that we are speaking of "an *idea* of the self which must necessarily underlie its infinite practical *demand*" (Fichte 1982, p. 244 [FW: I, 277], italics added). But this just leaves us with the puzzle of why Fichte in the earlier passage attributed absolute *being* to the self, and of how an idea which does not (yet) possess an object, can lend authority to a practical demand.[13]

I will come back to this, but for the moment the point is just that Fichte draws a direct connection of foundational issues in the Wissenschaftslehre with Kant's concept of practical postulation, while seeming to depart from the pattern of Kantian practical postulation. Rather he seems to have in mind and see the need for some *development* of Kant's notion – Fichte seems to envisage some sort of reflexive structure in which "ought" and "is" double up and validate one another.

(2) This supposition is borne out in the "new presentation" of the Wissenschaftslehre (*nova methodo*) (Fichte 1992). Here Fichte tells us that the Wissenschaftslehre begins, as all philosophy must, with a postulate, but it is one "that is grounded in an *Act* [*Thathandlung*] and not in a *fact*", where "Thathandlung" means: "what occurs when I let my I act within itself and observe what happens", namely the construction of a world, "a continually progressing synthesis" (Fichte 1992, pp. 109–110 [FW/GA: IV, III, 344–345]).[14] We might briefly wonder if Fichte wants us to understand by postulate anything more than is in-

---

13 The ambiguity concerning ontological commitment, again in connection with the concept of a practical postulate, is present also in Fichte's account of human freedom in his review of Creuzer, where he describes 'manifestation of absolute activity in the determination of the will' as a *Postulat* of the moral law (Fichte 1971, p. 293 [FW: VIII, 413]), and recommends that the question of whether we should think of this activity which supplies the 'real ground' of empirical acts of will as 'the *cause*', the *Ursache*, of the will's being determined, should be answered negatively: the sufficient ground of determinations of the will is not to be identified with 'an actual real ground' (Fichte 1971, p. 294 [FW: VIII, 414]). For a general discussion of the issue of the Wissenschaftslehre's ontological status, see (Gardner 2007).

14 Alternative specifications of the primary postulate are given: 'that this free activity of his I is that principle that cannot be derived from anything else' (Fichte 1992, p. 95 [FW/GA: IV, III, 335]); 'Construct the concept of the I and observe how you accomplish this' (Fichte 1992, p. 119 [FW/GA: IV, III, 349]). Later the postulate is added that: '*The I appears outside of itself, as it were, and makes itself into an object*' (Fichte 1992, p. 138 [FW/GA: IV, II, 44]).

volved in the basic Euclidean geometrical case,[15] but all such doubts are removed when he later writes: "Moreover, the scope of Kant's practical postulate is too narrow, for he limits it entirely to belief in God and immortality; but we will see that consciousness in its entirety is included within this postulate." (Fichte 1992, p. 298 [FW/GA: IV, II, 139])

The postulate to which Fichte is referring here is Kant's claim that "I ought to do something; therefore, what I ought to do must be possible" – which is equivalent, Fichte says, to his own claim that the I must effect, within my thinking and my willing, a transition from determinability to determinacy.[16] So the operative conception of postulate here is not just a postulate in the basic Euclidean sense but explicitly tied to Kant's moral theology. Fichte attributes Kant's not having presented his philosophy as a whole under the rubric of a transition from Ought to Is, i.e. as a set of postulates, to the order in which the *Critiques* were composed; to have done so would have required Kant to go back and laboriously revise his critique of theoretical reason. In other words, had Kant begun with a treatment of the I "as it is for itself", instead of treating it as an "accident" of "sensible, objective thinking", then he would have arrived at the postulates of the Wissenschaftslehre.

(3) In the 1804 lectures, Fichte attempts to recast the Wissenschaftslehre in terms that will show it to possess the virtues claimed for Schelling's identity system; that is, he wishes to show that his own system is no merely one-sided, merely subjective idealism, but that it grasps as much of the absolute as can be thought possible. Fichte proceeds by playing off different formulations of realism and idealism against one another, in a way that leads to their successive refinement and finally to the insight of non-objectified being, "a being in pure act" which is "self-enclosed oneness with itself" (Fichte 2005, p. 116 [FW: X, 206]).[17] This concludes the first of his two major tasks.

---

15 Fichte draws the analogy with geometry, (Fichte 1992, p. 110 [FW/GA: IV, III, 344–345]), no doubt with Beck (whom he has just been discussing) in mind.

16 More exactly, Fichte describes Kant's principle as analytic, and his own as synthetic (Fichte 1992, p. 297 [FW/GA: IV, II, 138–139]).

17 'simple, pure being as absolute, self-enclosed oneness' (Fichte 2005, p. 120 [FW: X, 212]), 'an unconditionally self–enclosed, living oneness' (Fichte 2005, p. 147 [FW: X, 245]) which we do not go *toward*, for the reason that we ourselves *are* (in) it; our insight is that 'being itself is an absolute I', or We (Fichte 2005, pp. 117 and 120 [FW: X, 207 and 212]), because it is not just already construct*ed* but self-construct*ing* (Fichte 2005, p. 122 [FW: X, 214–215], which refers back: the being which we had insight into 'constructs itself, and … is only in this self-construction'). This being is 'entirely *of itself, in itself, and through itself*', where this '*self*' involves no antithesis (of subject and object) because it is 'grasped with the requisite abstraction purely inwardly … as I am most fervently conscious of grasping it' (Fichte 2005, p. 116 [FW: X, 205]).

The second task, which we are set as soon as the first is completed,[18] is to "deduce from the first part, as necessary and true appearance, everything which up to now we have let go as merely empirical and not intrinsically valid" (Fichte 2005, p. 121 [FW: X, 213]), what Fichte calls "factical existence".[19] And the difficulty we face here is that of avoiding an irrational gap, *hiatum*, of the kind that confronts us, Fichte claims, when we consider the relation of consciousness to objects:[20] the relation of pure being to appearance should not reproduce the "inexplicable and inconceivable" character of that relation.

Fichte's first step towards a solution is to hypothesize a relation of "Sollen", staked on the condition of our own cognition into the essence or ground of being: *If* the cognition – the "absolute insight" (Fichte 2005, p. 125 [FW: X, 218]) – that we achieved in completing the first task is to be possible, *then* being *should* (es *soll*) construct itself in a way that allows it to make itself known to us. Fichte calls this the *ideal* self-construction of being (Fichte 2005, p. 123 [FW: X, 215]). He then asks us to reflect on the essence of this *Sollen*, and says that:

> ... an inner self-construction is expressed in the '*should*': an inner, absolute, pure, qualitative *self-making* and resting-on-itself ... It is, I say, an 'inner self-construction', completely as such: *nothing else* supports the hypothetical 'should', except its inner assumption entirely by itself and without any ground [die innere Annahme durchaus von sich selber und ohne allen aüssern Grund] ... 'Inner assumption *entirely by itself*' I have said: hence a creation from nothing, producing itself as such. A 'resting on itself' I have said, because ... it falls back into nothing without this continuing pursuit of inward, living assumption [innerlich lebendigen Annahme] and creation from nothing. Hence it is the self-creator of its own

---

18 The transition from the first to the second takes place in Lecture 16. The part of the text which I am concerned with in what follows runs from this point in Lecture 16 to Lecture 21 inclusive.
19 (Fichte 2005, p. 122 [FW: X, 214]): 'being's factical existence in the form of external, objectifying existence'. Fichte specifies the target in different ways: 'if we wanted to come to something more than the one being, for example to the latter's way of appearing ... primordial appearance; and so consciousness' (Fichte 2005, p. 128 [FW: X, 222]); '... if appearance is to arise' (Fichte 2005, p. 146 [FW: X, 245]); 'this entire manifold as it occurs empirically ... to present appearance in general and as such' (Fichte 2005, p. 147 [FW: X, 246]); we seek to explain *a priori* appearance and its 'principle of the manifold' (Fichte 2005, p. 147 [FW: X, 246]), 'the resolution of the puzzle of the world and of consciousness' (Fichte 2005, p. 151 [FW: X, 251]).
20 Not, note, merely spatially outer objects, but all states of affairs which are taken to obtain, to be matters regarding which there is *truth*, including our own *Denken*, in so far as we have Cartesian certain consciousness of thinking: see (Fichte 2005, p. 111 [FW: X, 199–200]).

being and the self-support of its duration. (Fichte 2005, p. 125 [FW: X, 219], translation modified)[21]

Fichte is referring here to an act which is *normatively* conceptualized but expresses an *ontological* ground, an ontologically *creative* ground.

The crux of Fichte's argument – on which rests the anti-skeptical force of the Wissenschaftslehre, as well as his claim that its idealism is (*pace* Schelling's criticisms) a higher realism – is his claim that we can convert this hypothetical *Sollen* into "something categorical and absolute", because it can be regarded, not merely as a condition for our cognition, but also as a *principle of pure being* itself (Fichte 2005, p. 126 [FW: X, 219]). The antecedent – If we are to have insight, then ... – falls away, Fichte argues, leaving just the consequent: Being must construct itself as factical existence or appearance.[22] As Fichte puts it, the ideal self-con-

---

[21] Again: the *should* has 'been illuminated for us as an absolute that holds and sustains itself out of itself and through itself *as such*, on the condition that it exists', whereby 'we have a categorical insight into the unchangeable, unalterable nature of the "*should*", an insight in which we can completely abstract from [its] outward existence' (Fichte 2005, pp. 131–132 [FW: X, 227]); the *should* is 'self-producing and self-sustaining' (Fichte 2005, p. 134 [FW: X, 230]); 'the "should" is the basic principle for everything' (Fichte 2005, p. 135 [FW: X, 231]).

[22] Explicating this move occupies Fichte throughout Lectures 17–21. Fichte's argument for the conversion of the conditional necessity (*if* there are to be appearances of which we have cognition, then being *must* ...) into an unconditional necessity (being *must* ...) is not easy to make out, but its nerve is undoubtedly the conception of the former as an instance of *Sollen*, the importance of which for Fichte cannot be overstated: he refers to it as what differentiates his system from all those which have gone before (Fichte 2005, pp. 148–149 [FW: X, 248]). The task is to 'eliminate' its 'hypothetical status', putting us in possession of the *Sollen* as a 'self-supporting principle' (Fichte 2005, p. 130 [FW: X, 225]). Fichte says that 'the most secure means is to look it straight in the eye', whereby it loses itself or evaporates in insight into pure being (Fichte 2005, p. 130 [FW: X, 225]). In one place, Fichte describes the search for the ground we are seeking as itself displaying the reality of what we seek – 'in order to state the true result of your desire ... just to arrive at your demand', there must be an '*original seeing*' (Fichte 2005, p. 135 [FW: X, 232]). The idea seems to be that the conversion is achieved by an alteration of, or abstraction from, *form*, which leaves just the pure awareness of *content* (Fichte 2005, p. 144 [FW: X, 242–243]): the imperatival normative form of the *Sollen* falls away, leaving just *insight*; we 'let go of the proposition's form', viz., of presupposition (Fichte 2005, p. 149 [FW: X, 249]). This is supported by the places in which Fichte claims that our insight into pure being takes us to a point from which we can grasp its differentiation into contrasting forms (real and ideal) as merely downstream features, which change nothing regarding its essential content and identity; allowing *is* and *ought* to be regarded as, to put it empirically, different aspects of one and the same thing.

Another strand in the text concerns our own reflexive appreciation of our presence in our reflections *as knowers*: Fichte tells us to remember that the condition in the antecedent (our having cognition) is *actually* satisfied, not in the sense of any assumed determinate cognition –

struction of being encompasses also its *real* self-construction.²³ And once the *Sollen* has been grasped as categorical, not merely hypothetical, Fichte refers to it as a *postulate:* he talks of the "postulate of the *absolute necessity* in the pure, *positive in-itself*" (Fichte 2005, p. 142 [FW: X, 240]), "the postulate that inner being ... must construct itself" (Fichte 2005, p. 147 [FW: X, 246]), "the absolute postulation of genesis", "the 'should [Soll]' is a postulation ... and a postulation is a genesis" (Fichte 2005, p. 155 [FW: X, 256]).

1.2 Schelling

Schelling's early writings take up Kant's concept of practical postulation in close association with Fichte, but with several differences. For one thing, Schelling tells us explicitly that that is what is he doing – self-consciously appropriating and revising Kant's conception. There are however also substantive points of contrast with Fichte, of which the first two are these. First, whereas for Fichte,

---

Fichte's is not a regressive argument in that sense – but in the sense that we are *candidates* for possessing knowledge, beings for which the minimal and indeterminate possibility of knowledge is assured by the very fact that we can ask what, whether, and how, we can know anything; this allows us to grasp that we 'know ourselves in' the presupposition, and *are* 'knowing' (Fichte 2005, pp. 151, 153 [FW: X, 252, 253]).

Also important is Fichte's idea that we can and must in our reflection shake off the thought that the *Sollen* has validity merely relative to *us*, meaning that being's obligation (so to speak) to construct itself for *our* sake becomes being's obligation to construct itself for its *own* sake. The sort of normativity that Fichte has in mind by *Sollen* must be something like what we grasp in practical consciousness (a normative demand that is fulfilled by a doing), and not the thinner normativity of theoretical reasoning. It cannot be the latter alone, because in that case Fichte's references to *doing* as opposed to *saying* would make no sense, and no progress would therefore be made with the anti-skeptical task of validating the presuppositions of theoretical reason: Fichte argues that the *enactment* [*Thun*] in the *should* is revealed to be categorical, even though its *saying* is hypothetical (Fichte 2005, p. 142 [FW: X, 239]).

As I understand it, when Fichte describes the Sollen as insight into 'genesis' (absolute genesis; genesis of being, and being as genesis), we do not just grasp that something's *being the case* is a condition of the fulfilment of a mere demand of ours, but that the demand inheres in being itself: we grasp being *as* having-to-be, as subject to its own self-addressed imperative, so to speak; at the very least we can abstract from the distinction of our own reflection and reason itself (Fichte 2005, p. 152 [FW: X, 252]). This insight is reformulated (from Lecture 19 onwards) in terms of the identity of light (or pure reason) and being (Fichte 2005, p. 144 [FW: X, 243]), where light is characterized in terms of a 'von' (genetic grounding).

23 'The distinction between being's *real* and *ideal* self-construction that we made earlier ... is now completely annulled' (Fichte 2005, p. 138 [FW: X, 235]).

at least prior to 1804, the attraction of the practical postulates begins and ends with their unification of Freedom and Nature, for Schelling it lies not only in their doing this but also, and more importantly, in their *thereby* taking us to the highest concept or Ideal of Pure Reason. Second, and connectedly, Schelling disposes of any equivocation concerning ontological commitment.

In the Appendix to his 1797–98 *Abhandlungen zur Erläuterung des Idealismus der Wissenschaftslehre*, Schelling spells out the reasons why "the first principle of philosophy must be *simultaneously theoretical and practical*, i.e., a *postulate*" (Schelling 1994, p. 134 [SW: 1, 446]),[24] "neither theoretical nor practical alone [but] *both* at once [*beides* zugleich]" (Schelling 1994, p. 135 [SW: I, 448]). The principle of philosophy cannot be theoretical, Schelling asserts, without surrendering *ab initio* to dogmatism, nor however can it be practical, since practical propositions are mere imperatives. But in the concept of a *postulate* we find the theoretical and practical united, in so far as it concerns a "primordial construction" in inner sense, which is theoretical in form but which borrows its compelling force ("zwingende Kraft") from the practical sphere (Schelling 1994, pp. 134–135 [SW: I, 447–448]).

This conception is preserved intact in Schelling's 1800 *System of Transcendental Idealism* (Schelling 1978, p. 33 [SW: III, 376]):

> There is no possibility of our principle forming the basis of both theoretical and practical philosophy if it be not itself at once theoretical and practical. Now since a theoretical principle is a *theorem* [*Lehrsatz*], while a practical one is a *command*, there must lie something in the middle between the two – and this is the *postulate* which borders on *practical* philosophy, since it is simply a *demand*, and on *theoretical*, since its demand is for a *purely theoretical construction*. Where the postulate gets its coercive power from, is at once explained by the fact that it is used for practical demands. Intellectual intuition is something that one *can* demand and expect; anyone who lacks the capacity for such an intuition *ought* at least to possess it.

The reasons Schelling gives here are therefore of a *meta*philosophical kind, and prescind from the consideration that we have in fact located, thanks to Fichte, the particular and uniquely appropriate content for the postulate which the system of philosophy requires. The Fichtean content of the postulate which in fact

---

24 I focus on this text because it brings to a conclusion the early series – *Über die Möglichkeit einer Form der Philosophie überhaupt* (Schelling 1980a), *Vom Ich als Princip der Philosophie* (Schelling 1980), and *Philosophische Briefe* (Schelling 1980b) – and summates Schelling's views at the end of this first crucial phase of his development, with close reference to Fichte. Schelling's conception of absolute cognition dates from *Vom Ich* (Schelling 1980), but it is not until the 'Antikritik' that Schelling refers to it as a postulate (Schelling 1982, [SW: 242–244]).

provides the first principle of philosophy is: "what is *undemonstrable* and *primordially intuitable* [*Undemonstrierbaren, ursprünglich Anzuschauenden*]" (Schelling 1994, p. 133 [SW: I, 444]), which Schelling says is equivalent to the intellectual intuition which reveals to us the origin of self-consciousness (Schelling 1994, pp. 102, 116, 135 [SW: I, 401, 420, 448]).

These characterizations stand in rough agreement with Fichte, as his position stood in the Jena Wissenschaftslehre.[25] But Schelling's further insight is that there is an alternative to Fichte's strategy of focussing on the *Sollen* in order to reach the point of identity of the theoretical and practical. On Schelling's alternative, we can lay direct claim to intellectual acquaintance with that which resolves itself immediately for *reflection* into distinct, theoretical and practical factors, but which *in itself* is neither, and so can be *both*.[26] The absolute postulate discloses the "*original identity of the theoretical and the practical in us*", and it represents for practical reason the 'absolute state' to be achieved, but it can do so only because our intuition attains, as Schelling puts it in Plato's language, "an intuition of its archetype in the intellectual world" (Schelling 1994, p. 111–112 [SW: I, 413–415]).[27] Fichte's *ought* is retained but demoted: for Schelling it is not that *as* which we grasp being-in-itself, as Fichte has it in 1804 (Fichte 2005), a *ratio cognoscendi* and *ratio essendi*, but merely the basis on which we are entitled to postulate the *universal validity* of our intellectual self-intuition (Schelling argues: since all are capable of heeding the moral law, all possess the capacity for such intuition) (Schelling 1994, pp. 112, 113, 116, 134 [SW: I, 414–415, 416, 420, and 446]).

Schelling thereby removes, as I said, the ambiguity regarding the ontological significance of the absolute postulate. And he takes care to explain how this is

---

25 In particular, with how Fichte presents the Wissenschaftslehre in the Second Introduction (Fichte 1994a).

26 Schelling defines a postulate as 'the requisite of a *primordial* (transcendental) construction', without reference to the primacy of practical reason, (Schelling 1994, p. 137 [SW: I, 451]). At this stage, Schelling takes Fichte to share this concept of a postulate: see (Schelling 1994, p. 137n [SW: I, 451n]).

27 See also (Schelling 1980b, p. 180 [SW: I, 318]). Such a point is not merely the node of coordination of practical and theoretical reason, but lies *above both*. Schelling does not draw attention to this departure from Fichte, and it is obscured by the fact that so much of what Schelling says – concerning theoretical philosophy as 'presupposing' practical philosophy (Schelling 1994, p. 101 [SW: 399]), and of the necessity of grasping oneself as pure autonomy, freedom, etc. – seems to merely recapitulate Fichte. The derivative character of the practical, for Schelling, is nonetheless reaffirmed at (Schelling 1994, p. 114 [SW: I, 417]) – the absolute postulate 'contains the first reason for the practically universal postulates' – and (Schelling 1994, p. 124 [SW: I, 433]): the primordial *Sollen* has its ground in knowledge itself.

possible. Propositions which *predicate* existence are theoretical,[28] Schelling says, but there is another mode, he argues, in which existence is grasped in transcendental cognition, to which must correspond a distinct sense of existence – "Seyn" as opposed to "Daseyn".[29] "Seyn" is what the neither-theoretical-nor-practical absolute postulate is concerned with. Thus what threatens to be, as Schelling notes, a "paradox" – namely that one cannot say of the self *qua* "principle of all reality" that it "*exists*", since it "possesses none of the predicates that attach to things" – is resolved by saying that the self is *being itself*, "es das *Sein selbst* ist" (Schelling 1978, p. 32 [SW: III, 375–376]).[30]

The further point to be emphasized – which I will come to later – concerns the importance of Kant's moral theology for guiding Schelling to his conception of a postulate, which is not just a distillation from his reading of Fichte.

2 The problems of Kant's moral theology

2.1 First responses to the moral theology

In order to grasp how exactly Fichte and Schelling's uses of the concept of a practical postulate relate to and emerge from Kant, we need to go back to an earlier point in the historical story and consider the first wave of responses to Kant's moral theology.[31]

To an impartial observer of early Kant reception, Kant's moral theology would have appeared by the early to mid-1790s to have emerged from the intensive discussion which it had provoked as at least highly problematic, and this outcome would moreover have been taken as putting a question-mark over the coherence and integrity of Kant's philosophy as a whole. The reasons why the

---

[28] '… ein Satz, der ein Daseyn aussagt', (Schelling 1994, p. 134 [SW: I, 446–447]). And see (Schelling 1994, p. 136 [SW: I, 449]): 'a proposition predicating an *existence* [der ein *Daseyn* aussagt] is diametrically opposed to the very spirit of philosophy'.

[29] Schelling's position is made clear in an important footnote on the ontological argument and existence of God in *Philosophische Briefe* (Schelling 1980b, p. 174n [SW: I, 309n]): we are to distinguish the *actual* (*Wirklichen*) and the *existing* (*Daseyenden*), from *being* (*dem Seyenden*); Descartes and Spinoza spoke of *absolutes Seyn*, which our 'empirical age' misapprehended in terms of the pure concept of *existence* (*Daseyn*).

[30] This supplies also Schelling's answer to the question, which we might raise, of how a *demand-for-a-construction* can avoid falling asunder into two components, (i) the demand, and (ii) its object, the theorem.

[31] For a more detailed account, see (Gardner 2011), which this section of the paper summarizes and draws on.

moral theology held such importance for the fate of the Critical system are both historical and systematic. Reinhold had made strident claims for the moral theology as the solution to the Aufklärung's longstanding difficulty in reconciling reason and religion, claims which matched Kant's own statements on the topic; and the specific difficulties which had been identified in criticism of the moral theology had, as Kant's critics took pains to emphasize, direct implications for one's understanding and evaluation of the transcendental project as such.

One set of objections to Kant's moral theology concerned the claims regarding the relation of morality and happiness which Kant makes in the course of arguing that there exists an antinomy of practical reason, which finds its unique resolution in the theological postulates of personal immortality and the existence of God. These problems are of a relatively low-level sort, and were adequately resolved by Kant's defenders through elucidation of what is meant by positing the highest good as a necessary object of will which is nonetheless not a condition of validity of the moral law. Fichte's *Kritik aller Offenbarung* provides such elucidation (Fichte 1978, §§ 2–3). The objections which are of much greater interest concern two different matters: first, Kant's account of the *relation of theoretical and practical reason* involved in practical postulation, and second, the *epistemic status and ontological commitment* of the theological postulates.

Regarding the first of these, the point was hammered home again and again by Kant's critics – inclusive of Flatt, Feder, Schulze, Wizenmann, though many others could be cited – that Kant's invocation of what he calls the primacy of practical reason to rationalize the sanctioning by theoretical reason of the propositions which practical reason claims as "practical cognitions" of the supersensible, fails to achieve coherence. The objection was formulated in different ways, but the common element is a complaint that Kant's move from a *need* of practical reason to a holding-true, "Fürwahrhalten", violates the independence and autonomy of theoretical reason.

The most forceful statement of the second difficulty is found in Jacobi's *Ueber das Unternehmen des Kriticismus* and then again in *Von den göttlichen Dingen* ((Jacobi 1968, pp. 175–195) and (Jacobi 1968a, pp. 340–378)). These are relatively late texts – respectively 1801 and 1811 – but I will concentrate on them because they articulate in incisive and amplified terms things that anti-Kantians such as Wizenmann and Schulze had been saying in the 1780s and 90s.

2.2 Jacobi

1. In *Ueber das Unternehmen des Kriticismus*, Jacobi reapplies to Kant's postulates the same type of criticism that he had applied previously to Kant's claim of empirical realism in the supplement, "On Transcendental Idealism", to his *David Hume* (1787) book (Jacobi 1994, pp. 331). According to Jacobi, the difference between the two cases, which are otherwise parallel, concerns merely *which faculties* are involved, with reason occupying in the case of the practical postulates the place occupied by the understanding in empirical knowledge.

The objection is that Kant's own account of the subjective genesis of the ideas of reason, not merely fails to positively endow them with epistemic authority, but makes it *impossible* to regard them as having any cognitive significance whatever. It is impossible, Jacobi says, to have an "honest, wholehearted confidence" in reason's ideas of God, freedom and immortality, since we are on Kant's account "clearly instructed by the origin, the constitution and the inner essence of these ideas" that they are only "Fictionen" – they arise in us only because they are necessitated to do so by the conceptual operations of the understanding, as needed in order to provide bounds for its extension, and so *can only* be taken as deceptive horizons, not as things existing for and in themselves (Jacobi 1968, pp. 100–103).[32]

Kant's claim that religious belief is rationally necessitated by moral consciousness thus requires, so Jacobi argues, theoretical reason to set aside its commitment to truth, and in any case leaves us only in the peculiar reflective position of knowing that our subjective constitution *compels us to endorse* certain representations, ones which, Kant's own theory of that constitution instructs, are for us necessarily without objective significance. And since the final end, and ultimate justification, of the entire Critical undertaking, according to Kant himself, was precisely to *save* the three practically significant ideas of reason, we can conclude from his failure in that broader endeavour, Jacobi claims, that the Critical project as such runs aground. And so – Jacobi tells us, drawing an even broader, more sweeping conclusion – must any attempt to philosophize on the basis of mere concepts in abstraction from divine intuitional input (Jacobi 1968a, p. 192).

---

32 As Jacobi puts it in (Jacobi 1968a, pp. 376–378): If reason relates only to the understanding, and this only to sensibility, and if cognition ascends only gradually from appearances to ideas, then Kant is right, against Plato: the ideas are then expanded concepts of understanding, without provable objective validity, and if their Kantian deduction is correct, then there is nothing more perverse than to proceed from ideas.

In the later text, *Von den göttlichen Dingen*, Jacobi – on the search for ever deeper diagnoses of the pathologies of philosophical reason – offers an extended reconsideration of the moral theology in light of *post*-Kantian idealism. This text is of particular significance for the case I am trying to make, since here Jacobi expresses the view – at a relatively late point, after German Idealism has developed into a mature state – that the moral theology functioned as a logical trigger for the German Idealist development.

Kant himself, Jacobi declares, is thoroughly innocent of anti-theistic intentions. Yet Kant bears an indirect responsibility for Fichte and Schelling, the twin "daughters" of Critical philosophy, since their philosophies are merely consistent applications of his principle that only what the subject has *produced*, or *constructed*, can the subject *cognize* (Jacobi 1968a, pp. 351–352).[33] This principle doubles with another: that *wissenschaftlicher Beweis* is required for all claims to knowledge.

According to Jacobi, the practical postulates represent Kant's endeavour to salvage the ideas of God, freedom and immortality in the face of these principles. The reality of the objects of the ideas of reason was for Kant, Jacobi thinks, wholly axiomatic, a basic conviction, but Kant's commitment to *Wissenschaft* precluded the epistemology which (given the impossibility of a theoretical proof of God's existence) this conviction entailed, namely Jacobi's own epistemology of immediate revelations of reason, since to affirm such original cognitions would be to affirm truths without the possibility of proof. Kant was thus forced into the compensatory strategy of raising up practical reason, rendering cognition of the objects of reason *mediate*, in order to preserve at least the *appearance* of proof (Jacobi 1968a, pp. 351–367).[34] Had Kant followed to its logical conclusion his principle of the necessity of construction for the conceptual grasping of objects, then he would have arrived at the position of Fichte – a nihilism which dissolves being into productions of thought – and ultimately at the atheistic materialist

---

[33] The *Kern* of Kant's revolution is that we grasp (*begreifen*, *einsehen*) an object only in so far as we have it come into our being in thought, are capable of creating it in our understanding (Jacobi 1968a, p. 351; restated on p. 354). Jacobi may be reading Kant in the light of J. S. Beck and Fichte, but he is of course right that the principle is one which Kant accepts: 'we can only understand and communicate to others what we ourselves can *produce*' (Kant 1999, p. 482 [AA 11:515]). See also Reflexionen 2394, 'Wir sehen nichts ein, als was wir machen können' (Kant 2005, p. 42 [AA 16:344]) and 2398, 'Wir begreifen nur, was wir selbst machen können' (Kant 2005, p. 42[AA 16:345]).

[34] As Kant lowered reason in theoretical philosophy, he raised it up in the practical part, and so was twice right, and twice wrong; Kant failed to combine his double right into a single, simple and complete one, but rather remained split, ambiguous and equivocal (Jacobi 1968a, pp. 364–367).

naturalism of Schelling.³⁵ Kant avoided this catastrophe only at the cost of equivocation; the correct response to his predicament would have been to abandon his commitment to the necessity of *wissenschaftlichen Beweis* (Jacobi 1968a, pp. 365–366).

2. Whatever we make of Jacobi's argument, it is hard to deny that the practical postulates from Kant's texts without a clear and determinate ontological status. Strictly there are two issues here: whether or not it is *required*, for Kant's purposes, that the postulates be ontologically committed; and whether or not in any case Kantianism has the resources to *provide* for it. Jacobi affirms the first and denies the second,³⁶ while anti-realist interpreters of Kant deny both ((Forberg 1912), and in our day, (Neiman 1994, Ch. 4)). But what matters for pres-

---

35 As Jacobi plots the historical story in *Von den göttlichen Dingen* (Jacobi 1968a, pp. 372–394): Kant's philosophy was orientated from the outset towards the defence of science in the sense of empirical knowledge, and so he prioritized the understanding over reason. Understanding falls, however, under the shadow of reason: it cannot help wanting to view all things transcendently, and in relation to a single principle. Reason does in fact have, *intuitively*, transcendent knowledge, but understanding cannot allow this. What it does instead is to *substitute* for reason's original intuitive knowledge certain ideal constructs that are indeed also products of reason, but which are made up of abstractions derived from the understanding, and which have no content of their own. These abstractions then eclipse the *actual* knowledge that reason has: because reason is unable to recognize the knowledge that it genuinely has in the abstractions that have been constructed for the sake of the understanding, it ends up treating its original ideas as mere illusions. Fichte followed suit, but reconstructed the whole of nature *a priori* from logic. The fact that the resulting reconstruction has no content of its own, and needs to derive its content from the material details of nature, led inevitably to its conversion into a form of materialism; Schelling made the necessity of this move explicit. Thus Kantianism reaches the same result as Spinoza. In sum, on Jacobi's account, philosophy arrives at naturalism either directly, along Spinoza's route, or *via* a circuitous transcendental excursus: transcendental philosophy is bound to resolve itself into naturalism, either because it gives priority to empirical knowledge claims, or because, even when does it not do so, its commitment to pure *a priori* thought, as against intuition and *Gefühl*, leaves its constructions without any reality or content, and in order to correct this deficiency, it must surrender itself to nature.

36 The ontological problem is restated by (Adorno 1973, p. 391): 'What Kant alludes to with respect to freedom would apply to God and immortality as well, only more so. For these do not refer to any pure possibility of conduct; their own concepts make them postulates of things in being, no matter of what kind. These entities need a "matter", and in Kant's case they would depend entirely upon that visuality whose possibility he excludes from the transcendent ideas. The pathos of Kantian intelligibility complements the difficulty of ascertaining it in any way ... The concept of the intelligible is not one of a reality, nor is it a concept of something imaginary. It is aporetical, rather.' Adorno shares Jacobi's view of the moral theology as representing a crux of the Enlightenment project: see the extended discussion in (Adorno 1973, pp.361–408).

ent purposes is that, although of course the practical postulates qualify by Kant's official lights as cognitions, the Kantian conception of a practical cognition does not allow a confident answer to be given to the question whether or not the objective reality of practical cognitions as they figure in the moral theology, involves the same robust degree of reality as theoretical reason is able to secure for empirical objects and to think for things in themselves. And this indeterminacy derives from two sources, corresponding to each of the criticisms levelled against the moral theology: from their being grounded in practical reason, and so doubtfully capable of truth; and from their being products of autonomous self-relating reason, and so doubtfully capable of objective reference.

On Jacobi's account, Kant's postulates thus represent an unhappy compromise between recognition of the unshakeable character of the root convictions of natural consciousness, and commitment to the necessity of proof and consequently to the principle which identifies cognition with construction (and which, *per* Jacobi, strips them of ontological commitment). One does not need to accept Jacobi's full diagnosis, however, in order to concur with his assessment of Kant as operating with two models which are in tension with one another: first, of practical reason in its pure form as a *higher form of cognition*, which *grasps the supersensible* with full ontological import;[37] and second, of practical reason in the narrow, plain sense of a power directed to *producing actions*.

The ambiguity that we encounter when we attempt to get the practical postulates into focus – when we try to work out exactly what they commit us to, and what entitlements to knowledge they provide us with – bears a close resemblance, which is certainly not accidental, to the peculiar duck/rabbit effect that Jacobi famously discovered in transcendental idealism: Just as reflection on transcendental idealism from its *inside*, where empirical reality seems secure, leads us *out* to a standpoint from which the doctrine appears, on the contrary, ontologically nihilistic, so similarly the standpoint from which the moral proofs appear effective gives way to a standpoint from which they appear to have gained nothing for practical reason.

---

[37] And which even, like Jacobi's *Glaube*, enjoys a degree of immediacy, in so far as Kant's justifications of the postulates are intended not as deductions but merely for the defence of antecedently formed convictions, spontaneously generated by the moral disposition.

3 The systematic connection

3.1 Kant's augmented sense of a practical postulate

Now I want to try to state the systematic connection in the terms that I promised at the outset.

The concept of a postulate as it emerges from Kant's moral theology is an *augmented* conception, which needs to be distinguished from the *generic* sense of postulate derived from Aristotle via Euclid. The generic sense – which is the sense that Kant intends in the Postulates of Empirical Thought chapter of the first *Critique* – is that of a proposition advanced without proof, which we are invited to accept on the basis that nothing speaks against it, and that it promises to lead to results which will recommend the proposition to us.[38]

Kant's *augmented* conception of a practical postulate incorporates this meaning but has additional, weightier features. It comprises, first, a rationally necessary cognition possessing a distinctive kind of *a priori* warrant, which is neither that of a Kantian deduction nor that of the Kantian *Faktum der Vernunft*, but which emerges uniquely from the *practical* point of view, when (and only when) it reflects on and attempts to coordinate itself with theoretical reason, i.e., when it broaches the standpoint of *reason as a whole*. Second, it occupies an intermediate, *bridging* position in relation to theoretical and practical reason, and on account of this dual citizenship, expresses the unity of Freedom and Nature in a manner which sets it apart from other claims in the Critical system. Third, the practical postulates supply *ideas of reason* with *objective reality*, furnishing end-points which fulfil, rather than boundaries which restrict, human reason: the theological postulates represent the ground of realization of the highest good, which is the highest idea of *practical* reason, and they restore to our cognitive stock the Ideal of Pure Reason, the highest idea of *speculative* reason. They comprise therefore the points in the Critical system where it comes closest to satisfying the Principle of Sufficient Reason.[39]

---

[38] The helpful definition from the *Philosophisches Wörterbuch* (Schmidt 1974, p. 521), is quoted in (Wallner 1985, p. 297n10): '… a demand, an assumption necessitated by material or logico-intuitive (*denkerische*) reasons; lacks strict "proof", but must be posited and made plausible on the basis of facts or for systematic or practical considerations'.

[39] Whether and to what extent theoretical reason's concept of God is redeemed is considered by Kant in Section VII of the Dialectic of Pure Practical Reason, (Kant 1996 [AA 5:137–141]). Here Kant affirms that, notwithstanding the impossibility of any increase in our theoretical knowledge of God by way of practical cognition, the Highest Good allows for – because it presupposes an omniscient, all-beneficent, omnipotent being – the determinate thought of a supersensible

It is in consequence of these features that the practical postulates exhibit the ontological ambiguity which so exercises Jacobi. There are in Kant two vying construals of what it is to *be* a practical postulate. On the one hand, a practical postulate is grasped in terms of its objective referent, an extra-subjective state of affairs specified by the content of a true judgement – a practical postulate is a claim about *how things are*. On the other hand, practical postulates have the character of self-directed *acts*, *commitments*, or *undertakings*, in virtue of which no object (over and above the act itself) is in play – a practical postulate is something that an agent *does*. The intended fusion, but actual collision, of these two construals is manifest when Kant writes that the morally upright man "may well say: I *will* that there be a God, that my existence in this world be also an existence in a pure world of the understanding ... that my duration be endless" (Kant 1996 [AA 5:143]). The emphasis on the first-person practical standpoint, and the continuity of *believing* with moral *doing*,[40] may seem to shelter Kant from the charge that practical cognition of the supersensible violates Critical strictures on transcendent metaphysical knowledge, but at the same time it implies an identification of postulation with mere intra-subjective manipulation of representations, "belief-states", with an exclusively practical end in view, making "honest, wholehearted confidence" in their truth impossible.

3.2 The German Idealist development of Kant's conception

1. *The strategy.* One reaction to Kant's quandary is to embrace the second horn of Kant's dilemma, and to *identify* religious faith with sheer moral striving – the strategy formulated (under Fichte's influence) by Friedrich Karl Forberg (Forberg

---

'*original being* [*Urwesens*]', a 'first being [*ersten Wesens*]' and 'author of the world possessed of the *highest perfection* [Welturhebers von *höchster Vollkommenheit*]' (Kant 1996 [AA 5:139–140]). If this leaves it uncertain whether all elements of the speculative concept of God including that of *ens realissimum* are in play and have been underwritten, the Canon of Pure Reason in the first *Critique* leaves no doubt concerning the objective reality of reason's transcendental Ideal and idea of a necessary being: see (A814–816/B842–844), where Kant says that the moral order leads to the conception of nature as a system of ends originating from an idea, and hence to a '*transcendental theology* – a theology which takes the ideal of supreme ontological perfection ... the absolute necessity of one primordial being'. The speculative concept of God is, therefore, validated (subject to all of Kant's usual qualifications) by means of the practical postulates.
40 In this light it may be said that the mere *propositions* that God exists and that I have an immortal soul (not even, *qua* their logical connections with objects of pure practical reason) are not postulates, but *become* so only as and when I *do* something, viz., postulate their objects in consequence of my moral will.

1912). Another response, which defines the German Idealist reception of Kant's moral theology, is to take the concept of a practical postulate as specifying a *target* – in other words, to view Kant as having at least identified what needs to be provided. On this account, Kant is to be regarded as exactly right about the postulates to the extent that he supposes claims *of such a sort* to be necessary for a system of Critical philosophy, but as having failed to show *that* and *how* Critical philosophy makes them possible. On this view, the Kantian system has overreached itself in the moral theology, yet has done so with all justification. The concept of a practical postulate would thus represent for *progressive* post-Kantians a problem to be solved, and which is to be solved by more idealism rather than less. The value of Kant's practical postulates for German Idealism consists accordingly not in their provision of any philosophical doctrine but in their giving a *forward-looking* definition to the problems of Kantianism – they project the *kind* of philosophical move required in order for those problems to be resolved.

Such a strategy can be held to to take full account of the criticisms levelled by Kant's critics, while drawing an opposed conclusion. According to Jacobi and others taking the side of *Glaube*, the hopelessly compromised, *ersatz* faith offered by Kant's rational religion displays in gross form the futility of the Copernican endeavour to make the subject the ground of all normative claims. At the other extreme, according to Kant's rationalist critics, if the moral theology works, then it can only be because it shows the unavoidable necessity of confidence in the spontaneous products of pure reason; so it leads us back to where we were before the Copernican revolution.[41] On the German Idealist construal, both of these outcomes can be avoided by redeveloping – by, as Schelling puts it, by an *intensification* of – the concept of practical postulation. On this account, practical postulates represent what might be called background, or second-level, transcendental conditions, extrapolated from the front-line conditions of possibility of objects, the conditions which figure in the conclusions of transcendental proofs and which constitute the objects which they condition. Practical postulates – or what began as such in the Kantian system – would accordingly comprise *conditions of the conditions* which directly make objects (theoretical and practical) possible. They would satisfy Critical strictures and retain a claim to being properly transcendental, while having potentially the same *reach* as the intuitions of reason to which early modern rationalism laid claim: they would comprise, as it were, pure reason rehabilitated, purged of dogmatic contamination. The postulate strategy thus holds out the promise – already intimated in

---

[41] This is the implication of Johann August Eberhard's critique of Kantian philosophy – see (Eberhard 1793 and 1799) – and, in a different way, of Maimon's.

Kant's claim for a "practico-dogmatic metaphysics" – of recouping, on properly Critical grounds, the sphere of speculative metaphysics.

This claim of logical continuity is supported if we look at Kant's essay, "What Does it Mean to Orientate Oneself in Thinking?" (1786) (Kant 1996b [AA 8:137–139]). Here Kant is trying to walk a straight path between Jacobi's *Glaube* and the dogmatic rationalism of Mendelssohn, in the context of the Pantheismusstreit. Kant is required accordingly to show that the Critical philosophy delivers claims regarding the supersensible which are more than notionally distinct from those of dogmatic metaphysics, yet at the same time sufficiently robust to satisfy a theist. To this end Kant refers to, as he puts it, "*the right* of reason's *need* [*das Recht* des *Bedürfnisses* der Vernunft]", where he means reason in *general*, as opposed to simply the rights and needs of *practical* reason. And Kant affirms that the notion of a right based on a need extends to speculative reason as well:[42] theoretical reason has, Kant says, a legitimate need to take the *existence* of an original and highest being as the ground of all possibility; reason needs not just to "take the concept" of an unlimited being as the ground of the possibility of all things, but to presuppose "its *existence*" – "so geht dieses Bedürfniß auch auf die Voraussetzung des *Daseins* desselben" – and to do so in the mode of holding it true, *Fürwahrhalten* (Kant 1996b [AA 8:137–138]).[43] This existential assumption goes beyond, Kant again makes clear, the mere regulative use of reason.[44] But, Kant adds immediately, the necessity here is merely "subjective" and yields "only a necessary *presupposition*", since, he reminds us, a *need* of reason should not be mistaken for an *insight* (that being the mistake of the dogmatic rationalist) (Kant 1996b, [AA 8:138n]).

This of course recalls the acute difficulty pinpointed by Jacobi – what can it mean to talk of a necessary presupposition incorporating an ontological claim and possessing truth, which is nonetheless to be regarded as *merely* subjective? – but the key, *new* point which has come to light here is Kant's recognition that there is need for something, some principle, to lie *behind* practical reason. Such a principle could not derive its authority from the moral fact of reason, but would instead provide a general *principle of warrant* for taking reason to have at least potential ontological significance, and the principle of the primacy

---

42 The passages in question are at (Kant 1996b [AA 8:137–139]).
43 Compare the later discussion in (Kant 2000 [AA 5:402]), where existentially committed belief is not affirmed.
44 The regulative use of theoretical reason – 'Erfahrungsgebrauche unserer Vernunft' – is what Kant has been describing in the preceding paragraph (Kant 1996b [AA 8:136–137]), and it does not require that the right of reason's need be invoked.

of practical reason would be only a special form of this principle.[45] In this light, the Fichte-Schelling construal of a highest postulate – to which I will now return – represents the next step that needs to be taken, *if* the Kantian theory of the rights of reason is to be differentiated from that of the dogmatic rationalist, *and* to meet Jacobi's objection that it results in mere fictions.

2. *Fichte.* The augmented sense of practical postulate matches what we saw in the 1804 Wissenschaftslehre, where Fichte affirmed an ultimate point of identity between ontology and normativity, a point where being is grasped *as Sollen*, which reflection on empirically determined consciousness cannot attest to the reality of, and which therefore cannot be legitimated as a front-line condition of possibility of objects,[46] but which we are bound to presuppose in its background, as an "upstream" or second-level transcendental condition. The crux of this argument, we saw, lies in the idea of an imperative or practical judgement, a *Sollen*, that testifies to the reality of (by containing insight into) its own presupposed, theoretically conceived ground: which represents exactly the target defined by Kant's employment in the moral theology of the concept of a practical postulate.[47] So the Wissenschaftslehre can be held to have done what Kant showed *needs* to be done for the sake of the moral theology, but failed to actually *do*, and it has moreover taken up the problems of the moral theology in a generalized form, yielding a *general* solution to the problem of transcendental proof. As Fichte puts it, in 1804 (Fichte 2005), what we have grasped is that in the case at hand "the bare possibility of this presupposition shows its truth and correctness" (Fichte 2005, pp. 144–145 [FW: X, 243]).[48]

---

45 K. F. A. Schelling quotes a lecture fragment from 1803 (Schelling 1988), in which Schelling describes Kant as positing as many reasons as he wrote *Critiques*: 'one may ask him: Where is the Reason of these Reasons?' (Schelling 1988 [SW: V, viii]).

46 Hence Fichte's emphasis on the problematic, hypothetical, merely presuppositional character of the *initial* assumption of the *Sollen*: we 'present [it] only hypothetically as a declaration of pure consciousness ... which we append to being only mediately as an inference' (Fichte 2005, p. 122 [FW: X, 215]).

47 These are defined, in the *Jäsche Logic* (Kant 1992, [AA 9:86–87]), as 'theoretical' (because they express not 'what ought to be' or 'a possible free action', but rather 'what is') but not 'speculative' (because imperatives can be 'derived from them').

48 We began with 'a mere *presupposition*, grounding the process of our proof regarding the essence of the absolute, but itself based on nothing', but 'this presupposition proves its *correctness* simply by its mere possibility and facticity' (Fichte 2005, p. 148 [FW: X, 247]); 'this presupposition is now proven by its facticity and possibility' (Fichte 2005, p. 150 [FW: X, 249]); 'we immediately proved the legitimacy of this presupposition by means of its bare possibility and facticity' (Fichte 2005, p. 154 [FW: X, 254]).

The 1804 Wissenschaftslehre, I suggest, resolves the ambiguities of the Jena Wissenschaftslehre, which, we can now see, were inherited directly from Kant: Fichte's difficulty in determining whether or not the absolute self has *being*, or is merely an *idea*, the projected object of our striving, reproduces the difficulty that Kant's critics identified in determining whether or not the theological postulates can be thought to have objective reality.[49]

3. *Schelling*. Again, Kant's augmented sense of postulate is continuous with what we find in Schelling in the writings I discussed earlier, and also, even more clearly, in his *Philosophische Briefe*, written slightly earlier than the *Abhandlungen*.

This text consists of a critical response to Kant's moral theology and a mediation of Kant and Spinoza.[50] The two tasks are intimately connected. The mediation of Kant and Spinoza requires above all, on Schelling's account, that we understand the distinction of criticism from dogmatism correctly. And for two reasons he chooses Kant's moral theology as the territory on which to pursue

---

[49] This bears on the issue explored in (Ameriks 2000). In so far as Fichte is construed as pursuing a global strategy of attempting to vindicate epistemological propositions on moral grounds by extending drastically the scope of the principle of the primacy of practical reason, the foundation of which lies in the fact of pure practical reason, it is right to wonder if the *Faktum der Vernunft* can bear the considerable burden imposed upon it. If it cannot, then it must be concluded that the Wissenschaftslehre reproduces the weaknesses of Kant's moral theology on a larger scale – which was in fact just the complaint of Schelling after his break with Fichte, and of Hegel (as discussed below; see notes 93 and 94). Whether or not this is a correct estimate of Fichte's Jena position, it is clear that in the 1804 Wissenschaftslehre, at least, he does not lean on the principle of the primacy of practical reason as Kant left it: here Fichte aims to solve the problems surrounding the idea that practical reason has authority for theoretical reflection, which he perceives as bound up with general problems attending the transcendental method. Providing some evidence that Fichte had taken the lesson of Kant's critics and was attuned from the very outset to the problems attending practical foundationalism – whether or not the Jena Wissenschaftslehre made a good job of it – see the opening of 'Praktische Philosophie' (Fichte 1971b, [FW/GA: II, III, 181–182]), and (Breazeale 2004, pp. 67–68), suggesting that the Wissenschaftslehre be viewed as a response to the manifest strain of practical postulation, as revealed in Fichte's *Kritik aller Offenbarung*.

[50] As noted earlier, Schelling was exposed to argument concerning the relation of Kantian philosophy to Christian belief at the Tübingen Stift. Henrich 1997 argues for the key role of Immanuel Diez in articulating dissatisfaction, on 'radical Kantian' grounds, with the attempts of Storr and his school at an accommodation of Kant's philosophy with Christian orthodoxy. Schelling's abreaction to Christianized Kantianism is evidenced in his letter to Hegel, 6 January 1795; in (Frank/Kurz 1975, pp. 117–120). The *Philosophische Briefe* are doubtless targeted above all against the Christian appropriation of Kant, but the scope of Schelling's discussion goes far beyond what is required to challenge claims for the agreement of Kantianism with revealed religion.

this aim: first because it is the part of Kant's system which has been most conspicuously perverted by religious conservatives, who have misunderstood the distinction of criticism from dogmatism; and second because it is, at the same time, the part of the system in which the *spirit* of Kantianism comes closest to receiving open expression.

Schelling presents accordingly a detailed critique of the moral theology, the upshot of which, however, is not abandonment of practical postulation, but its *reinstatement*, in the form of absolute cognition grounded on *freedom* – which is the real ground of criticism's distinction from dogmatism, and the true respect in which criticism represents a philosophically higher position. Schelling describes the two systems as distinguished by the different *spirit* of their practical postulates, freedom supplying that of critical postulates (Schelling 1980b, p. 190 [SW: I, 333]). Kant's theism having been disposed of, practical postulation is re-associated with the anti-theism of Spinoza, whose realism it absorbs, counter-balancing Kantian idealism.[51] And it is also associated by Schelling with tragedy: in an anticipation of the general view of art taken in the 1800 *System* (Schelling 1978), Schelling describes the state of mind of the tragic protagonist, which tragic art allows us to enter into, as a unification of opposites – of man *vs.* world, subject *vs.* "absolute object", freedom *vs.* necessity, and so on. Tragedy is thus an alternative form which philosophy's absolute postulate, or intellectual intuition, may take (Schelling 1980b, p. 157 [SW: I, 285]).

The argument of Schelling's *Philosophische Briefe* centres on his repudiation of the, as he sees it, pseudo-Kantian strategy of positing a *weakened* theoretical reason, the "system of weak reason" (Schelling 1980b, p. 161 [SW: I, 290]).[52] In addition to generating the paradoxes exposed by Jacobi and other Kantians (Schelling 1980b, pp. 159 and 191n [SW: I, 287–288 and 333n]),[53] the strategy makes no sense since, once a new field of cognition has been opened up by

---

51 In an elevated form, of course, that goes beyond the naively dogmatic.
52 The view of the relation of theoretical and practical reason taken here is explained earlier in *Vom Ich*. Here Schelling observes that 'Kant's theoretical philosophy is not connected with the practical by a common principle. His practical philosophy does not seem to be one-and-the-same structure with the theoretical; instead it seems to be a mere annex to his philosophy as a whole and, what is more, an annex wide open to attacks from the main building' (Schelling 1980, pp. 65–66 [SW: I, 154]). The remedy for this disunity is to translate the practical back into the theoretical, by grasping that practical cognition is *non-objectual:* 'To be sure, according to Kant, practical philosophy leads into the supersensuous domain because, in its turn, it annihilates everything that is theoretical and reestablishes what is intuited intellectually ...' (Schelling 1980, pp. 99–100 [SW: I, 201–202]).
53 Conclusions cannot be drawn from mere needs, and if they are drawn, then they require theoretical support (Schelling 1980b, p. 158 [SW: I, 286–287]).

an "intensified [verstärkten]" practical reason, theoretical reason has every right to take possession of what has been discovered; indeed, theoretical reason may be regarded as itself *transformed* by intensified practical cognition (Schelling 1980b, pp. 158–159 [SW: I, 287]). Moreover, the "system of weak reason" fails to refute dogmatism, but merely demonstrates its indemonstrability (Schelling 1980b, p. 164 [SW: I, 295]), leaving dogmatism sufficiently intact to threaten to destroy the practical foundations of the moral theology.[54] What is needed is a conclusive, prior victory over dogmatism in the *theoretical* sphere, and this demands that we proceed to a higher point than that of the *Critique of Pure Reason*. In short, the moral theology demands that we re-engage with questions in theoretical philosophy – in fact, with the highest question of all, that of the existence of the world, the egress of finite beings from the absolute (Schelling 1980b, pp. 164, 174, 177 [SW: I, 294, 310, 313–314]),[55] which subsumes the lower-level questions of the relation of subject and object, and of the possibility of experience. But it *also* tells us how those questions should be addressed, namely through a further augmentation of the concept of a practical postulate, which we should now conceive as a "*productive* realization" on the part of the practical faculty, by which the system of freedom *obtains reality* (Schelling 1980b, p. 171 [SW: I, 305]): "the theoretical question necessarily becomes a practical postulate" (Schelling 1980b, p. 175 [SW: I, 311]).[56] And this practical postulate also represents, Schelling claims, Spinoza's true (albeit inadequately expressed) insight.[57]

---

[54] A 'breath of dogmatism would overthrow your house of cards': (Schelling 1980b, p. 161 [SW: I, 290]).

[55] As an assertion of the absolute in human knowledge, it is 'groundless' and 'can have no further ground' (Schelling 1980b, p. 173 [SW: I, 308]).

[56] Schelling adds an explanation for why reason should *appear* weak: the 'absolute freedom in you ... makes the intellectual world inaccessible to every *objective* power' (Schelling 1980b, p. 195 [SW: I, 340]).

[57] Spinoza framed his insight, Schelling claims, in terms of merely analytic propositions: (Schelling 1980b, pp. 173–174, 178, 181 [SW: I, 309–310, 315, 319]).

The critique of Kant's moral theology in this text has many elements. I have referred already to (1) the alleged incoherence of the moral theology regarding truth and practical reason, and (2) the allegedly misguided strategy of weakening theoretical reason. Schelling's view is that the relevant properties of cognitive strength – capacity or incapacity to grasp the supersensible – cannot be localized to particular 'forms' of reason: if practical reason can grasp the supersensible, then this must be true of theoretical reason as well; practical reason testifies to theoretical reason's capacity to do the same. If the concept of God is not theoretically legitimate, then practical reason is not entitled to employ it (Schelling 1980b, p. 158 [SW: I, 286]). But several other important charges are also laid: (3) To the extent that the moral theology allows itself to be appropriated by dogmatism, this is because it is grounded on what has been conceived in abstract

4. The favourable and unfavourable treatments of practical postulation that we find in the German Idealists can be regarded as two sides of the same coin. If we look at the series of German Idealist treatments of Kant's moral theology – the list of writings I gave at the beginning – we see a progressive reversal of estimate concerning its value. At the outset, in 1792, Fichte endorses the moral theology and extends the scope of the practical postulates that emerge from the antinomy of practical reason to include revelation and transcendental idealism itself. At about the same time Hegel subscribes to the moral theology as a framework for developing his thoughts about religion, morality, and their regeneration. Later Schelling criticizes the detail of Kant's moral theology, dismissing Kant's antinomy of practical reason and the theistic resolution thereof, but proposes an overhauled, Spinozistic version which he claims captures its true spirit. Finally, in the *Phenomenology*, Hegel declares it a "whole nest" of "thoughtless contradictions" (Hegel 1977a, § 617, p. 374 [HW: III, 452]).[58] On the account I

---

terms as a mere *method*, which as such (like all methods) is necessarily *neutral* between dogmatism and criticism. The merely *methodological* conception of practical postulation which is deployed in the moral theology is thus inadequate (see note 124 below). (4) The moral theology is ethically limited and aesthetically null. To posit a 'moral god', a God *'under moral laws'*, in order to guarantee our indestructibility, is to annihilate the possibility of the sublime; sublimity belongs to tragedy, which allows that we may perish in the struggle with 'the immeasurable'. The positing of a moral god 'keeps the world within bounds', and interposes something between the world and myself, with the result that my intuition of the world is 'restricted', and that the 'abandonment' of myself to the world which marks tragedy – our confrontation with 'the immeasurable' – becomes impossible. Nor is the moral theology compatible with beauty, the proper principle of which is 'reciprocal yielding in contest', again the prerogative of tragedy. Moral theism thus has no 'aesthetic side': it negates the possibility of aesthetic value (Schelling 1980b, p. 157 [SW: I, 284–285]). (5) The moralized conception of God is in any case destroyed once we, having achieved practical cognition of God, reflect on what God's reality involves, namely, the transmoral reality of Spinoza's God *sive* Nature. Thus Schelling talks of destroying the moral theology once we retrace our steps (Schelling 1980b, p. 160 [SW: I, 289]). (6) The highest good, conceived as 'rewarding happiness', is a 'moral delusion', an incoherent *'assignat'* (Schelling 1980b, pp. 183–184 [SW: I, 322–323]). Properly interpreted, the highest good is a beatitude identical with absolute freedom (Schelling 1980b, pp. 184–185 and 187–188 [SW: I, 324 and 328–329]).

Specific criticism of Kant's theological postulates is also contained in *Vom Ich* (Schelling 1980, pp. 96–97 [SW: I, 197–198]), in *Abhandlungen* (Schelling 1994, pp. 137–138 [SW: I, 451–452]), where Schelling claims that Kant's claims concerning God and immortality fail to qualify as postulates, and in (Schelling 1927–59), which refers scathingly to Kantians who reintroduce by the back door of philosophy what has been expelled from the front, and again insists that deeming a concept a practical postulate cannot circumvent the theoretical question 'nach dem letzten Grund der Realität' (Schelling 1980b, SW: I, 476).

58 Restated in the *Encyclopedia Logic*, § 60 (Hegel 1975, pp. 90–91 [HW: VIII, 141–142]).

have suggested, this may be seen as a matter of using, and finally kicking away, a philosophical ladder: once everything necessary had been extracted from Kant's moral theology, there remained nothing to say about Kant's practical postulates beyond indicating how they fall short of the *desiderata* of systematic unification which they themselves implied, and which the new post-Kantian idealism claimed to meet.

This conception of the moral theology as defining the conditions of adequacy for post-Kantian idealism is reflected in the way that it recurs in the internecine strife of German Idealism. Schelling and Hegel, in the *Differenzschrift* of 1801 and *Kritisches Journal* essays of 1802 (Schelling 2000, pp. 371–374 [SW: V, 112–117]),[59] deploy against Fichte objections which follow closely the pattern of those that had been put a decade previously to Kant's moral theology – Fichtean idealism is, in effect, charged with reproducing its incoherences in magnified form.[60] The theme returns in the late Schelling's Hegel critique: Hegel's "pure-rational" philosophy, Schelling maintains, grinds to a halt at exactly the same point as Kant's postulate of God's existence, that is, before the transition has been made from mere ideation to actual existence.[61]

6. To recapitulate, and to return to the material discussed in the first part of this paper, we can see how, under pressure from the two objections to the moral

---

[59] The charge that Fichte's idealism reproduces the limitations of Kant's philosophy as displayed in the moral theology is made in (Schelling 1984, p. 22 [SW: IV, 326]), and (Schelling 1988, p. 54 [SW: II, 72]): the validity of subject-object identity is restricted by Fichte to subjective consciousness, and the absolute is reduced to the mere '*object* of an endless *task*, an absolute *demand*'; Fichte, like Kant, excludes absoluteness from speculation and seeks to reconnect it with the deepest subjectivity only through action and faith; Schelling refers to passages in the *Grundlage* where Fichte identifies absolute unity with the object of an Idea understood merely as '*something that ought to exist*'.

[60] Schelling, letter to Fichte, 3 October 1801 (Frank/Kurz 1975, p. 162): 'in order to *uphold your system*, one must *decide* at the outset to proceed from Seeing [Sehen] and to have no more to do with the Absolute (the truly speculative), roughly in the way that, in Kantian philosophy, the moral law must come first and God last, if the system is to hold up' (my translation).

[61] In passages from the late *Philosophy of Revelation*, Schelling returns to Kant's postulate of God's existence. This he now interprets as a *demand* 'for an extension' of philosophy which Kant was unable to follow through: lacking any concept of theoretical philosophy that is not that of a 'mere science of reason', Schelling says, Kant was forced to conceptualize it as a demand that 'only had significance for action [*die Praxis*]', whereas its true and proper fulfilment lies in 'positive philosophy' (Schelling 2007, p. 191 [SW: XIII, 146]). Schelling directs this same point against Hegel, whose 'rational', 'pure-rational' philosophy reproduces the limitations of a subjective moral need ('subjektive oder moralische Notwendigkeit') which demands the reality of God in a form (namely: as 'das Überseiende') which it cannot accommodate (Schelling 1977, p. 135).

theology, Kant's problematic notion of practical postulation evolves in German Idealism in three stages:

(i) In Fichte's Jena Wissenschaftslehre, the concept of a postulate remains practical in Kant's sense of invoking the principle of the primacy of practical reason, but it is, crucially, disconnected from the highest good and antinomy of practical reason analyzed in Kant's second *Critique*. This is shown by the way in which, we saw, Fichte in the Wissenschaftslehre *nova methodo* identifies what he calls "Kant's postulate" – in the singular – not with any proposition or doctrine sanctioned *by* the principle of the primacy of pure practical reason, but with that principle itself.

(ii) Then, in the move from the Jena to the 1804 Wissenschaftslehre, postulation remains thought through and as *Sollen*, but the *subject* of obligation – that which *soll* – is no longer the *Ich*, but *being* – the absolute – itself. The *Sollen* in application to the absolute no longer has a determinately moral character. Fichte thereby brings himself partially into line with Schelling, but remains separated from him by his insistence that *Sollen* provides the exclusive route to, and is equiprimordial with, absolute *Seyn*.

(iii) In Schelling's conception, the *Sollen* is side-lined, in so far as it is adduced merely in order to provide the basis on which we are entitled to postulate the *universal validity* of our intellectual intuition. This might seem to make Schelling's notion of postulation theoretical rather than practical, but he continues to affirm also its intrinsic practical significance, and this is readily intelligible, since it is for Schelling an *expression* – and not a *representation* – of freedom: Schelling's absolute postulate supplies the immediate ground of moral consciousness, which it therefore implicates.

The resulting notion, whether we take Fichte's version or Schelling's, preserves all three of the original Kantian features – rationally necessary cognition, which reflects the standpoint of reason as a whole, and realizes its highest ideas – with the differences that, because postulation has been released from its subservience to the highest good, the first objection is disarmed – philosophy's postulates are conceptually autonomous, not instrumental – and the ontological ambiguity has been removed – the existential commitment is unequivocal.

Fichte and Schelling's positions, as they stand at the end of this development, can of course be stated without reference to Kant's moral theology, but this eventual conceptual independence does not detract from the fact that the development and formulation of the notion of absolute postulation was undertaken in light of their perception of the philosophical *potential* of Kant's practical postulates. If we want to locate the point where German Idealism comes closest to explicitly acknowledging this debt, while at the same time affirming the self-sufficiency of the newly developed notion and its ultimate conceptual independence from its Kantian ancestor, then the place to look is Hegel's *Differenz* essay and *Glauben und Wissen*.[62]

4 Contrasting post-Kantian developments

In order to throw into relief the distinctive way in which Fichte and Schelling pursue Kant's conception of practical postulation, we may contrast their treatments of the practical postulates and moral theology with those of three other post-Kantians, namely Jakob Sigismund Beck, Jakob Friedrich Fries, and Novalis.

---

[62] See the account of Kantian faith as reflection's relation to the Absolute (Hegel 1977b, p. 100 [HW: II, 31–32], and (Hegel 1977, pp. 94–96, 156, 178, 187 [HW: II, 329–332, 395–396, 418–419, 428–429]) – moral faith is recognized as the highest point reached in the Kantian system, the point where it comes closest to the Absolute. This assessment endured: in a letter to Duboc, 30 July 1822, Hegel writes: 'However, besides the other merits of the Kantian philosophy, I still wish to point out how interesting and instructive it is to see in Kant's so-called postulates not only the necessity of the Idea but also the more precise definition of it' (Hegel 1984, p. 492 [*Briefe*, Bd. II, 1813–1822, no. 422, p. 327]). In the 'Postulates of Reason' section of the *Differenzschrift* (Hegel 1977b, pp. 111–112 [HW: II, 42–44]), which follows the discussion of transcendental intuition, Hegel exhibits a complex ambivalence regarding the concept of a postulate: the Idea itself cannot be postulated, but its intuitional complement is postulated by Reason, yet not in opposition to the Idea, though 'this whole manner of postulating' is also, viewed from another angle, merely due to the fact that one-sided reflection has been taken as a starting point, the effect of which is distorting, since reason thereby appears 'needy'. The upshot, I suggest, is that when Hegel describes Reason, liberated from reflection, as 'positing absoluteness', 'both Idea and Being', he might just as well have called it an absolute postulate. It is noteworthy, in this connection, that in the Lectures on the Philosophy of Religion Hegel affirms that religious consciousness proceeds, as Kant and Fichte maintain, via the necessity of a *presupposition*, while insisting that this presupposition is not merely subjective; its appearance as merely 'the activity and so forth' of the subject is only one 'moment' (Hegel 1824, pp. 212–214 [HW: XVII, 269–270]).

Hegel's position in these texts, from 1801 and 1802, is related to the intellectual development exhibited in the Jugendschriften in the following way: In the course of the 1790s, after initially affirming the unqualified adequacy of Kant's moral theology in the 1793 Tübingen essay on religion (Hegel 2002), Hegel discovers the problem (as he perceives it) that Kant is stuck with a flat opposition of Ought to Is. This problem is made explicit in the later *Spirit of Christianity* text (Hegel 1996), but at this point Hegel either does not perceive it as a deep metaphysical problem in its full generality or is without the means to address it. Schelling's identity philosophy provides Hegel with this means, allowing him in the 1801–02 essays to reject the moral theology from a standpoint that has surpassed it.

4.1 Beck

Beck's proposal is that Kant's theory of empirical knowledge be construed as a *theory of postulates*, and even more fundamentally, that the very transcendental *Standpunct* of Critical philosophy itself be regarded as defined by and around a single postulate, of what he calls "original representing", *ursprüngliche Vorstellen*. On Beck's account, the application of the categories – in for example the subject-predicate synthesis, whereby something permanent is posited as underlying the empirical manifold – presupposes (indeed, consists in) an "*activity [Handlung]* of objective relation", "*original attribution [ursprüngliche Beilegung]*", "*original procedure (or use) of the understanding [ursprüngliche Verstandesverfahren]*". This activity, whereby the category of for example substance is given application, is one that, we discover, *must* be performed if we are to satisfy the imperative "Conceive of being presented with an object!" or "Produce the synthetic unity of consciousness!" or "Represent originally!"[63] The categories are thus reconstrued as determinate functions realized in acts, as modes of *Vorstellen* as opposed to *Vorstellungen*, our consciousness of which is what gives our representations objective reference (and at the same time generates the "I think" of the objective synthetic unity of apperception). By treating application of the categories on the model of a geometer's acts of mental imaging in compliance with postulates, Beck aims to give transcendental claims the same degree of certainty and perspicuity.

Beck's early letters to Kant suggest that he was motivated originally to develop this theory by the difficulties that he considered created by Kant's definition of intuition in terms of "immediate relation to an object", which, Beck supposes, contradicts the Transcendental Deduction's claim that the categories are necessary for objectivity.[64] Beck's full view, however, which he develops in two books in 1796,[65] is that recognition of an original use of the understanding in "original representing" is strictly required for a correct understanding of *all* core Kantian notions – including the absolutely basic notion of "the possibility of experience", as Critical philosophy understands it – and that without it Kantianism becomes dogmatic. Dogmatic Kantianism is what results when transcendental phi-

---

[63] 'Stelle ursprünglich vor!', (Beck 1796b, § 9). These are alternative but according to Beck equivalent formulations of the *Postulat*.
[64] And not in the first instance, although this comes immediately to the fore, the problem of the thing in itself.
[65] Expounded in (Beck 1796a) and (Beck 1796b) and neatly summarized in his letters to (Kant: 17 June 1794, no. 630, [AA 11:509–511]) (Kant 1999, pp. 479–480), and (20 June 1797, no. 754, 12:164–169) (Kant 1999, pp. 512–515).

losophy is construed as a matter of discursive proof-giving, a methodology which is futile – since it leaves us with mere shells of philosophical concepts, to which no real sense or meaning attaches – and which provokes a new skepticism (which it is unable to answer). The presentation of the theory of experience in the *Critique of Pure Reason* follows a dogmatic route, Beck allows, but it does so only for heuristic purposes, in letter but not in spirit; Kant was obliged to begin within his readers' "dogmatic cast of mind", in order to lead them out of it (Beck 1796b, § 71).

Though his own intentions were limited to overhauling the exposition of Kant's theoretical philosophy without any alteration of its teachings, with a view to rendering it consistent and immune to skeptical attack, Beck's theory of a postulate of original representing departs from Kant in important, indeed, proto-Fichtean ways.[66] But while in some set of terms Beck's theory counts as a radical innovation, his employment of the concept of a postulate goes beyond that of Kant in the Postulates of Empirical Thought in only a limited respect. Kant claims in the Postulates chapter that the objective application of modal concepts involves a reflective, second-order appraisal of previously given objective cognitions: to say that an object is possible is to judge that the cognition of it is consistent with the principles of possible experience (Beck 1796b, §§ 49–52). Beck preserves this idea: to say that a certain category is necessary for experience is to say that the corresponding act must be performed if there is to be objective representation. The key element that Beck adds is the notion that, in order to undertake such an appraisal, it is necessary to *occupy the standpoint* of object-representation in a *non*-discursive, proto-phenomenological sense: Beck talks of the necessity of *transposing ourselves* ("sich versetzen") into the *situation* wherein all experience is generated.[67] In so doing Beck draws the Kantian sense of postulate back to its Euclidean root: in place of the mere *analogy* that Kant implies of the principles which govern the use of modal categories with the postulates of Euclid, Beck envisages geometrical cognition as a sub-instance of the very same *kind* of postulate-based cognition as, on his account, constitutes transcendental philosophical knowledge in general.[68]

---

[66] Note that, whether or not Beck's account eliminates sensation and sensibility in Fichtean fashion – the charge levelled by Schulz – and whether or not it improves Kant's situation overall, Beck (i) deprives Kant of his preferred retort to the charge of Berkeleyanism, and (ii) undercuts the non-empirical employment of the categories that Kant wishes to preserve.

[67] 'Ich ... suche meinen Leser in die Handlung selbst zu versetzen'; letter to Kant, 17 June 1794, no. 630 (Kant 1999, p. 480 [AA 11:510]). And see (Beck 1796b, § 91).

[68] '... this production of the synthetic unity of consciousness "the *original attribution* [*ursprüngliche Beilegung*]". It is this activity, among others, that the geometer postulates when he starts

Beck's notion of a postulate of original representing is thus clearly different from the notion of practical postulation employed in the moral theology. Indeed it might well be thought that on Beck's terms there *could not be* postulates in the sense of the moral theology, since postulation is tied by Beck to an *object's being given* in the synthetic unity of apperception, and the practical postulates certainly do not give objective reality to ideas of reason in that way. But in fact, and surprisingly, this is not what Beck says. Instead, Beck draws up an account of practical reason in an attempted parallel with his account of theoretical reason, maintaining that there is *also* a postulate of an "original use" of *practical* reason, whereby we conceive ourselves as non-natural causes capable of determining our wills independently of all natural influence. (Beck 1796b, Part II, §§ 208 – 233) The obvious problem with this strategy – which is forced on Beck by his agreement to follow Kant in matters of morality and religion, rather than handing them over to the *Glaubensphilosophen* – is the absence of any common feature, beyond the mere title, of the original theoretical and practical postulates: Beck gives no clue as to *how* an original act of the practical faculty can give rise to, or yield knowledge of, our existence as extra-empirical agents, in the way that an original act of the understanding can allow objects to be given. If practical postulation parallels theoretical postulation, then free causality ought to be phenomenologically immanent – which would convert practical reason into intellectual intuition (as well as undercutting Kant's identification of freedom with morality).[69]

---

his geometry from the proposition "Conceive of space"; and no discursive representation whatsoever could take its place for this purpose. As I see the matter, the postulate "To conceive of an object by means of the original attribution" is also the highest principle of philosophy as a whole', Beck to Kant, 17 June 1794, no. 630 (Kant 1999, pp. 479 – 480 [AA 11:509]). Note that Beck's concept of postulate, as my account has revealed, involves two separable elements: the (single) *imperative* that defines transcendental reflection and which demands a pre-discursive act (postulates as *per* Euclid, e. g., 'Represent an object!', which as Beck says (Beck 1796b, § 8) cannot be equated with a hypothesis; and the (plural) non-imperatival, theoretical, discursive *principles* that transcendental reflection leads us to grasp (postulates as *per* Kant's Postulates of Empirical Thought). The latter are discussed in some detail in (Beck 1796b, §§ 49 – 52). The connection of the two senses is nonetheless clear: postulates-as-principles are what result from the dissection and exhibition (Beck 1796b, § 9) of the original use of the understanding which the imperatival postulate commands.

69 The result is massively revisionary of Kant in several respects. If Beck is right that extra-natural freedom is involved in practical reason, then it must be epistemically prior to morality – perhaps in agreement with the *Groundwork of the Metaphysics of Morals*, Pt. III, but *contra* the *Critique of Practical Reason*. This indeed seems to be acknowledged, since in (Beck 1796b, § 215), Beck makes the Formula of Universal Law the expression of freedom, hence, presumably, epistemically derived from our knowledge of our freedom. Second, if Beck were correct, then

What Beck has specifically declined, with his attempted parallelism of theoretical and practical postulates, is the distinctive ambition of Kant's notion of a practical postulate to *straddle* the two spheres. It is no accident, therefore, that in Beck's own exposition of Kant's moral theology, no mention is made of postulates, and the distinctive and complex character of Kant's theological postulates, with all of the problems that surround them, gives way to the plain and simple identification of religious belief with *hope*, or an attitude of mere *confidence* that one will achieve one's moral goal.[70] Schelling's critique of Beck, in the 1797–98 *Abhandlungen* (Schelling 1994, pp. 112–119 [SW: I, 135]),[71] accordingly highlights and takes issue with the conservative character of Beck's revision of the concept of a postulate, which leaves the operations of the Verstand disjoined from the Ideas of Vernunft, and the latter outside the scope of theoretical cognition.

4.2 Fries

The interest of Fries in the present context lies in his showing how, while accepting the central thrust of Jacobi's critique of Kant's moral theology and of Critical philosophy in general, one might nevertheless attempt to rescue the Kantian system in the service of theistic ends. Fries aims to broker a reconciliation between

---

prima facie we would have cognition of ourselves as intelligible causes, and this would count as a piece of theoretical knowledge (it would be 'practical' only in the sense of being *facilitated* by willing). Beck attempts to head off this implication by saying that although we thereby conceive ourselves as intelligible entities with an intelligible character, 'all conception of the intelligible escapes us and is unintelligible' (Beck 1796b, § 217). But this is hard to understand: if an original use of understanding yields intelligibility, why should an original use of practical reason not do so? Again, Beck says in (Beck 1796b, § 228) that the concept of freedom has 'no theoretical, objective validity', because it is 'only an original use of reason', which has 'no original use of understanding for a basis', but it is hard to understand why it should need to have such a basis. In (Beck 1796b, § 214) Beck draws an analogy with the transcendental unity of apperception, but does not say what 'the original unity of practical reason' amounts to.

70 Beck says in (Beck 1796b, § 240) that the agent's supposition that he will attain his end of achieving a holy will and that nature will be consonant with a moral order leads him to *believe in* God, but that this belief does not connect with theoretical judgement, since it is nothing but a *confident* hope (Beck 1796b, § 241). In (Beck 1796b, § 249) Beck asserts that belief in God and immortality, resting on a morally good disposition aiming at a moral world-order, constitutes religion and favours morality, but leaves it unclear whether he follows Kant's moral proof.

71 Schelling objects that (among other things) Beck's postulate of primordial representation is merely theoretical and rests on a concept that it cannot make intelligible, viz. that of primordial representation (Schelling 1994, p. 118 [SW: I, 423]), and 'leaves practical philosophy without any foundation' (Schelling 1994, p. 121 [SW: I, 427]).

Kant and Jacobi, by recruiting Kantian resources to the defence of a philosophy of *Glauben* – to meet the demands, which Jacobi repudiates, of *Wissenschaft*, by giving a *wissenschaftlich* account of *Glauben* itself.

Fries takes it as given, in light of the criticisms of Schulze and Maimon, that in general so-called transcendental proofs *prove* nothing of ontological import: the Analogies of Experience for example show only that human reason has the *need to presuppose, das Bedürfnis vorauszusetzen*, the truth of their principles (Fries 1828, pp. xvii–xviii).[72] Kant's so-called moral proofs of the theological ideas are, in parallel, no more successful in getting us beyond mere necessities of representation: the arguments rest on the presupposition of moral consciousness, the necessity of which has merely factical, psychological status, and in any case they merely lead us in a circle (because, Fries claims, they show God, freedom and immortality to be in turn presuppositions of the validity of the moral law).[73] But instead of following Jacobi in rejecting wholesale the Critical endeavour,[74] Fries infers that transcendental enquiry should be reconstrued as what he calls "philosophische Anthropologie", that is, in the first instance, empirical psychology. What Kant's misunderstanding of his deductions as proofs brings us to see, Fries claims, here following Jacobi, is Kant's perpetuation of the rationalist dogmatic "prejudice", *Vorurtheil*, that cognition presupposes proof. Once this prejudice is overcome, we are able to return with full confidence to the immediate convictions of natural consciousness, and these include, *per* Fries, the truth of Kant's practical postulates: "we defend the rights of belief [Glauben] primarily by showing that knowledge, too, arises only subjectively in reason" (Fries 1989, p. 69).

Fries' reconstruction of the Critical philosophy salvages therefore a large quantity of Kantian doctrine, including Kant's theism, while sacrificing entirely its foundations. This, on Fries' view, is the proper lesson to be learnt from Jacobi's critique of Kant. The practical postulates are absorbed into sub-spheres of immediate cognition, initially into the province of *Glauben* and subsequently into the sphere of affective or aesthetic cognition that Fries calls *Ahnung*. Kant's insight that moral consciousness provides sufficient attestation of the re-

---

[72] See also (Fries 1812, pp. 31–37) on Kant.
[73] In *Wissen, Glaube und Ahndung*, Fries rejects the arguments that Kant gives for the theological postulates on a number of grounds. In the chapter 'On the Eternal Good' (Fries 1989, pp. 83–87). Fries describes the religious beliefs that Kant recommends as psychologically impossible, rejects Kant's formulation of the highest good, and denies the coherence of supposing infinite time to be sufficient for the attainment of complete virtue; later he rejects the priority of freedom over the theological postulates (Fries 1989, p. 90).
[74] See Fries' criticisms of Jacobi in (Fries 1812, pp. 38–53).

ality of the supersensible objects is generalized to all purely intellectual representations, and the propositions in Kant's theological postulates are upheld in a form which renders them immune to the objections levelled against Kant's moral theology, since Fries has abandoned the attempt to derive them from an antinomy of practical reason.

4.3 Novalis

The concept of practical postulation allows us to also specify the parting of ways within the post-Kantian development of the Romantics from the systematic idealists. This is clearest in Novalis.[75]

Novalis arrives through reflection on Fichte at the idea that intentional, propositionally articulated consciousness is dependent on a source which can come before us only in the shape of feeling. Whereas Fichte supposes it possible to step behind the scenes of natural consciousness and reverse its inverted image of reality, Novalis relinquishes the idea that we can achieve a cognitive grasp, of the sort claimed by Fichte, of the non-conscious ground of our subjectivity. Our proper relation to this absolute ground, after we have freely renounced it from the standpoint of cognition,[76] Novalis conceives instead in terms of *activity* – the activity of, as he puts it, seeking "connection [Verknüpfung]" with the whole, "*enlargement [Verganzung]*", of the subject's compass to a whole.

What Novalis has in mind by enlargement-and-connection-to-a-whole is the *Romantisierung der Welt*, which includes theoretical enquiry into nature – in appropriately *naturphilosophisch* forms – but only as a subsidiary component. It is not, therefore, equivalent to the extension of our *cognition* to the whole of nature, on the model of the Kantian understanding.[77] Nor, however, is it practical in the usual sense, since it consists not in our changing the world, but in our being changed *by* the world. Novalis says that we thereby manifest "the absolute ground of all grounding", the "freedom" in the ground, and become aware of our own "absolute freedom". This awareness, and the activity which makes it possible, constitute furthermore a *negative* cognition of the absolute ground, which is *given to us* "insofar as we act and find that what we seek cannot be attained

---

[75] I focus on a key passage from the *Fichte Studies*, Group V, no. 566 (summer 1796): (Novalis 2003, pp. 167–168).
[76] After '*interruption* of the drive towards knowledge of the ground' (Novalis 2003, p. 168).
[77] Novalis talks of extending understanding through imagination, 'Der durch die Einbildungskraft ausgedehnte Verstand' (Novalis 2003, p. 168).

through action": the "negatively known absolute" is "known through action" (Novalis 2003, p. 168).⁷⁸

Finally, Novalis says that all of this "could be called an absolute postulate", and we can see why he does so. Romanticization is positioned, as we have just seen, mid-way between theoretical and practical reason. In addition, Novalis explains that he is offering the postulate of enlargement to a whole in place of "searching for *a single principle*" (which he compares to the attempt to square the circle). Since Novalis is thinking here of postulates as alternatives to principles, we might ask what the difference is – why cannot a proposition be both, as Fichte and Schelling assume.⁷⁹ The answer is that Novalis *also* thinks, as other passages in the *Fichte-Studien* make clear, that practical existence, when it achieves its higher (that is, romantic) forms, exceeds what can be comprehended.⁸⁰ Fichte thinks that the act which his absolute postulate enjoins can be grasped by philosophical reason – it can be observed, and modelled systematically in the Wissenschaftslehre. This is what Novalis denies. Novalis must of course agree that an imperative can *point* us in the direction of the required activity – I can think: Let me connect myself to the whole! – but the forms of activity which might satisfy the imperative cannot be determined discursively, any more than the concept of a work of art can determine the objects which satisfy it. The concept of an absolute postulate marks then, for Novalis, an *exit point* for philosophical reflection, not, as in Fichte and Schelling, the highest point within it.⁸¹

---

78 Novalis concludes the passage: 'Thus eternity is realized temporally in spite of the fact that time contradicts eternity' (Novalis 2003, p. 168). A model for this conception of infinite approximation to an end as equivalent to its ultimate realization is contained in Kant's moral theology, where it is claimed that our infinitely extended, posthumous striving to achieve holiness of will can be taken – by God – to *count as* its realization. The fact that Novalis compares negative practical cognition of the absolute ground with achieving eternity through time implies his awareness of this connection. See also (Novalis 2003, no. 54, pp. 38–39), concerning Kant's postulates, practical striving, and duration. For detailed discussion of the practical and aesthetic in Novalis, see (Kneller 2007).
79 In (Fichte 1992, p. 109 [FW/GA: IV, III, 343–344]), Fichte objects to J. S. Beck, who maintains a first postulate *rather than* a first principle, that he misconceives principles. (Schelling 1994, p. 112 [SW: I, 414]), affirms that the *Grundsatz* of self-determination is a postulate.
80 See (Novalis 2003, no. 89, p. 46), where Novalis says that 'the practical I' is only a 'postulate' of the 'theoretical I': we *represent* the practical I, and this representation is formed by taking the idea of the theoretical I and qualifying it as 'practical'; it 'borrows' the idea of the unconditioned, the purely free. The genuine practical I escapes representation and has only one expression: it 'commands pure and simple'. As soon as we *reflect* on its efficacy, it is found to be theoretical.
81 What Novalis is proposing really amounts to, then, is the (extraordinary and striking) thought that our lives – when lived romantically – *are* the solution to the basic problem of tran-

The same idea of transcendental questions as resolving themselves into problems of modes of living, and as receiving their answers in special forms of human life, and in aesthetic forms, is present in Hölderlin.[82] In this sense it is the German Romantics – and not, we saw, Fichte – who pursue the primacy of the practical to its ultimate conclusion.

4.4 The contrast

For all of their considerable differences, Beck, Fries, and Novalis share common ground. Beck and Fries both proceed from the view that Kant's deductions, as they stand, fail in their objective of furnishing proofs for transcendental propositions, and their respective proposals to repair Kantian epistemology proceed from this point: Beck aims to save transcendental proof by modelling it more closely on geometrical demonstration, and Fries to rescue transcendental claims by grounding them on facts of inner awareness. Analogously, Novalis regards

---

scendental philosophy. So transcendental philosophy resolves itself into the task of living: not in the way that Kant thinks that pure reason finds its fulfilment in moral living, but in the way that Jacobi thinks philosophy leads us to leap outside it. But even if, in one sense, Novalis brings transcendental philosophy down to earth, it is to be remembered that the mode of living which provides the answer to the transcendental question is at the same time raised up: it is romantisch, transcendentalized living.

[82] Hölderlin conceives the tragic as 'the metaphor of an intellectual intuition' (Hölderlin 2009a, p. 68 [Sämtliche Werke, Bd. IV.1, p. 266]). See also the Vorrede to Hyperion, Vorletzte Fassung, concerning beauty as the presence to us of Being in its true sense (Hölderlin 1957, pp. 236–237), and (Hölderlin 2009b), concerning the poet's realization of the necessity of striving and of conflict between two postulates, and the idea of 'pure poetic life'.

Hölderlin's exact view of the relation of the aesthetic to the practical is not easily determined, but it is clear at any rate that Hölderlin's aesthetic turn is directly continuous with his interest in Kantian practical postulation. Hölderlin rehearses and endorses the whole of the argument of Kant's moral theology in a letter to his half-brother, Karl Gok, 13 April 1795 (Hölderlin 2009, pp. 49–5) and (Hölderlin 1954, no. 97, pp. 162–164), and the letter in which he famously talks of infinite approximation as an aesthetic matter comes only a few months later to Schiller, 4 September 1795; (Hölderlin 2009, p. 62) and (Hölderlin 1954, no. 104, p. 181). The idea of a continuous development from moral postulation to the aesthetic, as the 'highest act of reason', is found also in the roughly contemporaneous Oldest System-Programme. Hölderlin's letter to Niethammer, 24 February 1796, talks of 'making the conflict disappear, the conflict between the subject and the object, between our selves and the world, and between reason and revelation,— theoretically, through intellectual intuition, without our practical reason having to intervene' (Hölderlin 2009, p. 68) and (Hölderlin 1954, no. 117, p. 203), which recalls the conception of absolute postulation in Schelling, with whom Hölderlin reports a recent meeting in the following paragraph.

Fichte's post-Kantian epistemology as unsuccessful, and invokes an affective or aesthetic substitute for the sought-after single principle. In all three cases, then, the proposed revisions involve a *rejection of the requirement of discursive demonstration*.

The turn to non-discursivity has implications for the treatment of the relation between the theoretical sphere of understanding and the practical sphere of reason. The connection between the two is supplied on Beck's account, we saw, by a mere thin parallel between theoretical and practical postulation, while Novalis envisages theoretical cognition as yielding at its limit to an aesthetic practice. Fries, by contrast, construes nature – apprehended as beautiful or sublime – as an indeterminate *Darstellung* accessible to aesthetic feeling (*Ahnung*) of the reality that we attempt to grasp by means of the ideas of reason. This preserves more of the structure of the Critical system – Fries at least agrees with Kant concerning the existence of a third category, intermediate between the theoretical and the practical – but it involves no *conception* of their unity and to that extent leaves the two spheres fundamentally distinct. Beck, Fries, and Novalis are therefore all united in abjuring the augmented sense of practical postulate, the notion of a single discursive claim which expresses the unity of the theoretical and practical reason, or of Verstand and Vernunft. In terms of the historical narrative that I am pursuing, these three thinkers represent points where (respectively) the concept of a postulate, the moral theology, and the conception of the practical as outstripping the theoretical, become central to post-Kantian philosophy, but in a way which does not conform to the philosophical strategy implied by the augmented concept of a practical postulate, and so they disembark from the German Idealist line of post-Kantian development.

The final observation to make is that Beck and Fries, whether or not their proposals succeed in resolving some of the problems facing Kantian epistemology, make no progress in resolving the problem, highlighted by criticism of the moral theology, concerning our need for assurance of the objective reality of ideas of reason. Beck clearly cannot provide this, for the reason given (and indeed he does not pretend to do so), and Fries' invitation to regard felt conviction of the reality of the ideas of reason as immediate cognition makes no obvious advance on Jacobi's *salto mortale*.[83]

---

[83] The precise problem reveals itself when the following question is raised: Granted Fries' account of how we come to *form* ideas of reason, namely through negation of the relational character of the spatio-temporal objects of our *Wissen*, how do we come to suppose them to have *objective reference*, i.e. to *believe* in their *reality*? The difficulty for Fries lies in reconciling (i) his commitment to explanation of all cognition in terms of subjective powers and processes (as *per* Kant, and as required by *philosophische Anthropologie*), with (ii) his affirmation of the

5 Conclusion

The preceding discussion has some bearing on the dispute concerning the metaphysical or non-metaphysical character of German Idealism.

Dieter Henrich has identified the long term historical importance of Kant's doctrine of postulation with (first) its contribution to the theological tradition which seeks to grasp God not metaphysically but through inner revelation, and (second) its role in the prehistory of pragmatism, laying the ground for Feuerbach and Nietzsche (Henrich 1960, pp. 187–188 note 1). This points to a sharp contrast with the German Idealists' reception of Kant's doctrine, where, despite the repudiation of Kant's theism, what stands out is the maintained connection of practical postulation with the Ideal of Pure Reason. As I have tried to show, while it is quite true that Fichte and Schelling detach the concept of a practical postulate from Kant's theism, they do not thereupon convert it into a mere general principle of rational belief in the manner of pragmatism.[84] Fichte and Schelling instead took Kant's moral theology as an incomplete model or preliminary sketch for a systematic structure intended to complete a metaphysical task with a distinctly early modern flavour, viz., the task of conceptually determining final ontological grounds. If we formulate the puzzle of German Idealism, as is often done, in terms of the question how the German Idealists could have considered it possible to restore metaphysics in the wake of Kant's Copernican revolution, the German Idealists' reception of Kant's moral theology helps us to see how it should be answered. In the perspective of Fichte and Schelling, it was never an option to hold apart the theory of rational belief from ontological commitments: to have negatively circumscribed the task at hand – to have defined philosophical reflection as concerned with epistemic and practical norms *in opposition to* metaphysics – would have led to the problems acutely visible in

---

objective reference of ideas of reason (as *per* Jacobi). The problem arises, therefore, even when Fries is allowed his claim that it is a mistake to aim at a discursive proof of objective reference. Fries is acutely aware of the difficulty – see (Fries 1989, pp. 70, 74–75) – for if it is not resolved, then Fries either falls prey to the objections levelled by Jacobi against Kant, or has added nothing to Jacobi.

[84] Schelling explicitly rejects the sufficiency of a methodological conception in the Fifth of his *Philosophische Briefe* (Schelling 1980b, pp. 168–171 [SW: I, 300–305]). His target comprises ('anxiously modest') Kantians who suppose that 'it is precisely the exclusive use of practical postulates that distinguishes the critical philosopher'. Schelling counters that, in general terms, method is precisely what is *shared* by opposing systems, and that when practical postulation is conceived as mere method, it does not contradict dogmatism but rather facilitates its *renewal*.

Kant's moral theology; what this portion of the Critical system showed above all, in their eyes, was the necessity of *completing* metaphysical enquiry.[85]

Bibliography

[FW]   Fichte, Johann Gottlieb (1845–46): *Johann Gottlieb Fichtes sämmtliche Werke*, 8 Bde. Fichte, Immanuel Hermann (Ed.). Berlin: Veit & Comp. and
Fichte, Johann Gottlieb (1834–35): *Johann Gottlieb Fichtes nachgelassene Werke*, 3 Bde. Fichte, Immanuel Hermann (Ed.). Bonn: Adolph-Marcus.
[FW/GA] Fichte, Johann Gottlieb (1964-): *Gesamtausgabe der Bayerischen Akademie der Wissenschaften*. Lauth, Reinhard/Jacob, Hans/Gliwitzky, Hans (Eds.). Stuttgart-Bad Cannstatt: Frommann-Holzboog.
[HW]   Hegel, Georg Wilhelm Friedrich (1970): *Werke. Auf der Grundlage der Werke von 1832–1845 neu edierte Ausgabe*. Moldenhauer, Eva/Michel, Karl Markus (Eds.). Frankfurt am Main: Suhrkamp.
[SW]   Schelling, Friedrich Wilhelm Joseph von(1927–59): *Schellings Werke. Nach der Originalausgabe in neuer Anordung*. Schröter, Manfred (Ed.). München: Beck.

Adorno, Theodor W. (1973): *Negative Dialectics*, London: Routledge & Kegan Paul.
Ameriks, Karl (2000): "Kant, Fichte, and the Radical Primacy of the Practical". In: *Kant and the Fate of Autonomy*. Cambridge: Cambridge University Press, pp. 187–233.
Beck, Jakob Sigismund (1796a): *Einzig mögliche Standpunkt aus welchem die kritische Philosophie beurtheilt werden muß*. Riga: Hartnoch.
Beck, Jakob Sigismund (1797): *The Principles of Critical Philosophy*. London: J. Johnson/W. Richardson/Edinburgh: P. Hill/Manners and Miller/Hamburg: B. G. Hoffmann.
Breazeale, Daniel (2004): "'Wishful Thinking'. Concerning Fichte's Interpretation of the Postulates of Reason in his *Versuch einer Kritik aller Offenbarung* (1792)". In: *Philosophy and Religion in German Idealism*. Ernst-Otto Onnasch/Willian Desmond/Paul Cruysberghs (Eds). Dordrecht: Kluwer, pp. 35–70.
Düsing, Klaus (1999): "The Reception of Kant's Doctrine of Postulates in Schelling's and Hegel's Early Philosophical Projects". In: *The Emergence of German Idealism*. Daniel O. Dahlstrom/Michael Baur (Eds.).Washington, D.C.: Catholic University of America Press, pp. 201–237.
Eberhard, Johann August (1793): "Dogmatische Briefe, 18–30". In: *Philosophisches Archiv* 1 (4), pp. 46–90.
Eberhard, Johann August (1799): *Ueber den Gott des Herrn Professor Fichte und den Götzen seiner Gegner. Eine ruhige Prüfung an das Publikum in einigen Briefen*. Halle: Hemmerle und Schwetschke.

---

[85] I am very grateful to members of the audience at the University of Aarhus, the University of Sydney, and the Oxford Post-Kantian Seminar, where earlier versions of this paper were presented, for comments and suggestions.

Fichte, Johann Gottlieb (1962): "Versuch eines erklärenden Auszug aus Kants *Kritik der Urteilskraft*". In: *J. G. Fichte: Gesamtausgabe*. Reihe II, Vol. I. Hans Jacob/Reinhard Lauth (Eds.). Stuttgart-Bad Cannstatt: Frommann-Holzboog, pp. 324–373.
Fichte, Johann Gottlieb (1971): *Die Wissenschaftslehre*, in *Fichtes sämtliche Werke*. Bd. X. Berlin: Walter de Gruyter, pp. 315–492.
Fichte, Johann Gottlieb (1971a): "Eigene Meditationen über ElementarPhilosophie", in *J. G. Fichte: Gesamtausgabe*. Reihe II, Vol. III. Hans Jacob/Reinhard Lauth (Eds.). Stuttgart-Bad Cannstatt: Frommann-Holzboog, pp. 1–177.
Fichte, Johann Gottlieb (1971b): "Praktische Philosophie". In: *J. G. Fichte: Gesamtausgabe*. Reihe II, Vol. III. Hans Jacob/Reinhard Lauth (Eds.). Stuttgart-Bad Cannstatt: Frommann-Holzboog, pp. 179–266.
Fichte, Johann Gottlieb (1978): *Attempt at a Critique of All Revelation*. New York: Cambridge University Press.
Fichte, Johann Gottlieb (1982): "Foundations of the Entire Science of Knowledge". In: *Fichte, The Science of Knowledge, with the First and Second Introductions*. Peter Heath/John Lachs (Ed.). Cambridge: Cambridge University Press, pp. 87–286.
Fichte, Johann Gottlieb (1992): *Foundations of Transcendental Philosophy: (Wissenschaftslehre) nova methodo (1796/99)*. Ithaca, NY: Cornell University Press.
Fichte, Johann Gottlieb (1994): "On the Basis of Our Belief in a Divine Governance of the World". In: *Fichte, Introductions to the Wissenschaftslehre and Other Writings (1797–1800)*. Indianapolis: Hackett, pp. 141–154.
Fichte, Johann Gottlieb (1994a): "Second Introduction to the Wissenschaftslehre". In: *Fichte, Introductions to the Wissenschaftslehre and Other Writings (1797–1800)*. Indianapolis: Hackett, 1994, pp. 36–105.
Fichte, Johann Gottlieb (2001): "Review of Creuzer's *Skeptical Reflections on Free Will*". In: *Philosophical Forum* 32, pp. 289–296.
Fichte, Johann Gottlieb (2005): *The Science of Knowing: J. G. Fichte's 1804 Lectures on the Wissenschaftslehre*. Albany, NY: State University of New York Press.
Forberg, Friedrich Karl (1912): "Entwickelung des Begriffs der Religion". In: *Die Schriften zu J. G. Fichtes Atheismus-Streit*. München: Georg Müller, pp. 37–58.
Frank, Manfred/Kurz, Gerhard (Eds.) (1975): *Materialen zu Schellings philosophischen Anfängen*. Frankfurt am Main: Suhrkamp.
Franks, Paul (2005): *All or Nothing: Systematicity, Transcendental Arguments, and Skepticism in German Idealism*. Cambridge, Mass.: Harvard University Press.
Fries, Jakob Friedrich (1989): *Knowledge, Belief, and Aesthetic Sense*. Cologne: Jürgen Dinter Verlag.
Fries, Jakob Friedrich (1812): *Von Deutscher Philosophie Art und Kunst: Ein Votum für Friedrich Heinrich Jacobi gegen F. W. J. Schelling*. Heidelberg: Mohr und Zimmer.
Fries, Jakob Friedrich (1828): *Neue oder anthropologische Kritik*. 2nd. Ed., Vol. 1. Heidelberg: Christian Friedrich Winter.
Gardner, Sebastian (2007): "The Status of the Wissenschaftslehre: Transcendental and Ontological Grounds in Fichte". In: *Internationales Jahrbuch des Deutschen Idealismus – Metaphysik im Deutschen Idealismus / International Yearbook of German Idealism – Metaphysics in German Idealism* 5, pp. 90–125.
Gardner, Sebastian (2011): "Kant's Practical Postulates and the Limits of the Critical System". In: *Bulletin of the Hegel Society of Great Britain* 63, 187–215.

di Giovanni, G. (2005): *Freedom and Religion in Kant and His Immediate Successors: The Vocation of Humankind, 1774–1800.* Cambridge: Cambridge University Press.
Hegel, Georg Wilhelm Friedrich (1975): *Encyclopedia Logic.* Oxford: Oxford University Press.
Hegel, Georg Wilhelm Friedrich (1977): *Faith and Knowledge.* Albany, NY: State University of New York Press.
Hegel, Georg Wilhelm Friedrich (1977a): *Phenomenology of Spirit.* Oxford: Oxford University Press.
Hegel, Georg Wilhelm Friedrich (1977b): *The Difference Between Fichte's and Schelling's System of Philosophy.* Albany, NY: State University of New York Press.
Hegel, Georg Wilhelm Friedrich (1984): *Hegel: The Letters.* Bloomington: Indiana University Press.
Hegel, Georg Wilhelm Friedrich (1996): "The Spirit of Christianity and its Fate". In: *Early Theological Writings.* Richard Kroner (Ed.). Chicago: University of Chicago Press, pp. 182–301.
Hegel, Georg Wilhelm Friedrich (2002): "The Tübingen Essay". In: *Miscellaneous Writings of Hegel.* Jon Stewart (Ed.). Evanston, Illinois: Northwestern University Press, pp. 44–71.
Henrich, Dieter (1960): *Der ontologische Gottesbeweis. Sein problem und seine Geschichte in der Neuzeit.* Tübingen: Mohr/Siebeck 1960.
Henrich, Dieter (1997): "Dominant Philosophical-Theological Problems in the Tübingen *Stift* During the Student Years of Hegel, Hölderlin, and and Schelling". In: *The Course of Remembrance and Other Essays on Hölderlin.* Stanford: Stanford University Press, pp. 31–54.
Hölderlin, Friedrich (1954): *Sämtliche Werke: Grosse Stuttgarter Ausgabe,* Bd. VI, 1te Hälfte, *Briefe.* Stuttgart: Kohlhammer.
Hölderlin, Friedrich (1957): *Hyperion. Die vorletzte Fassung,* in *Sämtliche Werke: Grosse Stuttgarter Ausgabe.* Vol. III. Stuttgart: Kohlhammer, pp. 235–252.
Hölderlin, Friedrich (2009): *Essays and Letters.* Harmondsworth: Penguin.
Hölderlin, Friedrich (2009a): "The lyric, in appearance idealistic poem …". In: *and Letters.* Harmondsworth: Penguin, pp. 302–306
Hölderlin, Friedrich (2009b): "When the poet is once in command of the spirit …". In: *and Letters.* Harmondsworth: Penguin, pp. 277–298.
Jacobi, F. H (1968): "Ueber das Unternehmen des Kriticismus die Vernunft zu Verstande zu bringen". In: *Werke.* Vol.3. Darmstadt: Wissenschaftliche Buchgesellschaft, pp. 57–195.
Jacobi, F. H (1968a): "Von den göttlichen Dingen und ihrer Offenbarung". In: *Werke.* Vol. 3. Darmstadt: Wissenschaftliche Buchgesellschaft, pp. 245–460.
Jacobi, F. H. (1994): "David Hume on Faith, or Idealism and Realism. A Dialogue". In: *The Main Philosophical Writings and the Novel 'Allwill'.* George di Giovanni (Ed.). Montreal/Kingston: McGill-Queen's University Press, pp. 253–338.
Jaeschke, Walter (1990): *Reason in Religion: The Foundations of Hegel's Philosophy of Religion.* Berkeley: University of California Press.
Kant, Immanuel (1992): *The Jäsche Logic,* in *Lectures on Logic.* Cambridge: Cambridge University Press.
Kant, Immanuel (1996): *Critique of Practical Reason.* In: *Kant, Practical Philosophy.* Cambridge: Cambridge University Press.
Kant, Immanuel (1996a): *Groundwork of the Metaphysics of Morals.* In: *Kant, Practical Philosophy.* Cambridge: Cambridge University Press.

Kant, Immanuel (1996b): "What Does it Mean to Orient Oneself in Thinking?" In: *Kant, Religion and Rational Theology*. Allen W. Wood/George di Giovanni (Eds.). Cambridge: Cambridge University Press, pp. 1–18.
Kant, Immanuel (1998): *Critique of Pure Reason*. Cambridge: Cambridge University Press.
Kant, Immanuel (1999): *Correspondence*. Cambridge: Cambridge University Press.
Kant, Immanuel (2000): *Critique of the Power of Judgement*. Cambridge: Cambridge University Press.
Kant, Immanuel (2005): *Notes and Fragments*. Cambridge: Cambridge University Press.
Kneller, Jane (2007): *Kant and the Power of Imagination*. Cambridge: Cambridge University Press.
Neiman, Susan (1994): *The Unity of Reason: Rereading Kant*. Oxford: Oxford University Press.
Novalis (2003): *Fichte Studies*. Cambridge: Cambridge University Press.
Schelling, Friedrich Wilhelm Joseph von (1927–59): "Ueber Offenbarung und Volksunterricht", in *Schellings Werke*. Manfred Schröter (Ed.). Vol. I. München: Beck, pp. 474–482.
Schelling, Friedrich Wilhelm Joseph von (1977): *Philosophie der Offenbarung 1841/42*. Frankfurt am Main: Suhrkamp.
Schelling, Friedrich Wilhelm Joseph von (1978): *System of Transcendental Idealism*. Charlottesville: University of Virginia.
Schelling, Friedrich Wilhelm Joseph von (1980): "Of the I as Principle of Philosophy, or On the Unconditional in Human Knowledge". In: *The Unconditional in Human Knowledge: Four Early Essays 1794–1796*. Fritz Marti(Ed.). Lewisburg: Bucknell University Press, pp. 59–149.
Schelling, Friedrich Wilhelm Joseph von (1980a): "On the Possibility of a Form of All Philosophy". In: *The Unconditional in Human Knowledge: Four Early Essays 1794–1796*. Fritz Marti (Ed.). Lewisburg: Bucknell University Press, pp. 38–58.
Schelling, Friedrich Wilhelm Joseph von (1980b): *Philosophical Letters on Dogmatism and Criticism*. In: *The Unconditional in Human Knowledge: Four Early Essays 1794–1796*. Lewisburg: Bucknell University Press, pp. 156–218.
Schelling, Friedrich Wilhelm Joseph von (1982): "Antikritik". In: *Friedrich Wilhelm Joseph Schelling, Historisch-Kritische Ausgabe*. Reihe I, Vol. III. Annemarie Pieper/Hartmut Buchner/ Wilhelm G. Jacobs (Eds.). Stuttgart-Bad Cannstatt: Fromann-Holzboog, pp. 177–197.
Schelling, Friedrich Wilhelm Joseph von (1984): *Bruno, or On the Natural and the Divine Principle of Things*. Albany, NY: State University of New York Press.
Schelling, Friedrich Wilhelm Joseph von (1988): *Ideas for a Philosophy of Nature as Introduction to the Study of this Science*. Cambridge: Cambridge University Press, pp. 43–55.
Schelling, Friedrich Wilhelm Joseph von (1994): *Treatise Explicatory of the Idealism in the Science of Knowledge*, in *Idealism and the Endgame of Theory: Three Essays*. Albany: State University of New York Press, pp. 61–138.
Schelling, Friedrich Wilhelm Joseph von (2000): "On the Relationship of The Philosophy of Nature to Philosophy in General". In: *Between Kant and Hegel: Texts in the Development of German Idealism*. George di Giovanni/ H. S. Harris (Eds.). Indianapolis/Cambridge: Hackett.
Schelling, Friedrich Wilhelm Joseph von (2007): *Grounding of Positive Philosophy*. Albany, NY: State University of New York Press.

Schmidt, Heinrich (1974): *Philosophisches Wörterbuch*. Stuttgart: Alfred Kröner.
Storr, Christian (1794): *Bemerkungen über Kants philosophische Religionslehre*. Tübingen: J. G. Cotta.
Timm, Hermann (1974): *Gott und die Freiheit. Studien zur Religionsphilosophie der Goethezeit*, Bd. 1. *Die Spinozarenaissance*. Frankfurt am Main: Klostermann.
Unkown (1995): "Oldest system-programme of German Idealism". In: *European Journal of Philosophy* 3, pp. 199–200.
Wallner, Ingrid M. (1985): "A New Look at J. S. Beck's 'Doctrine of the Standpoint'". In: *Kant-Studien* 75, pp. 294–316.

Günter Zöller
Homo homini civis.
The Modernity of Classical German Political Philosophy

> I propose therefore that we enquire into the
> nature of justice and injustice, first as they appear
> in the State, and secondly in the individual, proceeding
> from the greater to the lesser and comparing them.[1]

The following essay on the actuality of German idealist thought focuses on the specifically political conception of the human individual in the moral, social and political philosophy of Kant and the post-Kantian German idealists, placing their political thinking into the larger historical context of modern accounts of the relation between the citizen and the state. In particular, the essay draws on Kant, Fichte and Hegel for extracting a conception of selfhood that is mindful of the worth of the individual and attentive to its supra- and inter-individual existence in general, and its existence in political or civil society and the state in particular. Under conditions of classical modernity – and its sustained manifestation in Kant and German idealism – the individual human being, while being liberated from traditional communal ties that previously subjected it to religious, cultural and social control, is introduced into a novel existence as an independent, but integrated, "free" member of a society in which the individual is at once the subject and the sovereign, the ruler and the ruled, the origin and the object. Classical German political philosophy can be seen to make an original contribution to that tradition. Contrary to the stress on individual freedom in (political) liberalism, classical German political philosophy maintains the derivative, constituted character of individuality. Contrary to the emphasis on the primacy of the social in communitarianism, classical German political philosophy defends the normative independence of the individual.

The proposed reading of classical German political philosophy, which seeks to place Kant, Fichte and Hegel in the tradition of modern republicanism, begins – after preliminary reflections on the standing and success of classical German political philosophy – with Locke, Montesquieu and Rousseau, moves from there to the three chief representatives of classical German political philosophy[2] and concludes with a brief look at the democratic transformation of republican

---

1 (Plato 1960, Book II, 369a).
2 On Schelling's contribution to classical German political philosophy, see (Zöller 2014).

polity, as diagnosed and analyzed in Tocqueville's work on the early United States of America, and its repercussions for classical German political philosophy today. The methodological background of the proposed reading of classical German political philosophy is the close analogy drawn by Plato in the *Republic* between ethical matters pertaining to the individual and political matters concerning the city state (*polis*), in particular the prefiguration of individual character types by the corresponding forms of political governance. In a reversal of the original Platonic analogy, modern political philosophy – including classical German political philosophy – rather than employing the constitution of the just state to ascertain that of the just soul, conceives of the state on the model of the individual, and in turn reimports originally political categories – chiefly among them freedom, will and autonomy – to define and delimit the individual in its juridico-political as well as ethical constitution. The chief concern of the proposed reading is the republican configuration of the classical modern individual as a historical counter-example and systematic antidote to the late, post-classical reconfiguration – or disfiguration, as the case may be – of the sovereign, self-determined individual through representative mass democracy, consumerist mass culture and financially focused globalizing governance.

1 Classical German political philosophy

From mid- to late-nineteenth century neo-Kantianism and neo-Fichteanism through turn-of-the-century British neo-Hegelianism to recent Anglo-American retrievals of Kant and Hegel in neo-Aristotelian and neo-pragmatist contexts, the reception and effective history of Kant and the German idealists has tended to focus on epistemological and metaphysical issues, including the philosophy of mind and the theoretical foundations of volition and action. To be sure, there have always been appropriations of Kant, Fichte and Hegel for purposes of moral and political philosophy, from the Young Hegelians through the Austro-Marxists to Rawls and Habermas. But except for past and recent scholarly work in the history of philosophy devoted to Kant's ethics, Fichte's legal philosophy and Hegel's social philosophy, little attention has been paid in the further development of philosophical thought during the past two centuries to the lessons of Kantian and post-Kantian idealist thought in practical philosophy in general and in political philosophy in particular. When it comes to sustained reflection on the grounds and bounds of political association, philosophers have relied much more on early modern political thought on the social contract, from Hobbes through Locke to Rousseau, than on the original contributions of Kant, Fichte and Hegel on the distinction between law and morality and the non-empirical foundations of public law – a certain longstanding but narrowly focused interest in Kant's program for political progress toward perpetual peace notwithstanding.

To be sure, the past and present factual inactuality of the political philosophy of Kantian and post-Kantian German idealism is not without some justification. Juridico-political thinking in Kant, Fichte and Hegel is, to a large extent, marked by the tradition of natural law (*Naturrecht*) and reflects a preoccupation with supra-positive and essentially moral standards of political life that seem removed from the exigencies of efficient government in modern, increasingly pluralist and globally situated mass-democratic states that have their sovereignty challenged – economically, financially and militarily – from within and without. Moreover, the alternative meta-political positions of liberalism and communitarianism, with their matching extreme preferences for original individuality and primary sociality, respectively, seem to leave little room for a tradition of political thought that joins the focus on individual entitlements ("rights") with that of social obligations ("duties"), and that tends to view the state, rather than the pre-political individual or the praeter-political community, as the enabling condition for individual and social living and flourishing.

Most importantly, though, the political thought of classical German philosophy has suffered from an evaluative bifurcation that was introduced into the notion of freedom in general and political freedom in particular through Isaiah Berlin's influential distinction between "two concepts of liberty" (1958) – a negative concept reflecting the freedom from tutelage, interference and domination inherent in the British, essentially Lockean tradition, and a positive concept of freedom involving the imposition of law and order in the Romantic or expressivist tradition (Berlin 1990). But Berlin's typological disjunction, which is more the essayistic product of a brilliant historian of ideas than the argumentative conclusion of a political philosopher, underestimates both the presence of more-than-negative freedom in classical liberal thought from Locke to J. St. Mill and the role that negative freedom continues to play in Kant, Fichte and Hegel as the necessary condition rather than the excluded alternative for establishing and preserving "laws of freedom" (Kant).

Placed against the historical and systematic background of the related oppositions of liberalism and communitarianism and of negative and positive freedom, the political thought of German idealist philosophy emerges as a possible third way – a genuine alternative to a seemingly complete twofold disjunction and not some strange *Sonderweg* – for joining freedom and law, individual and society, liberation and commitment, self-reliance and solidarity, and entitlement and obligation in a normative assessment of the conditions and forms of life in the modern polity. With Kant tying freedom to self-legislation, Fichte grounding self-awareness in civic sociality and Hegel linking substantial freedom to ethical life (*Sittlichkeit*), a line of thought emerges that allows to think political or civic existence as the space for the emergence and exercise of a freedom *sui generis:* a freedom that is not the freedom *from* the political realm – apolitical freedom under the shape of the self-sufficient individual or the self-enclosed community – but the freedom *in*, *through* and *for* the political realm; a freedom that needs to be created and not only claimed, maintained and exercised, and a freedom that shapes and advances individuals beyond their particular preferences and local communities. In Kant's, Fichte's and Hegel's reflections on the relation between the individual and society, freedom takes on an eminently political sense. It is a civically constituted freedom that not only conjoins the individual and society, but co-constitutes the two. The individual comes to be a citizen and society comes to be civic all at once. No one is a citizen outside the *civitas*, and there is no *civitas* without citizens.

In their efforts to think the specifically political interdependence of the individual and society, Kant, Fichte and Hegel typically resort to the imagery of the organic body. Drawing on contemporary work about the constitution of living beings ("organization"), in which constituent parts ("organs") and whole ("organism") mutually condition each other,[3] Kant, Fichte and Hegel conceive of the polity as an entity exhibiting the phenomena of organic life, including generation, regeneration and degeneration. Earlier modern thinking about the constitution of the state, from Hobbes through Rousseau, had likened its mode of operation to the workings of a machine ("political machine", "mechanism") ingeniously construed, or at least so to be viewed, and reflecting the human-superhuman design of a mastermind responsible for its form and function.

By reconceiving the body that is the polity ("body politic", *Staatskörper*) of early modern times as a living body or animal, Kant and his idealist successors can be seen to lend new meaning to the Aristotelian phrase, "political animal" (*zoon politikon*), which no longer designates the individual human being as such, but rather the strange beast that is made up of them and makes them what they are. Once a monster risen from the sea and towering over the earth with unrivalled might ("Leviathan"), the macranthropic state – a superhuman being made up of each and every human being it comprises – in Kant & Co. has been framed and tamed, circumscribed and constricted by rules of its institution and constitution. For Kant, Fichte and Hegel, the body politic ceases to be the instrument of

---

[3] The *locus classicus* for a philosophical account of the living organism is Kant's *Critique of the Power of Judgment*, specifically its second part, "Critique of the Power of Teleological Judgment."

absolute rule that it had been thought to be and made to be with the advent of the sovereign territorial state in post-reformatory Europe and its Westphalian order.

Contemporaneous with the tremendous political upheavals of the late eighteenth and early nineteenth centuries – from the lasting success of the American Revolution and the pathological course of the French Revolution through the short-lived career of the Napoleonic empire to the restoration sought by the Congress of Vienna – Kant, Fichte and Hegel, each in their own way, rethink the civic relation between individual and society under a perspective of political freedom that seeks to ensure the twofold, correlated freedom of the individual as well as the state. A state fit for free individuals and individuals fit for a free state are brought together in a conception of political life inspired by, or reminiscent of, the classical notion of the commonwealth (*res publica*), the republican state – in short, the republic.

To be sure, neither Kant nor Hegel endorse a republican form of government, not to mention its democratic variant, as exemplified by fifth-century Athens and only to be sought again on the European continent in the bourgeois revolutions of the later nineteenth and early twentieth centuries. Moreover, Fichte's occasional portrayal of a future "Republic of the Germans" (*Republik der Deutschen*) is more a national dystopia than a political ideal. But while Kant and his idealist successors do not understand themselves as advocates of republicanism and democracy, they still tend to place their normative discourse about the inner and outer constitution of the state under the concept "republic" (*Republik*). Taken in a more generic sense, which finds expression in its extension to "Plato's republic" (*Platonische Republik*) (AA 3:247/4:201), the term "republic" for Kant and his idealist successors does not denote a particular structure of statehood (*Staatsform*), but a basic mode of government (*Regierungsart*).[4]

Moreover, the structurally, or virtually, republican state of the German idealists is not defined through the political participation of its citizens, which remains limited, if not minimal as partial and representative self-governance in the federal tradition of the Imperial constitution (*Reichsverfassung*). Rather, the German-idealist free state is republican in legal and ethical terms. In juridico-political terms, the German idealist republic is a state under the rule of law, and of supra-positive, "natural" law at that. The fabrication and application of legal rules is to be free from arbitrariness and inequity. The republican state is a state of law (*Rechtsstaat*). In ethico-political terms, the republic of the German idealists is a state of civically minded citizens who are able to free themselves

---

4 On the distinction, see (AA 6:338–342.)

from particular interests and narrow concerns to consider and further the common good. They are to be patriots "with a cosmopolitan intent" (*in weltbürgerlicher Absicht*), to adopt Kant's title phrase for his project of a political philosophy of history.

The essentially republican conception of the state in its specifically legal and ethical character, which unites the differently executed political philosophies of Kant, Fichte and Hegel to form a relatively coherent discourse about the civic relation between the individual and the state, is not without precedence in earlier modern political thought, and which influenced and shaped Kant's, Fichte's and Hegel's thinking about things political. In particular, the German idealists are indebted to Locke for his conception of natural, inalienable rights that bind the sovereign to the law, Rousseau for his conception of the supra-individual subject of the political process ("general will") and the generic personal identity of the political subject and the sovereign ("sovereignty of the people") that turns states from monarchical properties to civic institutions, and Montesquieu for his conception of republican solidarity ("virtue") as the spiritual, quasi-ethical basis of civically minded individual and social action.

The enterprise of addressing and assessing the politico-philosophical actuality of German idealism by way of tracing the political constitution of the individual and the constitution of the political individual in Kant, Fichte and Hegel therefore cannot be carried through outside and in abstraction from modern European political thought in general and English and French political thought in particular. The peculiarities as well as the potential of the contributions made by Kant, Fichte and Hegel to modern political philosophy only emerge in the context and by way of contrast with earlier eighteenth century political thought and its advances toward a specifically modern and quintessentially republican understanding of the relation between the individual and the state.

2 The Incorporated Individual

In the beginning, there was Locke. Hobbes had reacted to the endangerments of the post-reformatory era of religious conflicts and civil wars with a non-theological justification of absolute political power. While making political power depend on human agreement as opposed to divine covenant or dynastic entitlement, Hobbes had conceived of the contract instituting the sovereign power as essentially irrevocable and extensionally unlimited. Once put in place, stately authority, for Hobbes, was akin to the traditional divine right to rule, turning the absolutely ruled state itself, paradigmatically conceived as absolute monarchy, into a "mortal God". Yet the state so conceived and endowed with a power and authority that triumphed over each and every individual, save the monarch himself or herself, was not superhuman in origin. In fact it was the human being "writ large" – an individual designed on a larger scale than any factually given individual.

Moreover, on Hobbes' account, the super-human being that is the state, in addition to being an over-dimensioned human individual, is itself constituted of individual human beings. Strictly speaking, the Hobbesian state is but the sum-total of the subjects that make it up, albeit put into a shape and form that exceeds both their individual being and the sheer accumulation of their number, however large. For Hobbes, the state is the totalization of the individuals and their integration into a comprehensive whole to which they are at once subordinated, as under their absolute lord and master. The iconic expression of the relation between the state and the individual in Hobbes is the frontispiece of the original edition of the *Leviathan* with its pictorial rendition of the state as a giant towering over the earth and everything and everyone on it – a measure of might confirmed in the biblical quotation (from Job 41, 24) placed above the figure of the Leviathan declaring there to be no power over the earth that could be compared to him (*non est potestas super terram quae comparetur ei*) – and yet consisting of and constituted by its own subjects, which are shown as literally making up the body of the Leviathan in the manner of recursive individuality.

It was John Locke who, in reaction to the English end of absolute monarchical power in the "Glorious Revolution" (1688), which tied the British monarchy irrevocably to civil constitution and parliamentary politics and subjected governmental rule to (some) citizens' consent, tamed and domesticated Hobbes' monstrous state by further humanizing the state monster. Rather than having human beings give up their natural, pre-political freedom in the interest of survival and security, as in Hobbes, Locke made the state subservient to the immaterial and material concerns of its subjects that remained in possession of their rights, which now were conceived as both natural and unalienable. The formal expression of the dissolution of absolute political power was the separation of the executive and the legislative power in the state, with the former vested in a king bound by constitutional law and natural right, and the latter placed in the hands of a representative assembly (parliament) designed to convey, consider and conclude the claims and interests of the collective citizenry. On Locke's account, the primary function and the ultimate criterion of state governance is each individual's "property", with the latter term understood in a wide sense to include the individual's immaterial as well as material belongings, viz., life, liberty and possessions.

The pictorial, or rather metaphorical, reflex of Locke's constitutionalization of the monarchic state and of the legal entitlement of its subjects is the image of individuals undergoing "incorporation" – Locke's term – to constitute the state. Already in Hobbes the anthropomorphic conception of the absolute state had found expression in the notion of the "body politic" considered as a body of its own kind that is not physically individuated through matter in motion, but is rather immaterially and politically constituted through the self-submission of originally free but endangered individuals under a contractually created terrestrial Almighty. In Locke the Hobbesian generic reference to the (quasi-)bodily status of the state is specified further by means of the juridico-political notion of incorporation, which in turns draws on the life phenomenon of the intake of nutrition and the integration of previously independent substances into a larger, encompassing whole which they sustain and maintain. Under conditions of incorporation, self-enclosed individuals coalesce to form a non-physical but quasi-organic body of which they are the "members" – parts that belong to a whole that would not be whole without them. By having the individuals assemble, associate and arrange in an original contractual situation, Locke turns each individual into a sustaining member of a larger body that is not physical but political in nature – made up not of blood and flesh, but of citizen-subjects that bring into life and keep alive an entity which in turn serves to safeguard their individual properties (life, liberty, possessions).

It deserves mention that Locke's reliance on the notion of the body politic, while drawing on the organic imagery of the living body and its constitutive members, does not extend the bio-political analogy to include the functional differentiation of the parts of the body politic, as carried out in the *locus classicus* for the somatico-political analogy undertaken by Menenius Agrippa and documented in Livy's *History of Rome* (Book II, Chapter 32). In an effort to appease and reconcile the plebeians revolting against patrician rule, Agrippa had resorted to the simile of the bodily organs refusing to serve any longer the apparently idle stomach, only to bring about their own emaciation and to discover in the process that it was the stomach which had provided nourishment to them all along and not vice versa.

By contrast, Locke's focus throughout is on the genuine status of each full member of the body politic as equally free, but also as equally constrained by political law. Moreover, Locke goes to great length in ascertaining the conditions and the extent of the subjects' entitlement to rebel or revolt against a ruler who executes political power in violation of the natural rights of the subject-citizens. For Locke, the individual, transformed from a solitary bearer of natural rights into a civically functioning member of the body politic, is and remains a member equal to the other political individuals so constituted and is to be respected in his inalienable rights by the sovereign power that rules over each and all of them.

3 The Autonomous Individual

With Montesquieu, the Lockean revolution in political philosophy from divine rights of monarchical rule to natural rights of political subjects and civil laws of governance moves from the local stage of post-reformatory Europe to the global theatre of universal history. For Montesquieu all monarchical rule that is not in turn ruled by law, including past and present absolute monarchy, is despotic and inimical to political freedom. Moreover, for Montesquieu, the historical origin and traditional guarantor of political freedom is not monarchical governance, including that of modern, constitutional monarchy, but republican rule, especially in its aristocratic variety as the rule of a select group in the interest of the entire republic. Montesquieu contrasts the operative principles of despotic and monarchical rule – "fear" (*crainte*) and "honor" (*honneur*), respectively – with the republican principle of civic "virtue" (*vertu*), which instills loyalty toward the republican state into the political individual, making it transcend and control selfish interests and particular concerns in favor of the commonwealth (*res publica*).[5]

Rousseau takes up both Locke's focus on individual rights and Montesquieu's concern with the civically virtuous individual by making the politically constituted individual both the subject and the sovereign of the republic that is the state. Not only is the individual inviolable in his (or her) property and inalienable in his (or her) rights. The political individual is also the lawgiver whose will issues the very rules that govern him as well as the other citizens. To be sure, the legislative will of the political individual is not the arbitrary will of the particular human being, but a will that is mindful of the commonwealth and heeds the needs of the political whole rather than partisan interest. Nor is the politically considerate will ("general will"; *volonté générale*) identical with the aggregate will of the majority or even of all members of the republican state ("will of all"; *volonté de tous*). Rather, it is the normatively constrained will of the politically minded individual (Rousseau 1964a, Livre II, Chap. 2.).

For Rousseau the contractual entrance into the civil state involves the equivalent exchange of "natural freedom" (*liberté naturelle*), which is essentially physical and reflects the natural inequality among human beings, for "civil freedom" (*liberté civile*), which is essentially cultural and geared toward non-physical, "moral" equality. In the process, physically obtained and held "possession" turns into legally acquired and secured "property". Rather than loosing their freedom altogether, as in Hobbes' absolutist state, the citizens in Rousseau's re-

---

5 See (Montesquieu 1876, Livre troisième).

public retain or rather regain it under the guise of equally distributed entitlements and requirements. Rousseau also regards the establishment and acquisition of civil liberty as a condition for the possibility of "moral freedom" (*liberté morale*). The political liberation of the previously merely natural individual from the rule of the instincts and passions turns him into a "master of himself", who is obedient only to a law which he has prescribed to himself (Rousseau 1964a, Livre I, Chap. 8.).

Compared to Locke's liberal conception of majoritarian rule that seeks to balance individual pursuits, group interests and the common good by means of parliamentary decision procedures, Rousseau's radically republican politics of the general will may seem to allow, if not encourage, minoritarian dictates. The same move that promotes the political individual from subject to sovereign also transforms him from a particular individual to an individuation of republican virtue. Yet all is not Robespierre-in-the-making in Rousseau's political philosophy. In particular, Rousseau stresses the comparative independence of the political individual, whom he regards as an autonomous member of the body politic with a life and a will of his own. In addition to its specifically political identity as a sovereign-subject of the virtuous republic, the individual remains a free and responsible agent of moral conduct, his individuality being the result of sentimental education as much as political pedagogy.

With his distinction between the two capacities of the individual – an extra-political identity as a human being (*homme*) endowed with a particular interest (*interêt particulier*) and a political identity as citizen (*citoyen*) with a common interest (*interêt commun*) (Rousseau 1964a, Livre I, Chap. 7.) – Rousseau has formulated a genuinely modern, complex conception of the individual, specifically different from the ancient conception of political liberty and its associated vision of civic republicanism, which had defined the human being exclusively through his political role and function, reducing the human being to the citizen and leaving little room for personal freedom in the arrangements and choices of private life sought and cherished in modern times. In attributing to the individual a twofold body – one private and particular, one public and communal – Rousseau seeks to reconcile and combine ancient and modern liberty, private individualism and political republicanism.

4 The Generated Individual

Rousseau's lasting legacy to Kant's political philosophy, which is both a philosophy of political history and a philosophy of political law, was the notion of the human being as essentially free, viz., as free from instinctual tutelage and left to its own designs and developments and enabling the human being, individually and collectively, to be of his (or her) own making and destines it to become his (or her) own master.⁶ Rousseau had termed the basic human condition of openness for self-induced change, which could be change for the better but risked to be change for the worse, "perfectibility" (*perfectibilité*), thereby indicating the potential, even the calling of the human being for incremental improvement.⁷

Under the twin influence of Rousseau's cultural critique of political inequality in the second *Discourse* and Rousseau's philosophical foundation of a republican polity in *On the Social Contract*, Kant gave his political philosophy the form of a natural history of human freedom gradually leading human development from legal and political anarchy to the rule of law and the establishment of republican self-governance. Kant's decisive addition to the prior accounts of the politicized individual in Locke and Rousseau was the strict separation between the individual and the species level of human development, especially of human self-perfection. For Kant human progress, in particular progress toward civil rights and political freedom, does not occur at the level of the individual, within a given individual's life span, but is to be regarded as a spatially and temporally extended development at the level of the human species (*genus*; *Gattung*), involving different regions of the earth and extended periods of time as well as numerous retardations and relapses (AA 8:23).

On Kant's analysis, the human species is the subject of political progress in the twofold sense of being the target of such comprehensive change as well as the agent, albeit not a conscious and much less a self-conscious agent of political progress, but an agent manifesting the secret designs of a teleological process, which Kant attributes to a providentially conceived "Nature". In Kant the secret agent of history – of juridico-political history, to be precise – is supra-individual, but it is not superhuman. Rather, the super-subject of the history of legal and political freedom is human nature generically embodied and teleologically conceived. The particular propensity adduced by Kant as the clandestine conductor of human development is the human being's "unsocial sociability" (*ungesellige Geselligkeit*) (AA 8:20), a dual disposition that has human beings flee as much as seek each other's company – flee them in order to be able to live by their own individual designs and desires, and seek them in order to socially enlarge and enhance their limited individual faculties and forces (AA 8:20).⁸

---

6 On the Platonic conception of self-rule in Kant, see (Zöller 2010).
7 (Rousseau 1964b, Première Partie).
8 On Kant's account of cultural and specifically political anthropogenesis, see (Zöller 2011a) and (Zöller 2012).

Unlike Aristotle (and an entire tradition of political thought following him), who regarded the human being as being naturally social to the point of being naturally state-building or "political", Kant considers the human as originally both asocial and social, and views the interplay and interference of human asociality and human sociality as the mechanism – not to call it, the cunning – behind human political development, which results from inventive compromises sought and found between the two equally ineliminable tendencies in human conduct. Under conditions of each individual's asocial, even anti-social selfishness, rightfully supposed by everyone in everyone else on the basis of his (or her) own selfish self-experience, combined with the equally undeniable mutual dependence of human beings on each other, human beings are contrived to invent and implement modes of living together that balance the need for individual independence with the countervailing need for mutual support. The perfect expression of the sought after equilibrium of individual and society, to be reached over the course of human history, is the legally regulated plurality of individuals that is "civil society" (*bürgerliche Gesellschaft*) (AA 8:22), which is first to be realized at a regional level, in a territorial state of republican constitution if not governance, and eventually as a league of (nation) states that is to achieve the cosmopolitan scope of human history (AA 8:24 ff).

5 The Derived Individual

Kant's portrayal of the origin of human society in general and of political society in particular combines Rousseau's nostalgic vision of self-sufficient individual existence in the "state of nature" (*état de nature*) with Locke's liberal conception of the political or civil society as the defender of incorporated individuality. As in both prior philosophers, the individual in Kant occurs in a twofold guise as both the pre- and extra-political, natural individual, and as the socially constituted, political individual. Kant also shares with Locke and Rousseau the notion of the continued independence of the politicized individual, who is an integral part of the body politic, yet not a mere function of the whole but one of its constituent "members" without which the body, that is, the state ("republic") could neither arise nor last.

Kant's heir-apparent, Johann Gottlieb Fichte, went farther yet in tying individuality to sociality in general and political individuality to political socialization in particular. For Fichte there is no pre-social and, for that matter, pre-political human existence. Based on his post-Kantian account of self-constitutive I-hood ("pure I", "absolute I": *reines Ich, absolutes Ich*), Fichte regards individuality as systematically secondary to supra- or rather pre-individual, absolute subjectivity ("subject-object") and its proto-social manifestation as undifferentiated ego mass (*Masse des Bestimmbaren*).[9] The individual, natural as well as political, is derived from some pre-individual ground, alternatively figured as absolute I, We and absolute community.

Fichte takes great pains to reconstruct the constitution of individuality out of sociality. In particular, he depicts the primal scene of a human being with only potential practical rationality (will) undergoing a call or solicitation (*Aufforderung*) by an already rationally willing and acting individual, which initiates the emergence of self-conscious practical individuality in the socially nascent individual. On Fichte's account, a human individual emerges as such only among the likes of himself or herself (*seinesgleichen*). The practical parity between the soliciting and the solicited individual finds original expression in the mutuality of "recognition" (*Anerkennung*) between the two individuals by means of which they regard and treat each other as free individual beings that are to conduct themselves toward each other in consideration of the other's equal freedom (Fichte 1991, §§ 1–3),

In a further step, Fichte extends the reciprocity of recognition among the two individuals involved in the primary scene of social initiation into practical rationality to a plurality of free and recognized-to-be-free individuals. According to Fichte, the principle of the continued mutual recognition in inter-individual relations is the concept of "right" (*Recht*) and its codification as the "law of right" (*Rechtsgesetz*), according to which everyone is to limit the use of his (or her) freedom by the conception of everyone else's freedom (Fichte 1991, §§ 4–7). The formal framework for assuring the rule of right and law is the state, which Fichte regards chiefly as a "state of right" (*Staat des Rechts*).[10] It deserves mention that, unlike Kant, who subordinates the sphere of right and its political institution and preservation to the categorical imperative, Fichte maintains a strict separation between unconditional ethical obligation and the development of juridico-political principles and practices governed by prudence and shaped by history.

6 The Formed Individual

In Hegel's integrated moral social, legal and political philosophy, Kant's project of a political philosophy of history as the natural-cultural history of freedom,

---

9 On Fichte's transcendental philosophy of human sociality, see (Zöller 1998).
10 On Fichte's philosophy of law and right, see (Zöller 2011b).

and Fichte's two-tiered deduction of individuality from sociality and of sociality from civility, are taken up into a systematically grounded, historically informed and developmentally structured account of the individual, interindividual and supraindividual actualization of freedom. The almost exclusive focus, to be found in left and right Hegelians alike, on Hegel's quasi-religious defense of the state as the "actual God" (*wirklicher Gott*) and the "earthly divine" (*irdisches Göttliches*) (Hegel 2004, §§ 258 and 272 (*Zusatz*)) tends to obscure that the state in Hegel is at once an end and a means – the worldly end of all human endeavors and the enabling medium for each such endeavor. Rather than submerging the individual into the state, or even having the latter suppress the former, Hegel has the state generate and guarantee the individual in its personal, social and political existence.

In particular, Hegel considers the individual worthy of that name not the object of natural occurrence or social chance, but the result of "formation" (*Bildung*) and "work" (*Arbeit*) that turns a private person and his particular preferences into a public *persona* with a civic identity (Hegel 2004, §§ 187 and 196). The onto-political transition from the particular to the universal and from the merely private to the manifestly political is not to be seen as a curtailment of the individual. Rather, Hegel considers the individual's socio-political formation as a process that enriches the continued private existence of the individual with civic functions that lend meaning and purpose to an otherwise perhaps thoroughly productive, but ultimately pointless social existence.

Hegel conveys the continued social validity of pre- and extra-political life by subsuming the state, along with the other forms of social life, under the concept of "ethical life" (*Sittlichkeit*), thereby distinguishing as much as linking the private and the political, the personal and the public. Notoriously, Hegel differentiates human sociality into its natural, or quasi-natural, basis in the family, its artificial but equally essential sundering in the economic and professional spheres of civil society (*bürgerliche Gesellschaft*) and its reintegration in the complexly differentiated and systematically unified whole of the state (*Staat*).

By delegating the pursuits of needs and interests to an intermediate and transitional stage of social life, positioned between the natural and the political, Hegel has liberated the state, which is now the "political state" (*politischer Staat*) in an eminent sense, from the organization and oversight of business and commerce, and freed it for the specifically political task of maintaining peace within and without as well as lending a final orientation and an ultimate purpose to individual occupations in the "state of peace" (*Staat des Friedens*). On Hegel's assessment, the political constitution of the state involves the formation and function of politically charged individuals, chiefly among them the state officials (*Staatsdiener*), that serve the interests of the political whole and constitute the core of the state's middling estate (*Mittelstand*), located between the social opposites of the laboring and the landed parts of the citizenry, and serving to integrate and unite the multiform modes of manual, industrial and agrarian productivity (Hegel 2004, §§ 294f. and 297). Moreover, Hegel recognizes the need for a symbolic expression of the state's political identity through a figurehead provided by a hereditary monarchy limited by a constitution and checked by a representative legislative body.

But Hegel's pointed politicization of the individual, which includes treating the state as an individual in its own right (Hegel 2004, § 321), also leaves room, and even creates space, for the unfolding and flourishing of the individual in its particularity and privacy. Hegel explicitly rejects the dissolution of the individual into the state that he finds in the ancient world, especially in classical Greek political life, and epitomized in Plato's *Republic*, as incompatible with the modern sense of personal freedom and the intrinsic value of the particular individual. Under conditions of political modernity, freedom must be twofold – private and public, subjective and substantial, particular and universal, civically social and eminently political.

On Hegel's balanced view of the reciprocal political relation between individual and civil society, the state is the sole secure condition for obtaining particular ends and personal well-being, while in turn being tied to the individuals for achieving and maintaining its "effectiveness" (*Wirksamkeit*) (Hegel 2004, § 277). In an analogy that harkens to the episode from Roman republican history cited earlier and as preserved by Livy, Hegel likens the role of the individual to the status of the stomach in a living body, which at once maintains its independence and is elevated, in fact "sacrificed" (*sakrifiziert*), by being made to go over into the whole. Hegel returns to the religious metaphor of sacrifice – this time by drawing not on the Latin term but the corresponding German word – in his account of military life, in which the specifically modern form of bravery (*Tapferkeit*) is said to no longer consist in extraordinary acts of "personal courage", but in being prepared to give oneself over (*Aufopferung*) to service for the state, thereby performing the integration of the individual into the universal (*Einordnung in das Allgemeine*) (Hegel 2004, §§ 269 (*Zusatz*), 278 and 328)

The counterpart of Hegel's organicist conception of civic individuality is his political critique of the inorganic collectivity called by him variously "people" (*Volk*), "*hoi polloi*" or, more tellingly, if less flatteringly, "rabble" (*Pöbel*) (Hegel 2004, § 301). Hegel shares the contemporary distrust in the political maturity of the populace that does not know what it wants and is unfit to rule itself and share in the governance of the state. For Hegel, popular political participation takes place through "delegated individuals" in selective legislative chambers (Hegel 2004, §§ 308–313). In an analogous move, Hegel critiques the populist medium of public opinion (*öffentliche Meinung*; 471) for its lack of reflection ("mediation"; *Vermittlung*) in the process of political deliberation and decision making (Hegel 2004, §§ 317–319). By contrast, Hegel's political state, ostensibly a constitutional monarchy, takes on the traits of a republic of civically minded or, in Hegel's somewhat antiquated phrase, "patriotic" individuals who place their personal freedom in the service of the public good, and not because they are constrained to do so, but out of their "political mindedness" (*politische Gesinnung*) (Hegel 2004, § 268).

7 The Democratized Individual

Fichte's integration of the philosophy of right into a political philosophy of history had narrowed human political progress to the rule of law and dissociated legal equality from civic or political freedom, in effect advocating a return to authoritarian politics, albeit based on the authority of reason. Hegel's distinction of civil society and the political state had assured the personal freedom of the individual at the price of its separation from political freedom, in effect identifying the latter with supra-individual state authority. With Alexis de Tocqueville's political portrayal of the early United States of America, a form of governance came into view that was not only republican in nature, but democratic in its operation, involving the active participation of the political individual in representative self-governance at the local, state and federal level. Almost two and a half millennia after the Athenian experiment with popular rule, the name, "democracy" came to be reused not only as the designation for the deficient governance by the many, and by the many poor at that, but for a "democratic republic", and a republican democracy marked by widespread political participation of an increasingly wealthy populace.

Yet Tocqueville not only noticed the political liberation of an entire population, but keenly perceived the new forms of political life emerging among the citizens of the burgeoning United States. In particular, he noted the effects of radical, pervasive equality on the shape of civic life, which made individuals not only equally free but freely equal, and to that extent less individualistic than in traditional, pre-democratic society marked by distinction and rank. As a result, the democratic individual he encountered in the town halls and in the market places of the American federal republic seemed small to Tocqueville – free and equal but also less significant and less remarkable due to the sameness of everyone with everyone else. Tocqueville also noticed the reverse of individual diminution in the state's increasing power in ruling over and administering to the multitude of equal individuals, in effect foreshadowing the benign Leviathan that is the modern mass-democratic state:

> In a democratic community individuals are very powerless; but the State which represents them all, and contains them all in its grasp, is very powerful.[11]

Tocqueville's perceptive portrayal of the mixed blessings of participatory mass democracy lends a surprising actuality to the roughly contemporary politico-philosophical counterculture of German idealism with its dual commitment to personal and political freedom, and to particular individuality and civic responsibility. At the descriptive level, the political philosophy of Kant, Fichte and Hegel demonstrates the compatibility and even the mutual requirement of individual pursuits and common concerns. The former are as much the enabling material conditions of the latter, as the latter are the enabling formal conditions of the former. At the normative level, classical German political philosophy exhibits the practical need and the theoretical justification for a complementary, mutually enhancing cultivation of the free, self-determined individual and the free, self-determined civic whole ("state"). No free state ("republic") without free citizens, and vice versa.

In their specific approaches, the politico-philosophical thinking of Kant, Fichte and Hegel each adds a distinctive perspective to the theoretically claimed and practically called-for co-presence of the privately personal individual and the politically public individual in modern society. Kant's political philosophy of history focuses on the cosmopolitan, supranational project of civically ordered freedom at the intra-state and the inter-state levels. Fichte's political philosophy of right emphasizes the essential role of civic freedom for the emergence of free individuality. Hegel's political philosophy of ethical life adds a final focus reaching beyond the division of labor in modern society and the multiple purposes served by civil society to the singular and supreme end intended by the political state.

Almost two hundred years after the idealist speculations of Kant, Fichte and Hegel and the timely-untimely meditations of Tocqueville, the normative accounts of the classical German political philosophers and the descriptive assessments of the French political theorist merge to form the image of a political (counter-)culture and its cultivated (counter-)politics that seeks to fortify individuals against losing their personal freedom – and along with it their personal dignity – in conspicuous consumption and greedy commerce, and against abandoning their political freedom – and along with it their political dignity – in deferred

---

11 (Tocqueville 1999, Vol. 2, Ch. XII).

and delegated decision processes under the tutelage of appointed bureaucrats and elected party officials.

The republican intent behind the classical German political philosophers and Tocqueville alike calls for a strong and influential middle class – already identified by Aristotle as the strategic center and unifying element in the polity. But the political danger of modern egalitarian society does not spring from the much-bemoaned decline of the bourgeoisie, once the social bearer and promoter of material, scientific and artistic culture, but from the early demise of a citizenry that emerged only fairly late as a shaping political factor in the modern world and that is about to vanish again in the face of economic preferences and pressures as well as religious revivals and reinvigorations, both of which revert free citizens to willing victims of manipulation and superstition.

Bibliography

Berlin, Isaiah (1990): *Four Essays on Liberty*. Oxford: Oxford University Press.
Fichte, Johann Gottlieb (1991): *Grundlage des Naturrechts*. Hamburg: Meiner.
Hegel, Georg Wilhelm Friedrich (2004): *Grundlinien der Philosophie des Recht*. In: *Werke in zwanzig Bänden*. (Edited by Eva Moldenhauer and Karl Markus Michel). Frankfurt/M: Suhrkamp.
Rousseau, Jean-Jacques (1964a): *Du Contrat social*. In: Oeuvres Complètes Vol. 3 (Ed. by Bernard Gagnebin and Marcel Raymond). Paris: Gallimard.
Rousseau, Jean-Jacques (1964b): *Discours sur l'origine et les fondements de l'inégalité parmi les hommes*. In: Oeuvres Complètes Vol. 3 (Ed. by Bernard Gagnebin and Marcel Raymond). Paris: Gallimard.
Kant, Immanuel (1900 ff.): *Gesammelte Schriften* [=AA], Akademieausgabe. Berlin.
Montesquieu (1876): *De l'esprit des lois. Première partie*. In: Oeuvres Complètes de Montesquieu. (Ed. by Édouard Laboulaye). Vol. 3. Paris: Garnier Frères.
Plato (1960), *The Republic*. Trans. B. Jowett. New York: Random House.
Tocqueville, Alexis (1999): *De la démocratie en Amérique*. Paris: Flammarion.
Zöller, Günter (2001): "Die Bestimmung der Bestimmung des Menschen bei Mendelssohn und Kant." In: Volker Gerhardt/Rolf-Peter Horstmann/Ralph Schumacher (Eds.): *Kant und die Berliner Aufklärung. Akten des 9. Internationalen Kant-Kongresses (26. bis 31. März 2000 in Berlin)*. Berlin/New York: Walter de Gruyter, pp. 476–489.
Zöller, Günter (2010): "Autocracy. The Psycho-Politics of Self-Rule in Plato and Kant." In Edmondo Balsamão Pires/Burkhard Nonnenmacher/Stefan Büttner-von Stülpnagel (Eds.): *Relations of the Self*. Coimbra: Coimbra University Press, pp. 385–404.
Zöller, Günter (1998): *Fichte's Transcendental Philosophy. The Original Duplicity of Intelligence and Will*. Cambridge: Cambridge University Press.
Zöller, Günter (2011a): "Kant's Political Anthropology." In: *Kant Yearbook* 3, pp. 131–161.
Zöller, Günter (Ed.) (2011b): *Der Staat als Mittel zum Zweck. Fichte über Freiheit, Recht und Gesetz*. Baden-Baden: Nomos.

Zöller, Günter (2012): "Between Rousseau and Freud. Kant on Cultural Uneasiness." In: Oliver Thorndike (Ed.): *Rethinking Kant*, Vol. 3. Newcastle upon Tyne: Cambridge Scholars Publishing.

Zöller, Günter (2014): "'Hierarchie'. Schelling über Staat und Kirche in den Stuttgarter Privatvorlesungen". In: Lore Hühn/Philipp Schwab (Eds.): *Natur und Anthropologie. Zum 200. Jubiläum von Schellings Stuttgarter Privatvorlesungen*. Tübingen: Mohr Siebeck, pp. 279–297.

Zöller, Günter (2015): *Res Publica. Plato's "Republic" in Classical German Philosophy*. Hong Kong: The Chinese University Press; North American distribution: Albany, NY: State University of New York Press.

Zöller, Günter (2016): "Republicity. The Forensic Form of Life". In: *Yearbook for Eastern and Western Philosophy 1*, pp. 123–135.

II Themes from Hegel

Markus Gabriel
A Very Heterodox Reading of the Lord-Servant-Allegory in Hegel's *Phenomenology of Spirit*

Given the complexity of the argument to follow, which should stand or fall in its own right, I will refrain from extended commentary on other possible or actual overall readings of the influential chapter of Hegel's *Phenomenology of Spirit* that I will focus on in this paper. My paper is neither a survey of the recent literature on the topic, nor do I intend to place it in the context of recent trends in Hegel scholarship. However, before we get started with the actual work, let me just briefly note that the recent engagement with Hegel by John McDowell, Robert Brandom, and Robert Pippin in America and Pirmin Stekeler-Weithofer and Anton Friedrich Koch in Germany has led to very significant breakthroughs in our understanding of the philosophical stakes of Hegel's arguments.[1] Some of their pioneering work pertains to the arguments presented in my paper. The common denominator of this breakthrough is that this recent work is able to reconstruct Hegel's arguments in a manner which departs from Hegel's own form of presentation, as this is often almost indecipherable by our contemporary standards. Yet, there are at least two presuppositions widespread in these readings as far as the *Phenomenology of Spirit* is concerned I do not share, one *methodological* and the other more *substantial*.

The methodological assumption I reject is that Hegel presents *his* views in the *Phenomenology*, such as his views about sense-certainty, perception, and self-consciousness. In this book we do not find any of Hegel's views on these topics. Rather, he is discussing various attempts to give an account of truth-apt reference to objective states of affairs which all fail for interesting and systematically connected reasons. In presenting and discussing the structure of these failures Hegel at most presents his view about the nature of failures in phi-

---

[1] Cf. (McDowell 2009); (Brandom 1999); (Brandom 2007); (Brandom 2008); (Pippin 1989); (Pippin 2007); (Pippin 2011); (Stekeler-Weithofer 1992); (Stekeler-Weithofer 2005); (Koch 2006); (Koch 2008); (Koch 2011). In his interesting book on *Self-Consciousness* (Rödl 2007), Sebastian Rödl proposes a theory of self-consciousness that bears important relations to Kant and Hegel, even though he does not present his account in explicit discussion with theirs. As will become clear in due course, Rödl's account is closer to what is going in the *Science of Logics* where Hegel, or rather his interlocutor, is trying to repair the weaknesses of the *Phenomenology*-discussion of the topic.

losophy. Specifically, in the *Phenomenology* he argues that there is rational theory change in philosophy and not just an arbitrary or contingent exchange of opinions.[2] He supports this view about the nature of philosophy by showing how one failure needs to another failure which resolves some shortcomings of an earlier failure while at the same time generating new problems. The *Phenomenology* is, thus, a systematically constructed series of failed conceptions of truth-apt reference to objective states of fairs. No position within the *Phenomenology*, none of the famous shapes of consciousness, represents Hegel's theory of said reference. This is one of the sense in which the *Phenomenology* is an introduction to the standpoint of philosophy as science, that is, as a positive development of philosophical concepts. In my reading, I emphasize the feature of the project according to which we are dealing with a "presentation of appearing knowledge (Darstellung des erscheinenden Wissens)" rather than with Hegel's own philosophical knowledge-claims about the nature of conscious intentionality.

The *substantial* assumption of recent reconstructions that I do not share is that Hegel's project is the continuation of Kantian transcendental semantics and not (primarily) an engagement with metaphysics and ontology.[3] Hegel frequently expresses a variety of criticisms of Kant, particularly against his distinction between appearances and things in themselves, and he himself insists that there is no coherent way of thinking about conscious intentionality without admitting that we can unproblematically grasp things in themselves.[4] But I will set these historical details aside in order to present a somewhat detailed and very heterodox reading of a highly influential chapter of the *Phenomenology*, "Lordship and Servitude (*Herrschaft und Knechtschaft*)".[5]

---

[2] Thanks to Robert Pippin for insisting on this point in discussion.

[3] To be more precise, Robert Pippin who is often credite with a Kantian reading of Hegel does not exactly hold this view, as he believes that Hegel is Post-Kantian to the extent that he rejects the modern (Leibniz-Wolffian) dogmatic rationalist metaphysics attacked by Kant, but not metaphysics as such. This does not rule out an appreciation of earlier enterprises in metaphysics and ontology. On this see also (Gabriel 2007) and (Gabriel 2009). On Hegel's critique of Kant in light of the reading proposed in this paper see my (Gabriel forthcoming).

[4] This is, I take it, where McDowell's project of finding "intentionality unproblematic" is really continuous with Hegel. Hegel does not give up the idea of an independent reality to be referred to or thought about, but rather wants to think of that reality as precisely compatible with the fact of its availability to concept-mongering activities. Cf. (McDowell 2009, p. 3).

[5] For the sake of simplicity I will translate "Herrschaft" by "lordship" and "Knechtschaft" by "servitude" and, correspondingly, "Herr" by "lord" and "Knecht" by "servant." I hope that no particular bias of interpretation will be associated with this decision. The argument presented

The degree of heterodoxy of my paper can be determined by measuring the extent both to which the reading it suggests radically departs from the tradition and to which it manages to deflate Hegel's metaphors. By a "deflation" of metaphors, I mean the clear identification of the concepts Hegel refers to with the help of his metaphors. His metaphors are part of larger allegories he sets up in order to illustrate how "natural consciousness", that is, everybody who is aware of their awareness of something, is blinded by its homegrown picture-like representations, what Hegel calls "Vorstellung".[6] Deflationary readings of Hegel thus generally tend to be heterodox in the sense that they identify the non-metaphorical concept behind apparently metaphorical terms, such as "life," "desire," "master," "death," "satisfaction," "recognition," etc. A very heterodox reading such as the one sketched in this paper is, accordingly, *very* heterodox in the sense that it is *maximally* deflationary. In short, I believe that every single one of the expressions most cherished by the most influential traditions of commentary on the often so-called "master-slave-dialectic" is a metaphor for a concept, and that consequently certainly all orthodox readings are misled by metaphors.[7] To put it as bluntly as I can: all theories of life, desire, or social recognition that take themselves to be grounded in Hegel's *views* are only grounded in Hegel's *metaphors*. Interestingly, Hegel does not even use the word "Anerkennung" "recognition" a single time in the self-consciousness chapter of the *Phe-*

---

in the chapter should not hinge on a prior understanding of these terms, precisely because Hegel gives these terms a clearer meaning in his discussion of the underlying concepts.

6 For a discussion of the strengths and potential weaknesses of "allegorical interpretations" of Hegel in general see (Pippin 2011, pp. 14–15), n. 12. Hegel himself characterizes an allegory as "ein Ganzes, das durch äußre Attribute dargestellt wird" (Hegel 2008, p. XXX). On the concept of "Vorstellung" in the context of the philosophy of subjective spirit and the metatheoretical relevance of it see (Gabriel 2015). (Rometsch 2017) rightly points out that any reading on the traditional spectrum, from the "orthodox" social reading to McDowellian heterodoxy will rely on some allegorical claims, as any such reading will have to give a philosophical, conceptual meaning to Hegel's metaphors spread out over the texts.

7 Of course, some prominent vocabulary of the chapter, in particular, "self-consciousness" are taken at face value. One of my reasons for this is that they belong to the meta-vocabulary which is driving the development of the account from the standpoint of absolute knowing, that is, the standpoint of theory-construction which is precisely not taken in by the metaphors typically associated with the accounts of conscious intentionality discussed in the form of shapes of consciousness. Notice that the criterion of heterodoxy is defined in light of the orthodoxy, where the orthodoxy is represented by the social readings of the chapter. For an early criticism of the social readings as such see (Kelly 1966). Thanks to Michael Forster for making me aware of Kelly's work. For a nuanced discussion of various possible aspects which have be discerned in the lordship-bondage chapter see (Forster 1998, pp. 247–255).

nomenology, but there only speaks of recognizing, *Anerkennen*, which is an essential ingredient in his diagnosis of the failure of self-consciousness.

Before the games begin, I will first (1.) explain what I take to be the actual stakes of the argument of the *Phenomenology*. Hegel explicitly determines a goal and sets up rules that determine achievement conditions. If he either does not act according to the rules or does not reach the goal by legitimate steps, the argument fails. In other words, I will first broadly sketch what the "method" is. I will then (2.) reconstruct the introduction to Chapter IV of the book, which bears the title "the truth of self-certainty." In part 3. I will then reconstruct the argument of IV.A., the famous chapter on "Dependence and Independence of Self-Consciousness; Lordship and Servitude."

1 The Rules of the Game

First and foremost, we need to settle the meaning of "consciousness." Given what Hegel says in the Introduction, the meaning of "consciousness" can be pinned down as intentionality in the minimal sense of a state which is *about* something. "Consciousness" in Hegel simply means *aboutness*. "Knowledge," another term Hegel frequently uses in the Introduction, and famously claims to be a result of the *Phenomenology* (in "Absolute Knowledge"), presupposes intentionality. One cannot know what one cannot refer to at all. Knowledge is knowledge of something; it involves objects or facts that are not necessarily a relatum in the relation of aboutness. Trivially, some things we can know are not identical with being known – the state of knowing is at least not in all instances identical with what it is about, with the possible exception of the state of knowing what knowledge is. Any theory of intentionality has to account for the fact that intentionality can be a part of knowledge. This provides us with two constraints that are very important for the development of the book: objectivity and fallibility.

The *objectivity* of intentionality consists in the fact that it can be about objects that would have been the way they turn out to be when referred to, had no one ever referred to them. Ways objects would have been had no one referred to them I call "maximally modally robust facts."[8] Maximally modally robust facts are very objective, as it were, but of course objectivity is not defined by the fact that intentionality is about this or that particular kind of object. The objectivity of

---

[8] That there are such facts should be counted among the realist platitudes one has to accept when spelling out what it is to refer to a reality we do not produce by referring to it. For a more detailed discussion of this see (Gabriel 2008). For further discussion of the book in the light of the topics of this paper see (Koch 2012).

intentionality is a feature of intentionality and not of its objects. We will see in a moment why this is so.

The second constraint, *fallibility*, becomes important once we realize that intentionality is entangled with knowledge and that it can go wrong. There can be reference failures, and if there is a reference failure, any knowledge claim built on the instance of intentionality in question will be a false knowledge claim and not amount to knowledge. A knowledge claim can fail by being based on a reference failure. Here is a simple example: A famous clown approaches. We see something red on his face and believe that he is wearing his red clown nose and hence claim to know that a clown nose is approaching our position in space-time right now. However, it turns out that the clown is not wearing his nose today, but rather happens to be carrying a red ball in front of his nose for some reason.

We can think about all sorts of objects, some of which are involved in maximally modally robust facts, such as the formation of our planet.[9] Some other objects are not as robust. Some social objects, such as certain social roles are evidently constructed insofar as they would not exist had no one been around to have beliefs about them.[10] Trivially, higher-order beliefs involve some facts with a null degree of robustness, such as the fact that I have a belief about a belief. This will be crucial for self-consciousness.

To sum up, the basic entity under scrutiny is consciousness. And consciousness is a relation between something and what it is about, where the aboutness is the relation. Most saliently, intentionality is realized as an aspect of knowledge, that is, when we know something about something. In this scenario, there are two very general constraints on intentionality: It has to be objective and fallible.

The third and last constraint, *topic-neutrality*, derives from Hegel's post-Kantian concern to unify reason; it can be boiled down to the following chain of reasoning. It might seem that acts of referring to good food, to the Big Bang, to universities, to cats, and to the moon are structurally different in that referring to these different kinds of objects requires different kinds of activities. In this case, it might seem that there could not be a unified account of intentionality

---

[9] Here I using "object" in the wide or formal sense of anything we can have a truth-apt thought about. This includes events such as the Big Bang or the formation of our planet. Arguably, Hegel himself operates at a similar level of generality in the self-consciousness chapter, as he is discussing accounts of intentionality that try to break free of the model of perception as reference to particular, stable objects in a given scene.

[10] On the "ontological subjectivity" of social facts in contraposition to their "epistemological objectivity" see, of course, (Searle 2007) and (Searle 2011).

or an overall theory of intentionality. However, all entities in my fairly random list can be referred to and known about, and it is not evident why the difference in content should entail a difference in form. The post-Kantians Fichte, Schelling, and Hegel agree that we need a unified treatment of intentionality in order to avoid splitting reason or rationality itself into an indefinite number of capacities or faculties. A theory of intentionality should consequently be able to account for intentionality's topic-neutrality, that is, for the fact that we can refer to all sorts of objects and know about them by referring to them in whichever way is useful to accomplish the ends of intentionality, most particularly knowledge.

The *Phenomenology* is a succession of theories of intentionality. The criterion for accepting or rejecting a theory is defined by the three constraints: Objectivity, fallibility, and topic-neutrality. The starting point of the whole book, *Sense-Certainty*, for instance, accounts for its topic-neutrality by ontologically committing only to individuals. Everything we can refer to and thereby acquire knowledge about is an individual. Let us call this "rampant nominalism". These individuals exist anyway, they are maximally modally robust, and this is why we can be right or wrong about them. The theory breaks down for many reasons, the simplest being that it does not withstand self-application: Given that it claims that there is intentionality and given that it claims that everything there is is an individual, there is an individual that consists of an instance of reference, an instance of being referred to, and the instance of these two being relata of the relation of aboutness. Sense-Certainty is not capable of distinguishing these three individuals from any other three individuals: it is forced to think of relations as just more individuals, which triggers famous regresses reminiscent of Aristotle's third man argument and Bradleyian, British Idealism regresses.[11] The claim that everything we can refer to is an individual entails under self-application that any instance of reference is both itself an individual and can only consist of individuals if it has a structure at all. For this and many other pertinent reasons, *Sense-Certainty* fails. The goal of the *Phenomenology* is thus well defined: We are looking for a theory of intentionality, which accounts for its objectivity, fallibility, and topic-neutrality.[12]

---

11 Cf. (Horstmann 1984).
12 We cannot rule out in advance or *ad hoc* that this theory can be about itself. We are simply capable of developing a theory of aboutness, of having thoughts about aboutness, and of claiming knowledge about aboutness. As long as one accepts the three constraints, it is not necessary to argue that self-reference is essentially different from reference full stop, as this violates the constraint of topic-neutrality.

2 The Truth of Self-Certainty: Introduction

The chapter on self-consciousness deals with self-reference in the form of higher-order intentionality. The first part of Chapter IV. serves as an introduction of the concept of self-consciousness and culminates in a discussion of higher-order intentionality in the last two paragraphs (¶¶11–12). I will not be able to account for the origin of self-consciousness, which is the theme of the preceding chapter. This would take me more than one additional paper. All we need is the thin notion of consciousness according to which some subject S can think about some object or other. Let us take a look at diagram (D1), which is the minimal diagram of consciousness:

(D1) $S \rightarrow O$

The relation described by (D1) is asymmetrical in that the topic-neutral, fallible, and objective most universal form of intentionality has to allow for many instances in which what is referred to does not itself refer to anything, whereas the subject S, that which is about something, is introduced as a referrer.

Hegel calls the functional position of the O the "In-Itself" in order to emphasize the objectivity constraint, given that we must not rule out in advance that some Os are maximally modally robust. There can be different instances of this form: I think about the rain, you think about the number 4.

The first diagram of self-consciousness, the starting point of Chapter IV., is diagram (D2):

(D2) $S \rightarrow (S \rightarrow O)$

Initially, the idea of self-consciousness is to identify the syntactic object "O", that is, something in the object position, with non-intentional objects, that is, objects that are not themselves thought of in terms of intentionality. A non-intentional object is an object not endued with intentionality. Avoiding complication with traces, texts, or other kinds of symbols, let us add that as far as the self-consciousness chapter is concerned, intentionality is restricted to conscious intentionality. This, of course, immediately raises the question how the bracketed term can be in the object position of the second-level consciousness. How can consciousness of a non-intentional object be a (syntactic) object of self-consciousness without being a non-intentional object?

The other main problem at this stage is created by topic-neutrality. According to this requirement, the syntactic object O could also be an instance of consciousness. The only constraint for the embedded O is that S is some subject and O some object. In this case, we can have instances of the form: S thinks about himself thinking about the cat. One can also not rule out the following instance:

S thinks about himself thinking about himself. This is what Hegel means when he says, "that being-in-itself and being-for-an-other are here the same" (Pinkard ¶¶166[13]).].[14] The embedded In-Itself is itself a (D1) and a (D1) is an asymmetrical relation, a "für ein anderes Sein," as Hegel puts it.

Now the most important point at this stage, which Hegel makes explicit in ¶¶2, is that the following instance of (D2), (D2*) (where S is always she herself, the same subject, S_1):

(D2*)$S_1 \rightarrow (S_1 \rightarrow S_1)$

is motivated only by the fact that it cannot be ruled out by the overall form of self-consciousness. However, there are other instances of self-consciousness in the formal sense such as when S thinks about herself thinking about the house:

(D2**)$S_1 \rightarrow (S_1 \rightarrow O_1)$

or notably also when S_1 thinks about S_2 thinking about the house:[15]

(D2***)$S_1 \rightarrow (S_1 \rightarrow O_1)$

When Hegel says that for self-consciousness, "The distinction as an otherness is in its eyes immediately sublated" (¶¶167)[16] (¶¶2), this just means that self-consciousness with three S_1s, that is, (D2*), is only any old unmotivated instance of (D2). It is unmotivated insofar as there is no reason to privilege it over (D2**). Both are, however, motivated as instances of (D2), nothing more and nothing less. This entails that one cannot motivate (D2*) as an instance of (D2) without motivating (D2**) as an equally valid instance. This is why "Ich bin Ich" (I am I) does not suffice, a fact Hegel sums up in the following sentences:

> Since in its eyes the distinction does not also have the shape of being, it is not self-consciousness. Otherness thereby exists for it as a being, that is, as a distinguished moment,

---

13 All English Hegel references are from the forthcoming Pinkard translation, which, in addition to being the most recent translation, dispenses with many errors found in the long-standing Miller translation.
14 "...daß das Ansichsein und das für ein anderes Sein dasselbe ist" (GW 9:120).
15 Notice that the structure of self-consciousness rules out that one takes the relation itself as an object. To take the relation as an object is to take it as an object either as an instance: aRb or as a logical form: xRy, but never just as R. The reason for this harks back to the failure of sense-certainty referred to above. At this stage of the argument we already know that relations are not individuals, whatever else there may be, which is not yet settled. Due to the asymmetry of the relation it is also ruled out that the object refers to anything. If there is an object in the structure, it serves as a regress blocker.
16 "Der Unterschied" is "*unmittelbar* als ein Anderssein *aufgehoben*" (GW 9:104).

but, for it, it is also the unity of itself with this distinction as a second distinguished moment. With that first moment, self-consciousness exists as consciousness, and the whole breadth of the sensuous world is preserved for it, but at the same time only as related to the second moment, the unity of self-consciousness with itself (¶¶167).[17]

(D2*) happens to be an instance of self-consciousness as much as (D2**). Anticipating a bit, we can already call (D2*) "the lord" and (D2**) "the servant." The question then becomes how we can have a unified account of self-consciousness that explains how we can be both self-conscious of being conscious of any other object and self-conscious of being self-conscious. Now Hegel writes that the difference between the lord and the servant is (¶¶3), "The difference between its appearance and its truth" (¶¶167).[18]

Yet, both positions need to be reconciled in our overall theory of intentionality, as they both are instances of self-consciousness. As John Campbell writes in a similar context, general awareness or self-consciousness here needs to be reconciled with the fact that "there is no such thing as a particular type of awareness without the object being there to differentiate that exercise of awareness from any other."[19] The need to reconcile self-consciousness in general and its many particular instances in our overall theory is what Hegel calls "Begierde überhaupt" (desire in general/as such) (¶¶2). "Desire" does not refer to what we now would ordinarily call desire; it refers to the rationally motivated desire of the theorist of self-consciousness to present a unified account of the phenomenon under investigation. We need to keep in mind all the time that "self-consciousness" is the name for a theory of intentionality, and in particular, for a theory of intentionality explicitly accounting for the fact that we can refer either to objects that are not themselves intentional agents (such as mountains) or to objects that exhibit intentionality as an essential feature (like ourselves). Therefore, we can refer both to referring to non-intentional objects and to referring to intentional objects, as this is exactly what the theory of intentionality is doing.

In the next paragraph, ¶¶3, Hegel introduces the concept of "life" and adds it to the vocabulary. Arguably, "life" here refers to reduplication, which plays an important role later. The unity of self-consciousness, the general formula of (D2), subsumes independent instances of itself. These instances are independent inso-

---

17 "...indem ihm der Unterschied nicht auch die Gestalt des Seins hat, ist es nicht Selbstbewußtsein. Es ist hiemit für es das Anderssein, *als ein Sein*, oder als *unterschiedenes Moment*. Mit jenem ersten Momente ist das Selbstbewußtsein als *Bewußtsein*, und für es die ganze Ausbreitung der sinnlichen Welt erhalten; aber zugleich nur als auf das zweite Moment, die Einheit des Selbstbewußtseins mit sich selbst, bezogen" (GW 9:104).
18 "[der] Gegensatz seiner Erscheinung und seiner Wahrheit" (GW 9:104).
19 Cf. Campbell 2008, p. 654.

far as we have not derived any rule to differentiate them a priori by inspecting the formula itself. The point is that the fact that the servant can take any object whatsoever and refer to it, introduces an element of contingency. The objects we happen to be able to refer to cannot be known by inspecting the fact that we can in principle refer to them. Yet, whenever we successfully refer to an object we happen to encounter, an O, we repeat the same procedure. Hegel frames this point in ¶¶4–5 by saying that the unity of self-consciousness is infinite in the sense of not ruling out any object as an instance of an object to be referred to. There is no a priori limit to intentionality. Everything can be referred to. Yet, what happens to be referred to is often independent of this fact. Some objects might as well not have been referred to, which can easily be shown if we take into consideration the fact that if we happen to know something, this is mostly contingent: It was not necessary that we knew it and we might have not known it. Given that any instance of consciousness is itself an object we can refer to, consciousness itself remains independent of self-consciousness, even though this independence is embedded in our awareness of it. We are aware that we might not have been aware of being aware of object O. Being aware of O might entail that we can accompany it with an "I think", as Kant had it, but it does not entail that there actually is an "I think" attached to any thought, as this amounts to an actual infinity of higher-order thoughts.

In the following two paragraphs (¶¶6–7), Hegel argues that all of this gives us a more complicated theory structure, which he then works with in the lord-servant episode. This structure can be represented in a diagram, which has "two moments" as he calls it and can be drawn like this:

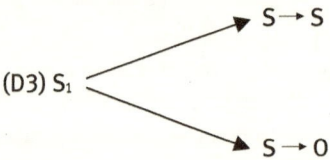

In words: We (the theorists of intentionality) are aware that we can either be aware of being aware or be aware of something else. Hegel names the disjunction "Gliederung" (a division into groupings) and the fact that an O is generated by the diagram "Gestaltung" (a taking shape).

However, nothing rules out that we are aware of being aware of the disjunction. In this case the upper branch of the diagram generates a fractal or self-replication. Let me just draw one further branch in order to keep things as simple as possible for the moment: (D3*).

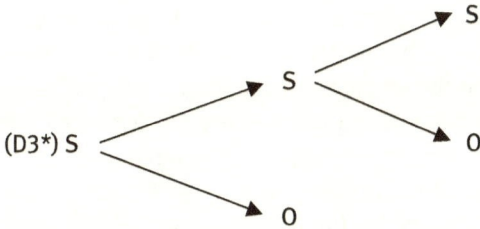

The opening of this tree is what Hegel calls "Auseinanderlegen", or elaboration, and he coins it as "Leben *als Prozeß*", life as a *process*. Hegel here plays with the fact that a *pro-cessus* literally means a coming forth from something and that it designates a movement.[20] The fact that we triggered an infinite progress or process is what Hegel calls "das Leben als *Lebendiges*," life as *living things*. The process moves through different stages and each instance is an instance of it, a "Lebendiges", a living thing. Immediately after introducing the distinction between life as process and life as a living individual Hegel writes:

> This estrangement of the undifferentiated fluidity is the very positing of individuality. The simple substance of life is thus the estrangement of itself into shapes and is at the same time the dissolution of these durably existing distinctions. The dissolution of this estrangement is to the same extent itself an estrangement, that is, a division of itself into groupings (¶¶171).[21]

The repeated pattern is a "genus", it is a repetition of the same in various instances. However, it is only a pattern for the theory of intentionality, which triggers all its instances by combining the minimal formula of self-consciousness with its legitimate applications.

¶¶8 – 10 contains a summary of what Hegel calls an "experience". An "experience" is the discovery by some theory of intentionality that its minimal formula has instances that do not meet some of the accepted constraints on a successful theory of intentionality. The concept of "experience" Hegel introduces in the *Phenomenology* denotes an insight into theory failure. The theorist of intentionality,

---

20 Just as a historical side-remark, it should be noted that Hegel here is engaging with the Neo-Platonist theory of conceptual content and its relation to the structure of what they call "life". For a fairly comprehensive discussion of Hegel's sources and his way of integrating them see (Halfwassen 2004).
21 "...dies Entzweien der unterschiedslosen Flüssigkeit ist eben das Setzen der Individualität. Die einfache Substanz des Lebens also ist die Entzweiung ihrer selbst in Gestalten, und zugleich die Auflösung dieser bestehenden Unterschiede; und die Auflösung der Entzweiung ist ebensosehr Entzweien oder ein Gliedern" (GW 9:106).

whom Hegel calls "consciousness" insofar as she instantiates her theory, and the "shape of consciousness" insofar as her whole theoretical edifice is concerned, is usually depicted as reacting to theory failure with rational theory change. Insofar as the theory change is rational, Hegel refers to it as a "determinate negation". In particular, *pace* Brandom's reconstruction of the terminology, it is important to emphasize that determinate negation is a name for rational theory change and precisely not an element in our overall semantics.[22] It does not mean that some expression only has content in contradistinction to some other expression and it is not even related to anything like the opposition between semantic atomism and semantic holism.

As I said, in ¶¶8–10 Hegel describes the experience of self-consciousness. He first introduces "das reine Ich" (the pure I) or "das einfache Ich" (the simple I) which is (D2). Self-consciousness only becomes aware of itself as an instance of (D2) by abstracting from the particularities of (D2*) to (D2*^{n}). It has to "destroy" (vernichten) "the independent object" (den unabhängigen Gegenstand) in the sense that it has to recognize any number of (D2*^{s}) as just more instances of (D2). The instances thereby come to depend on (D2); they are interpreted as its instances. Once the theorist manages to acknowledge this fact, Hegel speaks of "satisfaction" (Befriedigung). The famous satisfaction of self-consciousness is the identification of an instance of self-consciousness as such an instance by the self-conscious theorist herself. However, the problem triggering the experience is that all the (D2*^{s}) turn out to be independent instances of (D2) insofar as there is no overall rule privileging any (D2*) over any other. The (D2*^{s}) are independent, their order is not antecedently or a priori determined. In particular, this causes the following problem.

Let us say that self-consciousness is a fairly simple formal system consisting of axioms from a highly general theory of intentionality and some rules of inference, or rather substitution rules.

(AX1) Every instance of consciousness is fallible. (Axiom of Fallibility)
(AX2) Every instance of consciousness is objective. (Axiom of Objectivity)
(AX3) The theory is topic-neutral: Every legitimate instance of consciousness, every intentional subject, and every legitimate instance of objecthood, every object, has to be accounted for by the overall theory. (Axiom of Topic-Neutrality)

---

[22] Cf. (Brandom 2002, p. 49, pp. 55–57, p. 180, p. 194, p. 229). For further discussion see (Gabriel 2008, §14–15, pp. 374–401).

(AX4) The theory has to be consistent under self-application. If it takes itself as an object, this must not amount to paradox or contradiction. (Axiom of Self-Application)

At the stage of self-consciousness, we have two minimal diagrams:

(D1) S→O (Consciousness)
(D2) S→(S→O) (Self-Consciousness)

We also know that "→" is asymmetrical whenever it has an O on the right-hand side, for "objects" are defined as often being non-intentional in that they are not followed by a further arrow. If we have an object that is itself intentional, we write an S followed by an arrow.

If these are all the rules of the formal system, we cannot rule out that the system is incoherent.[23] In addition, we have no proof of its completeness. It might turn out incomplete, incoherent, or even explicitly self-contradictory if we can derive a theorem contradicting the axioms or if we can derive two mutually exclusive theorems. In self-consciousness the main problem is that it generates vicious infinite regresses on the one hand and arbitrary regress blockers on the other hand. The theorist is therefore confronted with the constant possibility of being undermined by an instance of (D2). If there is an instance with infinite complexities, the theorist cannot be satisfied, as she is not able to tell whether the instance at some point in its life, in its explicitation, turns out to be contradictory or not. Thus, Hegel concludes: "Self-consciousness attains its satisfaction only in another self-consciousness" (¶¶175).[24]

In contradiction to orthodox interpretations, Hegel is not speaking here about the success conditions of recognition, socially mediated self-awareness in human beings, the structure of the gaze of the other, the desire to make the other's desire one's own desire, or anything of this sort. Rather, he is saying why self-consciousness as an overall model for a unified theory of intentionality

---

[23] Hans Sluga has pointed out to me that it should already be clear at this stage that no theory of intentionality can be objective, fallible, and topic-neutral according to these constraints. However, Hegel is more charitable to the attempt to develop a universal theory of intentionality meeting all criteria. Yet, the major result of the *Phenomenology* is indeed that intentionality is the wrong paradigm for a relevant topic-neutral theory of all forms of thought, as he believes that in logical thinking about thought we need a different account of objectivity. The position of absolute knowing that defines the procedures of the *Science of Logic*-sequel to the *Phenomenology* will first attempt to give up fallibility. In logical thinking we cannot be fallible in the same way in which we are fallible with respect to maximally modally robust facts in general. This causes problems of its own evidently beyond the scope of a single paper.

[24] "Das Selbstbewußtsein erreicht seine Befriedigung nur in einem anderen Selbstbewußtsein" (GW 9:108).

fails. It fails for the simple reason that it cannot prove that it is complete and non-contradictory. It is only capable of accounting for some of its instances, in particular, for instances with certain self-referential implications. It cannot cover the whole ground and remains essentially incomplete. This is why Hegel writes that it can reach its satisfaction *only* in another self-consciousness. He presents this as the conclusion of an experience, as the peak of self-consciousness' failure and not as the celebratory moment of mutual recognition, or even as the class-free society of some utopian theorists. Self-consciousness as such winds up in contradiction, its satisfaction is incoherent, which is why there are many further steps and chapters in the *Phenomenology* leading to the insight that not all forms of self-consciousness or rather higher-order intentionality should be construed as bipolar intentional relations.[25] It is not capable of accounting for both the independence of some of its instances and for itself under self-application.

3 The Lord-Servant-Allegory

This famous-all-too-famous chapter discusses independence and dependence of self-consciousness. The first is called "Herrschaft" or "lordship" and the second "Knechtschaft" or "servitude." Before moving a little faster through the stages of the argument of the chapter, I would like to give a very close reading of the first paragraph in order to highlight just how far removed the orthodox readings are from the text itself. In the first paragraph Hegel distinguishes between "a recognized (ein Anerkanntes)" and "the movement of recognizing (die Bewegung des Anerkennens)". He explicitly says that self-consciousness is only a recognized insofar as it is in and for itself. By this he means that self-consciousness is itself just another object, a recognized. This point can be conveyed by a wordplay designed to convey the pejorative undertone of the German word "Anerkennung," which has the "An-" of "Angewohnheit" or "Anerziehen" as a prefix. It has the same meaning of the Latin ad- in attraction, which comes from ad- and trahere. A literal etymological translation of "Anerkennung" would be "Ad-Cognition" rather than "Re-Cognition." An alternative word-play would translate "ein Anerkanntes" as "a recognize-IT", an object of the attitude of ad-cognition. The point

---

[25] I disagree with Robert Pippin's rejoinder to my paper in recent discussions to the extent that I do not believe that Hegel presents his solution to the problems he raises in the *Phenomenology*. What it means that Hegel himself prefers a different account of the phenomenon of self-consciousness in a broader sense would be a different topic. In this paper I only focus on a particular chapter and its discussion.

is that "ein Anerkanntes" is a placeholder for whatever happens to appear in the object slot of the self-consciousness function, whatever satisfies the function. The concept of self-consciousness has instances in which an instance of self-consciousness is the object of an overall self-consciousness, for instance, in the case of the self-application of the theory itself. Hegel is structuring the chapter with the help of forks, as it were: Self-consciousness can be both of another object and of itself. Hegel constantly makes reference to the Neoplatonic theory of conceptual content as a theory of life, something represented by Porphyrean trees, which are still quite common when representing the relation between genus and its species. The concept of the genus thus opens a fork onto its species, which Hegel underlines with a very skillful and obvious alliteration in the second sentence of the first paragraph, which reads in German:

> Der Begriff dieser seiner Einheit in seiner **V**erdopplung, der sich im Selbstbewußtsein realisierenden Unendlichkeit, ist eine **v**ielseitige und **v**ieldeutige **V**erschränkung" (GW 9:109).[26]

Of course, there is a further twist to the poetry of the text, as the reduplication graphically underlined by the alliteration also refers to the "w" in the German word for self-consciousness, which is a reduplication of the v, a double v. We can now draw a particular (D3) diagram, the diagram of pure recognizing, $(D3^{PR})$:

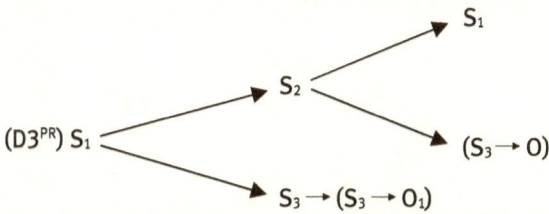

The sub-diagrams on the right-hand side are recogniz-ITS, they are merely Anerkannte. The overall diagram on the contrary represents "the movement of recognizing". Recognizing is taking something as an object of self-consciousness. The difference between cognition and re-cognition is that the latter is mediated by a further level of awareness. If I recognize something, I am aware of me being aware of it. Given that there are no restrictions on the identity of the subject, we can add a further level if S1 is aware of herself being aware of S2 being aware of O1. These are the instances of self-consciousness focused upon by

---

[26] "The concept of its unity in its doubling, of infinity realizing itself in self-consciousness, is that of a multi-sided and multi-meaning intertwining…" [¶¶178].

the classical readings of the chapter, for this is the structure of the gaze in Sartre's dating cafe: He is aware of being aware of her awareness of his hand: His hand moves slightly closer to hers. He is doing this with a high level of self-awareness pretending not to be aware of it, always watching in which way she is aware of the approaching hand, etc.[27] However, Hegel's interest here is not that there are these interesting instances of self-consciousness and what role they might play for the social life of self-conscious beings such as humans. Rather, he is discussing the structure of a formal system designed to model self-consciousness, and the system is threatened by the fact that it has the (D3*) as a regress-triggering instance. Hegel calls this instance "the movement of recognizing." Note that Hegel nowhere in the whole chapter uses the word "Anerkennung." He only ever speaks of "Anerkennen." You simply will not find recognition in the chapter, but rather only recognizing.

Of course, Hegel, or rather the theorist of self-consciousness with whom he is in dialogue, does not stop at (D3*). Rather, the first stage of the chapter, laid out in ¶¶1–7 indeed culminates in the celebrated, albeit widely misunderstood phrase: "They recognize themselves as mutually recognizing each other" (¶¶184).[28] Once again, this has nothing to do with Hegel's theory of recognition. It is another move introduced by the theorist of self-consciousness in order to prevent her system from inconsistency. The diagram of "mutual recognizings" or of the pure concept of recognizing looks like this:

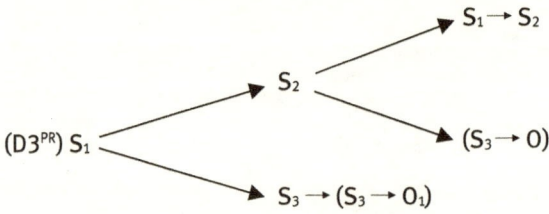

In this picture, S_1 recognizes S_2 as recognizing S_1 as recognizing S_2. Yet, this is only the beginning of the experience of self-consciousness in this chapter. It is the conclusion of the first stage of the presentation of self-consciousness. The rest of the chapter, in which the actual work is done, is divided into three more stages:

---

[27] Unfortunately, I cannot go into the details of my preferred instances of piling up levels of awareness in contemporary TV comedy as it has developed since the advent of *Seinfeld* and *Curb Your Enthusiasm*.

[28] "Sie *anerkennen* sich, als *gegenseitig* sich *anerkennend*" (GW 9:110).

Stage 2: ¶¶8–12: "The result of the first experience"
Stage 3: ¶¶13–16: The Lord
Stage 4: ¶¶17–19: The Servant

Hegel explicitly marks the transitions between these stages and sets them apart. He sums up Stage 2 by specifying "the result of the first experience", and then first develops the problem with the concept of the "lord", in order to conclude the chapter with an analysis of the problem with the concept of the "servant". There is neither any exegetical or *de dicto* clue to suppose that he is stating his preferred theory of self-consciousness nor any *de re* reason to believe that he ought to be doing this anywhere before "Absolute Knowing" – and it is possible that he is not even doing so in that chapter. Hegel is quite explicit about the level of reflection at which he presents the shapes of consciousness: They are theories of intentionality that we, that is, the phenomenological I – as it were, the narrator – of the text and we, the readers, observe as problematic and consequently have an experience characterized by a moment of failure and rational theory change. Let us go through the problems presented at stages 2–4 and see what really happens there.

Stage 2 (¶¶8–12)

The "pure concept of recognizing" displays itself first and foremost in the form of an inequality (Ungleichheit). "Gleichheit" (equality) is the German word for "partial identity", that is, identity in some, maybe in most respects. Some objects are partially identical or *gleich* if they share a sufficient number of properties and correspondingly are unequal if this condition is not met. The inequality here consists in the fact that, as Hegel states, one self-consciousness is merely a recognized and the other one is merely a recognizing. That is to say, when S_1 is aware of S_2, that particular awareness is not essential for S_1: She could be aware of all sorts of other things and happens to be aware of S_2. The same holds for S_2's awareness of S_1's awareness. S_1 and S_2 are merely individuals: "What comes on the scene here is an individual confronting an individual" (¶¶186).[29] By this Hegel means that they are random theorems of the formal systems. An "individual" here does not mean a person, it means an individual in the ontological sense of something below the level of generality of a genus. And Hegel's point here just is that there are different individuals, different instances of general awareness, whose existence seems to be utterly contingent. In this sense,

---

[29] "...es tritt ein Individuum einem Individuum gegenüber auf" (GW 9:111).

an individual merely confronts or rather stands in opposition to another individual. At the same time, they are paradigmatic instances of self-consciousness insofar as they instantiate the very structure of the theory as it has been developed. The theory of self-consciousness is a form of awareness that is aware of the fact that someone can both be aware of someone's awareness of someone's awareness of itself and be aware of someone's awareness of someone's awareness of some non-intentional object. To make this slightly simpler, it is sufficient to maintain that any theory of self-consciousness has to be able to account for self-awareness and awareness of non-intentional objects in the same terms, namely in terms of a topic-neutral theory of intentionality. In that sense, the forked arrow seems to be a paradigmatic form, the logical form of self-consciousness. However, no instance of (D3) exhausts its generative powers, its life. All instances are individuals falling under the concept (D3). But this means that we have a pure concept, (D3) and at least two instances. These two instances are independent of the fact that they are integrated into particular instances. They are independent theorems united in more complicated theorems, but themselves independent. In particular, Hegel identifies two building blocks or "moments" in (D3^{PR}):

> It is by way of that experience that a pure self-consciousness is posited, and a consciousness is posited which exists not purely for itself but for an other, which is to say, is posited as an existing consciousness, that is, consciousness in the shape of thinghood (¶¶189).[30]

We thus have a pure-self-consciousness, which corresponds to the upward structure of the pure concept of recognizing. It is the repetition of the tripartite structure of self-consciousness. Within this structure we find a subordinated element or moment, which are the various instances of $(S_x \rightarrow (S_y \rightarrow O_z))$. Hegel identifies them at the end of Stage 2:

> ...they exist as two opposed shapes of consciousness. One is self-sufficient; for it, its essence is being-for-itself. The other is non-self-sufficient; for it, life, that is, being for an other, is the essence. The former is the [lord], the latter is the servant (¶¶189).[31]

---

[30] "...es ist durch sie ein reines Selbstbewußtsein, und ein Bewußtsein gesetzt, welches nicht rein für sich, sondern für ein anderes, das heißt, als *seiendes* Bewußtsein oder Bewußtsein der Gestalt der *Dingheit* ist" (GW 9:112).

[31] "...als zwei entgegengesetzte Gestalten des Bewußtseins; die eine das selbständige, welchem das Fürsichsein, die andere das unselbständige, dem das Leben oder das Sein für ein anderes das Wesen ist; jenes ist der *Herr*, dies der *Knecht*" (GW 9:112).

Accordingly, Stage 3 deals with the lord and Stage 4 deals with the servant. In my interpretation of the reference of the anaphoric pronouns in the last sub-clause of the last sentence of ¶¶12, the lord and the servant are both moments, and they correspond to life on the one hand and being for another on the other.

Stage 3 (¶¶13–16)

The problem with the lord in the structure of the pure concept of recognizing is that there is "... A one-sided and unequal form of recognition" (¶¶191).[32] In other words, the lord is always a fork, a twofold awareness of some other awareness with another awareness as its object and of some other awareness with a non-intentional object as its object. The lord is aware of the servant who in some instances (where $S_x = S_y$) is only aware of being aware of a non-intentional object. The servant only works on ("bearbeitet es nur") the object, whereas the lord is aware of the servant's structure of awareness. At this point, Quine can provide us with further assistance. In ¶¶6 of *Word and Object* on "Posits and Truths" he comes to the following remarkable conclusion:

> Everything to which we concede existence is a posit from the standpoint of a description of the theory-building process, and simultaneously real from the standpoint of the theory that is being built.[33]

This corresponds exactly to the situation of the lord. The lord is a description of the theory-building process of the servant. From the standpoint of the servant, the object is real. Yet, the servant is built by the lord, and from the standpoint of the lord his object is a posit. In other words, the lord is aware of the ontological commitments of the servant and the servant merely holds them. What the servant accepts as real and out there, the lord recognizes as a posit, allowing him to withhold judgment, what Hegel calls "die reine Negation" (pure negation) and "Genuß" (consumption) (GW 9:113/¶¶190).

Yet, this amounts to the following tension in the theory. The lord on the one hand withholds judgment about a particular ontological commitment. On the other hand he has to force the commitment onto the servant. The servant is clearly wrong when he takes the object to be plain real in the sense of a non-intentional object embedded in maximally modally robust facts. His realism is not naïve in a good sense, but misguided. The overall structure of the lord's self-con-

---

[32] "...ein einseitiges und ungleiches Anerkennen" (GW 9:113).
[33] (Quine 1960, 22).

sciousness both commits him to there being a real object O and there not being such a real object O, but merely a posit. It is only real in the eyes of the servant who is wrong about this reality. The lord forces the commitment onto the servant and forces the servant to take the commitment literally. Yet, if there were no servant whatsoever, we would have to conclude that there is no truth-apt thought about non-intentional reality, which would be an untenable form of first-order idealism, according to which there are only objects if someone refers to them. This should not be the result of any theory of intentionality, as it plainly contradicts the objectivity constraint that Hegel refers to as "independence" in the chapter under consideration. The lord therefore fails.

Hegel could have stopped the chapter at this point. However, he adds another stage to the argument in order to give the theorist of self-consciousness one more chance. Here, as in the preceding chapters of the *Phenomenology*, Hegel's method is built on maximal charity. Given that the lord found objectivity to be problematic, the theorist of self-consciousness gets another chance to fix this problem by making good on the objectivity constraint. The lord is mistaken in privileging self-reference over reference to non-intentional objects. For him, the latter is "inessential". However, without the subordinated arrow pointing to reference to non-intentional objects, the different acts of self-reference or self-awareness could not be distinguished. The pure negativity of self-awareness freed from any external constraint cannot account for the fallibility and objectivity constraint, which is a well-known problem in theories of self-awareness based on the alleged incorrigibility of self-awareness together with the claim to privileged access. Be that as it may, for Hegel the problem of this constellation is that one has to be able to understand both the overall or general structure of self-awareness and how there can be many different instances of it: My being aware now of my being aware, your being aware now of your being aware, my now being aware of you now being aware, etc. What differentiates between these instances is trivially not their general structure, but rather the fact that they are always combined with some subordinated reference to some non-intentional object or other. The latter specifies the relevant realist truth-conditions. In precisely this sense Hegel claims that, "...the truth of the self-sufficient consciousness is the servile consciousness" (¶¶193).[34] "Truth" here just means objective truth-conditions. The servant provides the truth-conditions and therefore does all the work of distinguishing different instances of self-consciousness.

---

[34] "...die *Wahrheit* des selbständigen Bewußtseins ist demnach das *knechtische Bewußtsein*" (GW 9:114).

Stage 4 (¶¶17–19):

Accordingly, the theorist of self-consciousness insists in the last stage of the argument that this does not cause any problems for the view. However, servitude in turn has an experience presented in the last stage of the chapter. The argument hinges on servitude being another instance of self-consciousness. Servitude is embedded in the overall structure of (D3^{PR}). It is a subordinated form of consciousness, introduced by the general lord-structure. It is "im Herrn (in the lord)" as Hegel repeatedly puts this. In other words, it depends on prior theory decisions. It is introduced in the context of a theory of self-consciousness. This is its explanatory job, its *Arbeit*. Servitude serves a well-defined job. Yet, this job cannot be done without specifying it as an instance of self-consciousness. "However, by means of work this servile consciousness comes round to itself" (¶¶195).[35] For the logical form of the servant is an instance of (D2), for example,

(D2^S) $S_3 \rightarrow (S_3 \rightarrow O_1)$

Recall that the servant performs the conceptual task of individuating the lords. There are different lords only because the servant works on different non-intentional objects. These objects block both an infinite regress of adding self-consciousness to self-consciousness *ad infinitum* and the need for the overgeneralizing self-reference of the pure concept of recognizing. By referring to a non-intentional object, the servant instantiates a stable asymmetrical relationship terminating in an object. A servant is aware of being aware of an object. The awareness he is aware of is awareness of a non-intentional object. The object-awareness therefore has fixed truth-conditions. Hegel calls the higher-order awareness of the object-awareness an "Anschauung," an intuition, emphasizing the givenness of the object within the object-awareness. Yet, the intuition is not directly of a non-intentional object, but of a given instance of object-awareness. There is a difference between someone being aware of herself as being aware of, say, a tree, and someone being aware of a tree. This is brought out in English by some usages of "self-conscious." A self-conscious laugh is not just laughing about something, but is disturbingly aware of its conditions of laughing. An overly self-conscious thinker stands in her own way, like a skeptic who is not able to order a meal in a restaurant without constantly reassuring herself that she is not a brain in a vat. The self-conscious thinker of object-thoughts is threatened by "fear", the fear of the loss of the object, as the object has been introduced only in the relation of being referred to by fiat. It just happens to be there, in

---

[35] "Durch die Arbeit kommt es aber zu sich selbst" (GW 9:114).

front of someone's attention, as it were. It could be anything, independent of the truth-conditions the thinker projects from her point of view. This is why the servant continues paying attention to the object, he stabilizes the object within the repetitive acts of the lord for whom he does the service of being his principle of individuation.

The experience of the lord motivating the transition to the next chapter on the *Freedom of Self-Consciousness (Stoicism, Skepticism, and Unhappy Consciousness)* brings two thoughts together: "Dienst," or "service," and "Bilden." "Bilden" certainly does not mean "cultural formative activity," as Pinkard translates it. It means forming an image. We can translate this into the point that self-conscious awareness of some non-intentional object projects truth-conditions by having a propositional intentional content. If I am aware of being aware of the tree, my belief specifies the content that there is a tree in front of me. If I am wrong, I would still have specified this content, which justifies the cautionary use of "bilden." I project or imagine my truth-conditions by producing some propositional intentional content. Yet, this whole activity is part of the explanatory project of the theorist of self-consciousness. That means that every servant is only one instance out of many. Thus, there are many servants, many propositional contents associated with the same non-intentional object as well as many propositional contents associated with different non-intentional objects. Bearing this explanation in mind, the following quote should now be intelligible:

> Without the discipline of service and obedience, fear is mired in formality and does not extend itself to the conscious actuality of existence. Without forming an image, fear remains inward and mute, and consciousness does not become the "it" which is for itself (¶¶196).[36]

The theorist of self-consciousness is aware of the servant's awareness. She describes this awareness essentially as a contingent instance of some structure, as a theorem derived from the formal system. In this context, the theorist is warranted in positing indefinitely many servants, and thereby spreads "fear" over "the conscious reality of what is there". In other words, the combination of fear and service corresponds to the notion that there is an indefinite number of servants in reality itself. There has to be an indefinite number of servants for the simple reason that we can think of many thinkers thinking about all sorts of objects. In this sense we can associate many thinkers and their literal perspectives onto what there is with the objects. For any independent object,

---

[36] "Ohne die Zucht des Dienstes und Gehorsams bleibt die Furcht beim Formellen stehen, und verbreitet sich nicht über die bewußte Wirklichkeit des Daseins. Ohne das Bilden bleibt die Furcht innerlich und stumm, und das Bewußtsein wird nicht für es selbst" (GW 9:115).

there are many intentional subjects who could be aware of it at the same time and thereby take it for real. Reality is partially aware of itself, namely in the awareness of individuals being aware of non-intentional, unaware objects.

Hegel concludes the discussion of servitude with the claim that servitude does not get its quantifiers right: it cannot meet the universality-constraint of the theory according to which the theory of intentionality explains how everything can become the content of truth-apt thoughts, as anything, that is any determinate object or other, can be aptly described as whatever it is. He draws a distinction between the fact that the servant has "a meaning on his own (eigner Sinn)" and that this amounts to "stubbornness (Eigensinn)". The problem Hegel has in mind is that it is not possible to identify the universal conceptual form of self-consciousness with all the servants instantiating it, for the servants, just as the lords, are just more or less random instances. Piling up cases of self-consciousness does not satisfy the demand for a complete theory of intentionality. As long as the concept of self-consciousness in its relation to its various instances has not been derived from itself in the form of a universal rule, we have no proof for the completeness, non-contradictoriness, or even the overall coherence of the theory of self-consciousness. It remains an unprincipled form of free association,

> [...] a freedom that remains bogged down within the bounds of servility. To the servile consciousness, pure form can as little become the essence as can the pure form when it is taken as extending itself beyond the individual be a universal culturally formative activity, an absolute concept. Rather, the form is a skill which, while it has dominance over some things, has dominance over neither the universal power nor the entire objective essence (¶¶196).[37]

4 Concluding Remarks

On closer analysis, and with the help of an adequate method of translation, Hegel reveals himself to be a very meticulous and detailed conceptual analyst of various elements underlying potential and actual theories of consciousness in general, and self-consciousness in particular. As such theories are premised on theories of intentionality, of conscious reference and self-reference, Hegel is

---

37 "…eine Freiheit, welche noch innerhalb der Knechtschaft stecken bleibt. So wenig ihm die reine Form zum Wesen werden kann, so wenig ist sie, als Ausbreitung über das Einzelne betrachtet, allgemeines Bilden, absoluter Begriff, sondern eine Geschicklichkeit, welche nur über einiges, nicht über die allgemeine Macht und das ganze gegenständliche Wesen mächtig ist" (GW 9:115–116).

eager to reduce complex theories to such elements and give an account of their shortcomings.

The reading sketched here, therefore, makes sense of the very idea of a *Phenomenology of Spirit* as an account of apparent knowing, of illusory knowledge-claims that all fail for systematically related reasons. They are the wrong tools as they cannot achieve the level of universality needed for a theory of absolutely everything that is capable of first accounting for everything it is not, second for itself, and third for itself within the broadest domain possible, the domain of absolutely everything. If anywhere, Hegel develops an outline for the success conditions of such a theory in the *Science of Logic*, a science culminating in the absolute idea. However, on closer analysis, the *Science of Logic* also fails in interesting ways, and also does not claim closure. It remains "a realm of shadows", as Hegel says, and we need access to non-philosophical facts as the ultimate content to be accounted for by philosophy. The ultimate battleground for Hegelianism versus Post-Hegelianism thus is the *Realphilosophie* as it is presented in the *Philosophy of Right* and the *Encyclopedia*. Even though the last two centuries have seen a fight over this ground, I believe that we still have to settle the actual stakes of this debate by first presenting Hegel's arguments in detail, assessing their range, and then searching for systematic translations of his projects outside of logic and metaphysics, where I take him to still be among the very best philosophers of all time. I believe he ultimately fails in the *Realphilosophie* in ways that shed light on his project in logic and metaphysics, but this is another story, far too long for a single paper.

Bibliography

Brandom, Robert (1999): "Some Pragmatist Themes in Hegel's Idealism." In: *European Journal of Philosophy* 7. No. 2, pp. 164–189.

Brandom, Robert (2002): *Tales of the Mighty Dead*. Cambridge, Mass./London: Harvard University Press.

Brandom, Robert (2007): "The Structure of Desire and Recognition." In: *Philosophy and Social Criticism* 33. No. 1, pp. 127–150.

Brandom, Robert (2008): "Untimely Review of Hegel's *Phenomenology of Spirit*." In: *Topoi: An International Review of Philosophy* 27, pp. 161–164.

Campbell, John (2008): "Consciousness and Reference". In: Brian P. McLaughlin/Ansgar Beckermann/Sven Walter (Eds.): *The Oxford Handbook of Philosophy of Mind*. Oxford: Oxford University Press.

Forster, Michael (1998): *Hegel's Idea of a Phenomenology of Spirit*. Chicago: Chicago University Press.

Gabriel, Markus (2007): "Hegel und Plotin." In: Dietmar Heidemann/Christian Krijnen (Eds.): *Hegel und die Geschichte der Philosophie*. Darmstadt: Wissenschaftliche Buchgesellschaft.
Gabriel, Markus (2008): *An den Grenzen der Erkenntnistheorie. Die notwendige Endlichkeit des Wissens als Lektion des Skeptizismus*. Freiburg/München: Karl Alber.
Gabriel, Markus (2009): *Skeptizismus und Idealismus in der Antike*. Frankfurt/M.: Suhrkamp.
Gabriel, Markus (2015): "Hegel's Begriff der Vorstellung und das Form-Inhalt-Problem." In: Kazimir Drilo/Axel Hutter (Eds.): *Spekulation und Vorstellung in Hegels enzyklopädischem System*. Tübingen: Mohr Siebeck, pp. 7–27.
Gabriel, Markus (forthcoming): "What Kind of Idealist (if any) is Hegel?" In: *Hegel Bulletin*.
Halfwassen, Jens (2004): *Plotin und der Neuplatonismus*. München: C.H. Beck.
Hegel, Georg Wilhelm Friedrich (2008): *Vorlesungen über die Philosophie des subjektiven Geistes*. (= *Gesammelte Werke* 25. No. 1, ed. by Christoph J. Bauer). Hamburg: Meiner.
Horstmann, Rolf-Peter (1984): *Ontologie und Relationen: Hegel, Bradley, Russell und die Kontroverse über interne und externe Beziehungen*. Königstein: Athenäum.
Kelly, George Armstrong (1966): "Notes on Hegel's Lordship and Bondage." In: *The Review of Metaphysics* 19. No. 4, pp. 780–802.
Koch, Anton Friedrich (2006): "Die Prüfung des Wissens als Prüfung ihres Maßstabs. Zur Methode der Phänomenologie des Geistes." In: Jindřich Karásek/Jan Kuneš/Ivan Landa (Eds.): *Hegels Einleitung in die Phänomenologie des Geistes*. Würzburg: Könighausen & Neumann, pp. 21–33.
Koch, Anton Friedrich (2008): "Sinnliche Gewißheit und Wahrnehmung. Die beiden ersten Kapitel der Phänomenologie des Geistes." In: Klaus Vieweg/Wolfgang Welsch (Eds.): *Hegels Phänomenologie des Geistes. Ein kooperativer Kommentar zu einem Schlüsselwerk der Moderne*. Frankfurt/M.: Suhrkamp, pp. 135–152.
Koch, Anton Friedrich (2011): "Hegel: Die Einheit des Begriffs." In: Johannes Brachtendorf/Stephan Herzberg (Eds.): *Einheit und Vielheit als metaphysisches Problem*. Tübingen: Mohr Siebeck, pp. 177–198.
Koch, Anton Friedrich (2012): "Review of *An den Grenzen der Erkenntnistheorie*." In: *Philosophische Rundschau* 59, pp. 185–189.
McDowell, John (2009): *Having the World in View*. Cambridge, Mass./London: Harvard University Press.
Pippin, Robert (1989): *Hegel's Idealism. The Satisfaction of Self-Consciousness*. Cambridge/New York: Cambridge University Press.
Pippin, Robert (2007): *Recognition and Reconciliation. Actualized Agency in Hegel's Jena Phenomenology*. In: *Internationales Jahrbuch des Deutschen Idealismus* 2, pp. 249–267.
Pippin, Robert (2011): *Hegel on Self-Consciousness. Desire and Death in the Phenomenology of Spirit*. Princeton: Princeton University Press.
Quine, Willard van Orman (1960): *Word and Object*. Cambridge, Mass./London: Harvard University Press.
Rometsch, Jens (2017): "Why there is no 'recognition-theory' in Hegel's 'struggle of recognition': Towards an epistemological reading of the Lord-Servant-relationship". In: Markus Gabriel / Anders Moe Rasmussen (Eds.): *German Idealism Today*. Berlin/New York: DeGruyter, pp. 159–184.
Rödl, Sebastian (2007): *Self-Consciousness*. Cambridge, Mass./London: Harvard University Press.

Searle, John (2007): *The Construction of Social Reality*. London: Penguin.
Searle, John (2011): *Making the Social World. The Structure of Human Civilization*. Oxford: Oxford University Press.
Stekeler-Weithofer, Pirmin (1992): *Hegels Analytische Philosophie. Die Wissenschaft der Logik als kritische Theorie der Bedeutung*. Paderborn: Ferdinand Schöningh.
Stekeler-Weithofer, Pirmin (2005): *Philosophie des Selbstbewußtseins. Hegels System als Formanalyse von Wissen und Autonomie*. Frankfurt/M.: Suhrkamp.

Stephen Houlgate
Right and Trust in Hegel's Philosophy of Right

What is the principal aim of Hegel's philosophy of right? It is, in my view, to set out the true concept of *freedom*. Hegel was long accused of being a supporter of the Prussian Restoration, but, like Kant and Fichte before him, he is above all a philosopher of freedom.

1 The Arbitrary Will

In his *Elements of the Philosophy of Right* (1820) Hegel maintains that "the commonest idea we have of freedom is that of *arbitrariness* [*Willkür*]" (Hegel 1991, §15R) ((Hegel 1991) and (Hegel 1970)).[1] The arbitrary will, we are told, encompasses three different moments. The first is the "*absolute possibility* of *abstracting* from every determination in which I find myself" (Hegel 1991, §5R). This capacity for abstraction rests on the "pure reflection of the I into itself" or the "pure *thinking* of oneself" (Hegel 1991, §5). As creatures of nature we are determined in manifold ways by natural drives. In understanding myself to be a pure *indeterminate* I, however, I am conscious that my identity is not bound to these drives and that I can always separate myself from them.

Second, the arbitrary will includes the capacity, not just to distance oneself *from* one's natural drives, but to return *to* them and to identify oneself positively with one or other of them. In this case, the I is no longer passively determined by the drive concerned, but *lets itself* be determined by it.

Third, in giving itself a determinate character in this way, the arbitrary will retains the capacity to separate itself from the drive once again and to let itself be determined by a different drive. The I thus remains "indifferent" to the drive with which it has provisionally identified itself. It considers that drive to be "a mere *possibility* by which it is not restricted but in which it finds itself merely because it posits itself in it" (Hegel 1991, §7).

Understood in this way, the freedom of the arbitrary will consists in the capacity to *choose* in an unconstrained manner between one's drives (and their objects). Hegel does not deny at all that we enjoy this freedom. He believes, however, that it is inherently contradictory.

---

[1] Note that I have occasionally amended Nisbet's translation.

The freedom of the arbitrary will consists in determining oneself and not simply being determined by one's given nature. In order not to be determined by nature, the I abstracts itself from its natural drives and thinks of itself as purely indeterminate. This I, however, also gives itself a determinate character, so that it is free not just in a negative, but also in a positive way. Yet since it is indeterminate in itself, it turns back to its natural drives to find the determinacy it seeks. That is to say, the *indeterminate* I freely lets itself be determined by its *given* nature. In so doing, however, the I, in its unrestricted freedom, makes itself *dependent* on that given nature; but this dependence is at odds with the self-determination that it claims for itself.

How then is this contradiction to be avoided? This is possible, Hegel claims, only when the content affirmed by the free will is no longer simply *given* to it, and this happens when the free will has itself and its own freedom as its content and object. In this case, the indeterminate I lets itself be determined not by something else – by a drive that we are simply found to have – but by itself. The choosing will imagines that it is a truly self-determining will. Unfortunately, it can only choose from among the drives and objects that are available to it, and this is initially determined by nature, not by the will itself. The will casts off this moment of dependence, however, when it takes as its content its very own freedom. In this way, it achieves unambiguous self-determination, because it lets itself be determined purely by itself and its own freedom. "The absolute determination, or if one prefers, the absolute drive, of the free spirit" is thus, in Hegel's view, "to make its freedom into its object" (Hegel 1991, §27). We do not yet know what this will mean; we know, however, that the truly free will *must* take this form, for only in this way can it avoid the contradiction in arbitrary freedom.

2 Right as such

When freedom is understood as the object of the will in the strongest sense – that is, as an "immediate actuality" (Hegel 1991, §27), rather than something merely imaginary – it is understood as *right*. For Hegel, therefore, the essence of right is *freedom*; indeed, right is simply "the *existence* [*Dasein*] of the *free will*" (Hegel 1991, §29). The free will as such is something subjective. When this will is regarded as its own object, however, as something that exists *for* the will itself, it gives itself the form of right. Right is thus nothing but freedom, understood as an object, an actuality, for the will.

It should be emphasised that the free will *must* have its freedom as its content and object, if it is to free itself from dependence on what is given and relate only to itself. The will has no choice in the matter: if it wants to be truly free, it must make itself the object of its own willing. Right is thus freedom, understood not only as something actual and objective, but also as that which the will *must* will and affirm, if it is to be truly *free*. This moment of necessity belongs essentially to the concept of right. A right does not have the compelling force of a natural event or law; nonetheless, it demands recognition from the will. It confronts the will, therefore, with normative, not natural necessity. In the *Philosophy of Right*, Hegel points to this necessity in the concept of right by maintaining that "right is something *utterly sacred*" (Hegel 1991, §30). In the lectures of 1821/22 the moment of necessity is made more explicit: "People say that the will is free, because it can *choose*. Rational freedom, the will in and for itself, does not choose, but also has necessity. [...] Right is *necessary [Das Recht ist* notwendig]" (Hegel 2005, pp. 50, 56).

The modality of freedom in the usual sense is that of being able, of possibility: I am free, insofar as I *can* ... but do not *have to* .... In order to avoid the contradiction in this conception of freedom, however, the will *must* have itself and its own freedom as its object. This "must" is immanent in the free will: the truly free will is necessarily "*the free will which wills the free will*" (Hegel 1991, §27). Freedom understood *as* that which the will must affirm and respect is called "right". The truly free will must, therefore, will and affirm right. One *can* always violate right, because the abstract freedom of choice is not a fiction. Yet the concept of right itself *demands* that right be respected. Not to see this is not to understand what the word "right" means. It is to lack the proper concept of right and of true freedom.

The notion of right is, of course, not unknown to ordinary consciousness. Yet right is often understood as merely a "*limitation* of my freedom or *arbitrary will*" (Hegel 1991, §29R). According to Hegel, by contrast, true freedom does not consist merely in arbitrariness that is then limited by right, but in the free willing *of* right itself, a willing that freely submits itself to its own immanent necessity.

3 Abstract Right

Hegel endeavours, when he discusses a specific topic, to set aside unjustified presuppositions. In his view, this means that, to begin with, he may take up nothing but the bare matter itself in its simple immediacy. The truly free will in *its* immediacy relates immediately to itself in two ways.

On the one hand, it is conscious of being a finite subject with various determinate drives: "the *inherently individual* will of a subject" (Hegel 1991, §34). On the other hand, it is conscious of its freedom as an indeterminate, abstract I (Hegel 1991, §35R). Furthermore, it conceives of its freedom as *right* and so understands itself to be a *person*. A person, for Hegel, is a thus self-conscious individual, who understands his freedom to lie not just in the ability to choose, but in the capacity for right (*Rechtsfähigkeit*) (Hegel 1991, §36).

Personality as such is indeterminate in itself, since I know myself to be a person only insofar as I understand myself to be a pure, universal I. My personality – that is, my freedom, my right – is thus not bound to any specific drives or external objects. Like the arbitrary will, therefore, the person still enjoys the abstract freedom to *choose* this or that – the freedom that consists in being *able* to ..., in unconstrained possibility. Yet the freedom of the person is not reducible to that of the arbitrary will.

The arbitrary will identifies its freedom completely with the *ability* to choose. The person retains this freedom, but he also knows that this ability to choose is a *right* that must be respected. The modality underlying the freedom of the person is thus not mere possibility, but the necessity of possibility. The person *can* appropriate whatever he likes (as long as the limits set by the rights of others are respected). Yet he knows not only that he enjoys this freedom as a matter of fact, but also that he has the *right* to appropriate things (or not), as he sees fit. As a person, therefore, my freedom consists in the *rightful* possibility of choosing as I please – a possibility that must be respected by all. Consequently, the right of the person takes the form, for himself and for others, of an inviolable "*permission* or *warrant*" (*Erlaubnis oder Befugnis*) (Hegel 1991, §38) to appropriate things that are not already owned by someone else.

In the sphere of abstract right, for Hegel, arbitrary freedom is thus not just limited but also *secured* by right. The consciousness of right necessarily coexists, therefore, with the freedom of the arbitrary will. This means, as we have just seen, that persons have the right to appropriate things as they please, as long as they are not the property of another. Yet it also means that their very *willing and maintaining of right* is itself exposed to the contingency of the arbitrary will. A person is conscious that his or her freedom must be respected. But what guarantees that this freedom will be respected in fact? Nothing other than another person's arbitrary will. The necessity and actuality of right are thus dependent on the *contingency* of arbitrariness. The fact that in a contract two persons come together to exchange property rightfully does not alter the situation: rightful property simply becomes dependent on two contingent wills, rather than one (Hegel 1991, §81). Due to this moment of contingency, therefore, there is always the danger that persons will choose *not* to respect the rights they know they must respect, if such respect conflicts with their arbitrary will. This is the danger of wrong (*Unrecht*).

In merely abstract right, therefore, right is not yet present in its fully realized form. Right is freedom, understood as something actual and necessary; in abstract right, however, contingency undermines the necessity belonging to right, because the respect that is owed to the right of persons depends upon the arbitrary wills of those persons. Abstract right *must* be respected; yet it *can* happen that such right is not respected, and this possibility is logically necessary. Abstract right thus lacks true necessity, the necessity that holds sway in spite of contingency. In this sense, right is not yet fully realised in the sphere of abstract right.

4 Morality

The person sees his freedom embodied in the external *thing* that he appropriates and owns. In what Hegel calls the sphere of "morality", by contrast, freedom is actualised and acquires "existence" in and through the free will itself, that is, in *subjectivity* (Hegel 1991, §§106–7). The moral will does not just appropriate external things, therefore, but externalises itself and its freedom in its own *action* (Hegel 1991, §113). This will gives itself a particular, subjective content – an aim or purpose – and then carries it out in the external world (Hegel 1991, §§109–10).

Both the choosing will and the rights-bearing will are dependent in their freedom on what is given to them (their natural drives and the things around them). The purposes and intentions of the acting will are also determined in part by naturally given drives. Yet they are not merely found, but are formulated by the acting will itself. To this extent this acting, moral will demonstrates a more developed form of self-determination than the two wills that precede it.

Yet the moral will not only actualizes freedom and right in its action. Insofar as it is a subjective, individual will, it also *differs* from and stands in *relation* to right, which is something objective and universal (Hegel 1991, §108). In the sphere of morality, such right unites the abstract right of the person to property and personal security with the right of the moral subject to achieve satisfaction and well-being through its actions. This unity of abstract right and well-being, Hegel tells us, is the *good* (Hegel 1991, §129). Insofar as the moral will understands this good as something distinct from itself that nonetheless must be respected, it considers the good to be its *duty* (*Pflicht*) (Hegel 1991, §133). The moral will is thus necessarily subject to duty, because, on the one hand, it knows that it must affirm right in the form of the good, but, on the other hand, it considers the good to be something that stands over against, and binds, the subjective will.

The modality of moral freedom differs from that of abstract, rightful freedom, because moral freedom is subject to a "should" or "ought" (*Sollen*), rather than a simple "must" (Hegel 1991, §131). The must contained in abstract right is a normative, not a natural necessity: it does not have the power to force us to do something, but directs itself at our freedom. Specifically, it requires us to obey its command immediately without further reflection; and, as we have seen, the person obeys this command, and respects right, as long as doing so is in agreement with his arbitrary will. The should, by contrast, does not just demand immediate obedience, but directs itself at our subjective, *inwardly reflective* freedom. When I am conscious that I should do something, that it is my duty, I am conscious, not just of an immediate requirement that must be fulfilled, but rather of a demand that *I* have to fulfill through my *own* subjective freedom. To put it another way, a moral duty is not just something that must *be done*, but something that *I myself* am responsible for doing.[2] Indeed, the moral will considers it to be its right to take upon itself the responsibility for doing what duty commands and upholding right. In this sense, the moral will is characterised by a certain heroism: it always thinks that in the absence of its *own* activity right would not be actualised.

The moral will also presumes that it can determine by itself the content of the good. As is well known, Hegel believes that the concept of moral duty in itself is empty of content. Whether this is true of Kant's conception of duty, we shall leave to one side; Hegel shows, however, that duty, as it is conceived by the moral will that has emerged in the course of the *Philosophy of Right*, must be empty and without content. Since this concept of duty prescribes no specific duties, it falls, in Hegel's view, to subjective conscience to decide what the duty-bound will should do. Subjective conscience thus becomes the "power of *judgement* which determines solely from within itself what is good" (Hegel 1991, §138). Indeed, conscience claims for itself the *right* to exercise this power of judgement, for its sees itself as a "sanctuary [*Heiligtum*] which it would be *sacrilege* to violate" (Hegel 1991, §137R).

The moral subject who abides by his conscience is convinced that his actions are justified. Conscience, however, is something subjective; the moral subject thus always runs the risk that, even though he is convinced he is doing his duty, he actually gives free rein to his own subjective arbitrariness. In this case, the moral subject does not regress to the standpoint of the person, who consciously violates right when it conflicts with his arbitrary will; rather, he becomes an *evil* will that indulges its own, arbitrary inclinations while considering itself to be perfectly good and dutiful.

---

[2] This difference is obscured by Robert Brandom when he writes that "treating others as *selves*" at all means treating them as "ones who are *responsible* for their doings and attitudes" – which is not to say that Brandom would not draw the distinction. See (Brandom 2009, p. 3).

Hegel does not maintain that evil is unavoidable in human life, but he argues that the moral will runs the risk of becoming evil by claiming the right to determine purely by itself, through its conscience, what counts as the good. In the sphere of morality, therefore, the actualisation of right and the good is made dependent upon the subjectivity of the particular individual. This means that the good lacks true actuality and necessity, because its actualisation is exposed to *contingency*.

5 Ethical Life

Let us briefly recap. Arbitrariness is freedom understood as possibility: it consists in being *able* to choose, as one sees fit. Since the I that enjoys this freedom is utterly indeterminate, it finds determinacy only in what is *given* to it, namely natural drives and their corresponding objects. The freedom to choose is thus *dependent* on this given: however unconstrained such freedom may be, we can choose only what is available to us.

To free itself from such dependence, the free will must have itself as its object: it must be the "*free will which wills the free will*" (Hegel 1991, §27). Insofar as the free will has its own freedom as its object, it understands that freedom to be something actual and existent, not merely to consist in the possibility of selecting this or that. At the same time, the will understands its freedom to be that which it *must* will, to be something necessary for the will. When freedom itself is understood as the actual, necessary object of the will, it is conceived as *right*. The concept of right then determines the further logical development of Hegel's philosophy of freedom.

First, right is understood as something *immediately* actual and necessary, something that simply *must* be respected by the individual will. Understood in this way, however, right remains dependent on the arbitrariness of the individual, who can, if he chooses, violate right. Second, right is understood as something whose actuality and necessity is *mediated*. It is seen as something that is necessary, but that is actualised only in and through our own inner, subjective freedom. Right is here once again made dependent on subjective arbitrariness, though in this case such arbitrariness is convinced that it is in conformity with right, duty and the dictates of conscience. In both these cases, therefore, right is present in a form that lacks true actuality and necessity.

Only in *ethical life* (*Sittlichkeit*) is right something *truly* actual and necessary, and so present in its fully developed form. Ethical life, Hegel writes, is freedom as "the living good", as an "existing world" of objective laws and institutions (Hegel 1991, §§142, 144). These laws and institutions have "a fixed *content* which is necessary for itself, and whose existence [*Bestehen*] is exalted above subjective opinions and preferences" (Hegel 1991, §144). They thus constitute a "circle of necessity" (Hegel 1991, §145) that is no longer dependent on subjective arbitrariness, but that precedes and grounds it – a world within which subjective arbitrariness first arises and comes to expression. The concept of ethical life is introduced by Hegel, therefore, not just because it gives content to empty, contentless moral duty, *but because ethical life is the true actualization of right*. Indeed, ethical life is made necessary by the concept of right itself.

Ethical life has its actuality in the practical action of self-conscious subjects and does not lie, like external nature, outside of subjectivity: the institutions of ethical life are organisations of active *human beings*. Yet for the ethical individual, who grows up and is educated in these institutions, "the ethical substance and its laws and powers [...] *are* [*sind*], in the supreme sense of self-sufficiency" (Hegel 1991, §146). Ethical laws and institutions have the normative authority of right, so the individual knows that he must respect them; but they also constitute an *existing actuality*, in which the individual can participate, but which ultimately does not depend on *his* action or will. This point is important: the moral subject always thinks that the good is first realised through his own action. The ethical individual, by contrast, understands the good to be a reality that precedes him – one that he must sustain and can reform through his action, but whose independence he must also acknowledge and allow to hold sway.[3]

In the ethical world around him the individual sees other human beings who actualise right and the good in their actions. In such ethical human beings, acting in accordance with right and the good has become a habit or "*second nature*" (Hegel 1991, §151). They do what is good without further ado, without having at the forefront of their minds that it is their responsibility and duty to do so. Or, to put it another way, they actually *do* what is good, rather than just thinking that they *should* do so. Yet the ethical individual not only encounters a world of ethical human beings around him; he also actualises the good in his *own* habitual action. He knows, therefore, that freedom is a reality both in the world and in his own action.

The ethical individual, for Hegel, is thus a practical subject: ethical life is actualised in the *actions* of self-conscious individuals (Hegel 1991, §142). The relation of the ethical individual to the laws and institutions of ethical life cannot, however, be a purely practical one, for the individual relates to a world of freedom, right and reason, whose existence is objective and independent of his own

---

[3] Frederick Neuhouser writes that free individuals understand themselves to be "*re*-producers" of their institutions. See (Neuhouser 2000, p.87).

particular action. The appropriate relation for the individual to have to this objective, independent realm of freedom is a *theoretical* one, in which the individual *recognises* that the world around him is the embodiment of freedom.

According to the *Encyclopaedia*, the truly free will is "the unity of theoretical and practical spirit" (Hegel 2007, p.214 [§481]). Crudely stated, theoretical spirit is the knowing of what *is*. In the practical sphere, by contrast, something is brought *into* being by me. The will is obviously practical, insofar it brings about changes in the world through its actions. Yet insofar as the ethical will understands freedom to be something already existent and actual in the world, it is practical spirit that is mediated by a *theoretical*, cognitive relation to actualized freedom.

Recall that right is freedom, understood not just as possibility, but as something actual and necessary: that which the free will *must* will. Recall, too, that right must take the form of ethical life, if it is to be freed from dependence on the arbitrary will and to be something truly actual and necessary: the modality of right itself leads it from abstract right, via morality, to ethical life. As we have just seen, the appropriate relation for the individual to have to the actual, existing world of ethical life is a theoretical one: that of cognition. It follows from this that *right* itself in its fully developed form requires the individual to stand in a *theoretical* relation to it. The free will is always practical: it chooses, acts and produces. In the ethical sphere, however, such practical activity is subordinated to, and informed by, theoretical cognition of the actuality of freedom and right.

Note that in ethical laws and institutions the individual does not see an alien authority, but objective structures that guarantee and actualize his *own* freedom. "The subject bears *spiritual witness* to them as to *its own essence* in which it has its *self-awareness* [*Selbstgefühl*]" (Hegel 1991, §147). Such "spiritual witness", Hegel tells us, takes the form of *trust* (*Zutrauen*). The properly ethical individual thus *trusts* the laws and institutions of ethical life; indeed, his relation to them is "immediate and closer to identity than even *faith* or *trust*".

Trust, for Hegel, is "the consciousness that my substantial and particular interest is preserved and contained in the interest and end of an other" (Hegel 1991, §268). It is the feeling that my well-being and freedom are secured by that other, and that in relating to the other I am in fact relating to myself and my own essence. Such trust can remain naive and immediate, or it can "pass over into more or less educated insight" (Hegel 1991, §§268, 147R). The main point is that trust is an essentially *theoretical* relation to ethical life – a *knowing* of oneself in the other – that underlies the ethical actions of people. Ethical action is action grounded in the consciousness and recognition that right and freedom are indeed actualised in the world; this consciousness is our trust in the institutions of ethical life; action must, therefore, be rooted in trust, if it is to be truly ethical.[4]

Note that, for Hegel, true trust is not blind, but it is the immediate or educated *recognition* that right is actualised in the world. It is the understanding, in the form of *feeling*, that right and the good – which include my right and my well-being – are embodied in the laws and institutions around me. This point is crucial: trust and understanding are not at odds with one another, but true trust is itself a form of felt understanding and insight. Such trust is not merely peripheral to ethical life, for Hegel, but belongs to the very essence of ethical life, because it is the appropriate subjective relation to objectively existing right. In the spheres of abstract right and morality there can be no trust that right is actualised, because right has no properly independent existence, but depends utterly for its maintenance on the arbitrary will of the individual or the actions of particular subjects. In ethical life, by contrast, where right is something actual that precedes and grounds my subjective activity, the appropriate relation to right is above all that of felt recognition or trust.

This trust is itself a distinctive form of freedom that can be found only in ethical life (Neuhouser 2000, pp. 105, 111). For both the abstractly rightful person and the moral subject the actualisation of right depends on their will and their activity. The ethical individual, however, enjoys the freedom of seeing right already actualised in a world that is in an important respect independent of him. The ethical individual can thus, so to speak, relax and does not need constantly to take responsibility for actualising right, because his life is informed by trust in the existing institutions of ethical life. This freedom that consists in trusting the world around us and not always wanting to put the world right through my own efforts is to be found only in ethical life and is unknown to the bearer of abstract rights and the moral subject.

If, however, trust is to be the *consciousness* and *recognition* that right is actualised in the world, then the laws and institutions to which I relate must, indeed, actualize right: they must actually correspond to the trust I have in them. This means, among other things, that such laws and institutions must protect the abstract right to property and the moral right to freedom of action and particular well-being (Hegel 1991, §154). As I have stressed, ethical trust is not blind, but the immediate or educated *recognition* of the actuality of freedom. Trust can be such

---

[4] Neuhouser understands the relation between the theoretical and practical attitude in Hegel's concept of ethical life to be the other way around. The trust of individuals in the institutions of ethical life can, indeed, be conceived as "a theoretical stance", but "this attitude itself is derivative of their 'being-with-themselves' in their social institutions in a way that is more clearly practical in nature". See (Neuhouser 2000, pp. 105–6).

recognition and insight only if there is a reality there to recognise, that is, only if freedom in all its forms *is* actualised in the world about us. Those who are afraid of trust and always urge us to be vigilant in face of the state because they fear that trust will enable corruption among officials to flourish, misunderstand Hegel's concept of trust. True trust, as the felt *awareness* that freedom is realised in society, is possible only when freedom is indeed realised in society.

The actuality of freedom and right must, therefore, precede the trust we place in it, and, according to Hegel, the most important objective guarantee of public freedom is the *division of powers* (provided that this is taken in its true sense as a moment in an organically unified state) (Hegel 1991, §272R). This not only means that the executive and legislative powers must be distinguished from one another – something that Hegel thinks did not happen in the French Revolution, with devastating consequences.[5] It also means that local communities and corporations must be accorded legal recognition and rights in order to protect the state and those who are governed by it "against the misuse of power on the part of the official bodies and their members" (Hegel 1991, §295). The objective actualization of freedom also requires that the deliberations in the Estates' assemblies be public and that there be "freedom of public communication", including the press (albeit within limits set by right and law) (Hegel 1991, §319). All of this constitutes the objective condition of public trust. Such trust is, however, itself essential to ethical life and constitutes a distinctive form of freedom: the freedom of being and feeling at home in the world that is denied to the mere rights-bearing person and the merely moral subject.

I come now to my concluding remarks. What I wish to highlight here is the close connection, to which Hegel directs our attention, between right and trust. For Hegel, freedom consists in part in the ability to choose; true freedom, however, consists in the willing and maintaining of right. Right always has priority, in Hegel's view, over the unconstrained choices exercised by individuals. This right must encompass the rights of the person and of the moral subject, but its true actualization is to be found in the laws and institutions of ethical life together with the people in whom acting in accordance with the demands of right has become habitual and "second nature". If such people are to enjoy the full freedom of ethical life, they must be able to trust that their freedom and rights are secured by the laws and institutions under which and in which they live. They must also enjoy the freedom that lies in this trust itself and the feeling of being at home in the world that it involves. Hegel does *not* maintain that the citizens of every state in the modern world live in this trust: he is well

---

5 (Hegel 1923, p. 929): "for the whole power of the administration was placed in the legislature".

aware that there are bad states in which such trust is lacking (for example, the French Republic after 1792).[6] According to Hegel, however, a life without this trust cannot be a truly *free* life.

On the basis of Hegel's insight into the close connection between right and trust, we can identify two very clear dangers that people face in the modern world. The first is that our trust might be blind after all and not involve any recognition of what there actually is. In this case, we may well place our trust in institutions that do not merit it. Genuine trust, however, is an essential element of modern freedom, for Hegel. It is important, therefore, that modern states maintain the division of powers and protect themselves from public corruption by (among other things) publicising proceedings in the assemblies and according appropriate rights to local communities and corporations. It is also important that the press and education system make it possible for citizens to gain a proper understanding of the real political and social situation in which they live. Only under these conditions can the trust that citizens place in their laws and institutions become genuine trust, as Hegel conceives it, namely, the felt *recognition* that freedom is, indeed, realised in those laws and institutions.

The second danger is that we might refuse ever to place our trust in the institutions of ethical life, even when they do in fact merit it, and instead cultivate an attitude of perpetual vigilance and suspicion. Vigilance is certainly warranted when signs of corruption are evident. Such vigilance and suspicion are, however, not always well grounded and can degenerate into a self-sustaining "culture of suspicion", to use Onora O'Neill's term, that undermines the possibility of trust (O'Neill 2002, p. 57).[7] In this way, our zealous efforts to be alert and to avoid naivety threaten the very ethical life we claim to be protecting.

A life in which we trust our fellow human beings is not altogether without risk; but a life without genuine trust lacks an essential element of ethical freedom. Some see trust, especially that placed in the laws and institutions of the state, as nothing more than naivety. Hegel's insight, however, is that a life lived in a *trusting* relation to laws and institutions, that are themselves free of corruption, is one to which we all have an inalienable *right*.

---

6 (Hegel 1923, p. 930): "thus suspicion [*Verdacht*] reigns".
7 See also (Hegel 1991, §272R): "to make malevolence and distrust of malevolence the primary factor [...] is, as far as thought is concerned, characteristic of the *negative understanding* and, as far as the disposition is concerned, characteristic of the outlook of the rabble".

Bibliography

Brandom, Robert B. (2009): *Reason in Philosophy. Animating Ideas*. Cambridge, Mass.: Harvard University Press.

Hegel, G.W.F. (1923): *Vorlesungen über die Philosophie der Weltgeschichte. Zweite Hälfte*. Georg Lasson (Ed.), 2nd edition. Hamburg: Felix Meiner Verlag.

Hegel, G.W.F. (1970): *Grundlinien der Philosophie des Rechts oder Naturrecht und Staatswissenschaft im Grundrisse*. In: *Werke in zwanzig Bänden*, Vol. 7. Eva Moldenhauer/Karl Markus Michel (Eds.). Frankfurt am Main: Suhrkamp Verlag.

Hegel, G.W.F. (1991): *Elements of the Philosophy of Right*. Allen W. Wood (Ed.). Cambridge: Cambridge University Press.

Hegel, G.W.F. (2005): *Die Philosophie des Rechts. Vorlesung von 1821/22*. Hansgeorg Hoppe (Ed.). Frankfurt am Main: Suhrkamp Verlag.

Hegel, G.W.F. (2007): *Philosophy of Mind*. Oxford: Clarendon Press.

Neuhouser, Frederick (2000): *Foundations of Hegel's Social Theory. Actualizing Freedom*. Cambridge, Mass.: Harvard University Press.

O'Neill, Onora (2002): *A Question of Trust*. Cambridge: Cambridge University Press.

Robert Pippin
Hegel on the Varieties of Social Subjectivity

1

Hegel is well known for having claimed that philosophy is "its time comprehended in thought" (*ihre Zeit in Gedanken erfaßt*). The implications of this claim are immediately apparent in the Grundlinien der Philosophe des Rechts (GPR) that follows this claim in its Preface. That is, Hegel's Grundlinien is not a treatment of the institutions Hegel thinks constitutive of justice for anyone, anywhere, at any time. It is clearly an analysis of the modern understanding and realization of contract, crime, legal and moral responsibility, moral conscience, the modern, nuclear family, a market economy and modern political institutions. But it is also clearly neither an empirical social analysis of how such a society actually works, nor a pure normative assessment of these distinctive characteristics, measured against some trans-historical ideal.

Moreover, the GPR seems to be relatively self-contained. Hegel's argument for the incompleteness of Abstract Right and Morality as ways of understanding "right" (*Recht*) do not appear to depend on some elaborate historical theodicy, or on any claim about some comprehensive historical development. Or, if it is, that element appears separable in some way, not appealed to for any support in the body of the text itself. And the argument for such an incompleteness and for the more adequate comprehension of right within ethical life (*Sittlichkeit*) does not appear to rely on systematic considerations, requiring that we understand the account of "objective Geist" within the structure of "subjective" and "absolute" Geist, or as occupying some position within an encyclopedic account of all the possible philosophical sciences. (This is true although Hegel does say, also in the "Preface" to The Philosophy of Right, that that outline or Grundriss presupposes "the speculative mode of cognition." This is to be contrasted with what he calls "the old logic" and "the knowledge of the understanding" [*Verstandeserkenntnis*], a term he also uses to characterize all of metaphysics prior to his own. He makes explicit that he is referring to his book, The Science of Logic. But again, no such appeal to the details of a speculative logic seems explicitly called on to do anything in the inter-related claims made in the actual course of the Grundlinien itself.

This immediately raises the question of just how time-bound Hegel's account of *Recht* actually is, and, therewith, how we should understand the bearing of his account on our own time, a very different time of mass consumer societies, a globalized economy, very different marriage and divorce conventions, a highly commercialized and manipulable public sphere and so forth. Some have argued that, even so, there are enough points of determinate contact that some direct relevance is still possible. Some commentators refer to Hegel's account of the limitations of contractarian models of the state or to the limitations of liberal notions of rights protection, or his reasons for insisting on a state/civil society distinction. I will follow here another line of thought, highlighting instead the fruitfulness of his approach in general, and one unusual aspect of that approach, announced in my title.

But both aspects of his original and influential claim that philosophy has a historical-diagnostic task have proven difficult to understand. By the two aspects, I mean, first, exactly what is to be understood by the philosopher's "time," and, second, what does "comprehended in thought" amount to? Space is limited, so I will simply make a suggestion about each. There would seem to be a simple, clear answer to the former question. The covering name for the historical institutions and practices that attract Hegel's philosophical attention to a time is "spirit" (*Geist*) whether manifest in subjective, objective or absolute form, whether *Geist* is the subject of a unique kind of analysis, a phenomenology, whether understood as a *Weltgeist* or *Volkgeist*. For the sake of argument, let us stipulate that *Geist* refers to a collective mindedness, the forms of which collectivity, the "shapes of spirit"[Gestalten des Geistes" change over historical time. Further, any concrete shape of *Geist* is never treated by Hegel as some summary compilation of individually held attitudes, majoritarian views, or even as the direct object of intentional attitudes like beliefs. However, while there are similarities, *Geist* does not function in Hegel as something like a presupposed "form of life," as it might be found in Wittgenstein, or as "*Welt*" might function in the early Heidegger. Hegel clearly thinks it is possible to ascribe states and capacities to such a collective subject in a sense identical in many senses to the way we ascribe such states and capacities to individual persons. This goes well beyond the ascription of common, deeply presupposed commitments and assumptions and dispositions. We can even say that a historical form of *Geist* can be reflective about itself and its commitments, can come over time to greater and greater self-consciousness (for example, in and by means of its art works), and that it can be said to do things, for which responsibility can be ascribed. (This last is especially true of states that act in our name as citizens.) We can thus speak of a group agent, or of a social subjectivity. Such a postulation of a common mindedness is not a fiction, or a mere heuristic or theoretical posit. It has ontological status; there are such entities. Now of course, *Geist* cannot be said to behave in all ways like an individual subject or agent. It is not embodied in the same way, can be said to "have emotions" only in a highly metaphorical way (as in a collective hysteria or panic, or in moments like the French Terror). It has a past it carries forward and appeals to, but *Geist* does not remember its past as an individual does, and so on. Nevertheless, Hegel is willing to go very far in what he is willing to claim about such a collective subject, and we will consider one of his most ambitious and initially implausible claims soon.

Finally, when Hegel describes *Geist* as an "I that is a We," **and** a "We that is an I," [*Ich*, das *Wir*, und *Wir*, das *Ich* ist] he is committing himself to a dialectical relation between any such collective or group subject and the individual persons who are its participants. That is, such a collectivity is not possible except as constituted in some way by the attitudes and commitments of these participants. It would not exist were there not these attitudes and commitments. This does not reduce in any way the reality of *Geist* as *Geist*; such attitudes and commitments *do* achieve the status of collective agency. But the direction of dependence famously goes both ways for him. Individuals should not be understood as, ex ante, atomistic, self-sufficient origins of such commitments, as if *Geist* comes into being only as a result of constituting acts by spiritless (*geistlose*) atomic individuals. They are the individuals they are only as "formed" or *gebildet* always already within such collectivities. (So, Hegel will insist: "to take conscious individuality so mindlessly as an *individual* existing phenomenon is contradictory since the essence of individuality is the universal of spirit." [Die bewußte Individualität hingegen geistlos als *einzelne* seiende Erscheinung zu nehmen, hat das Widersprechende, daß ihr Wesen das Allgemeine des Geistes ist (Hegel 2013, § 304). This is expressed in full Hegelese, but in itself this is a very old idea, apparent in the philosopher equally as influential on Hegel as Kant; that is, in Aristotle's insistence that, considered outside the *polis*, a human being is not comprehensible as a human being. He is either a beast or a god. But Hegel's bi-directionality and historicity greatly complicates such a picture. This co-constituting mutual dependence is why Hegel can frequently say something that would otherwise be quite mysterious, that spirit, this social subjectivity, is "a product of itself." (Hegel 1978, pp. 6–7) (*Geist* is this co-constituting relation; the product of individuals who are themselves the products of their participation in *Geist*. *Geist* has no substantial existence apart from this mutual reflection.)

All of this just introduces the first of the two elements in Hegel's famous claim about the task of philosophy; *Geist* as "its own time." What could he mean by the second element: the *Geist* of its time "comprehended in thought"? Again a suggestion. Sometimes what he says sounds quite implausible. He will say that philosophy gives the form of necessity to what would otherwise appear merely contingent. When this is said about, for example, the development of the empirical sciences (Hegel 1971, § 12 A), it can sound as if Hegel wants to say that the actual course of that development could not have happened otherwise. If this is supported by a claim about a self-transforming, underlying metaphysical entity, "cosmic spirit," or "God," developing according to some necessary law of internal teleology, then the claim seems hopeless. At a more modest level, though (and this is how I think he wants to be understood), he could mean that a significant transition in art history, or political history, or religious history, a shift in collective ethical commitments, can be rendered intelligible by a philosophical account. This account is based on a form of practical contradiction that introduces a more familiar form of necessity, the form appropriate to: "he who wills the end <u>must</u> will, or necessarily wills, the means" (otherwise we have evidence that he has not willed the end). If a collective attempt to accomplish some goal can be said to learn collectively that commitment to that end is impossible without commitment to, let us say, a broader and more comprehensive end, then it must pursue such a new end or give up the enterprise. Or, if it develops that the means chosen actually make achieving the end impossible, then the means <u>must</u> be altered. They are not arbitrarily altered. They <u>must</u> be altered, on pain of practical incoherence. A philosophical account, assuming the rationality of such a teleological enterprise, can show this. It can give the form of (practical) necessity to what would otherwise seem contingent alterations. I said: "assuming the rationality of such a teleological enterprise." I meant to recall the Hegelian maxim announced in the Lectures on the Philosophy of World History: "To him who looks on the world rationally, the world looks rationally back" (Hegel 1971, p. 23). Here is yet another theme worth several independent lectures.

2

This raises again the question of the adequacy of treating a collective or a group agent as capable of such end-setting, practical rationality, and self-correction. To understand this, we now need a somewhat broader set of considerations. The broadest would involve the long history of treating collective entities as agents, or entertaining the possibility, but denying it, especially in legal contexts and in questions of liability. It extends at least back to Innocent IV in the thirteenth century, who left matters somewhat confused when he called corporate persons "ficta" or fabricated. He could have meant, and was taken to mean both, mere fictions, unreal, or he could have meant "artificial," not natural, but nevertheless real, not fictional. (He appeared most interested in whether such group agents, like the University of Paris, had a soul and so could be excommunicated. He concluded that they did not and could not be.) Those contemporary philosophers who have defended a robust view on the reality of group agents, like Philip Petit, have pointed out that as long as something can be said to satisfy the overall conditions for agency, whether as an individual or group, it should be counted as an agent, and ascriptions of purposes, representations, and reflective attitudes are appropriate. He argues that those conditions are three-fold and that they are met by many groups: the capacity to hold plausible purposes as a collective (and this means: purposes known to be held and pursued; such group agents must be self-representing agents, not just enterprises represented with a presumed purpose), the capacity to form reliable representations of reality and be responsive to what is represented, and the capacity to act reliably to advance those purposes according to those representations. This last involves the capacity to respond appropriately to what is learned in the course of such a realization, and to adjust activity in the light of learned difficulties or the discovery of incompatible commitments. Fulfilling these conditions is compatible with a wide variety of institutional embodiments, representative associations, or various steering mechanisms. Moreover, Petit goes on to argue that such groups cannot be said to be constituted by simple majoritarian vote, as if a group agent or *Geist*, were simply a *façon de parler*, a way of expressing what most people want or believe. Many valuable ends can only be achieved by participation in a group and the so-called "discursive dilemma" in legal theory has shown that it would irrational to participate in such a group if the only reflective, deliberative procedure were majoritarian, a mere sum of individual preferences. A situation can easily be shown to develop in which such a group would have to be committed to an end that is in fact rejected by all the members of the group in their individual role. The details of this argument (which depends on a series of disjunctive choices) need not concern us here. It is another way or arguing that a genuine group agency must be subject to some reflective procedure in a real process of coming deliberatively to form a view or voice, all in ways not limited to a merely summative procedure.

The lesson here is that what makes a group a group agent is that it posses a certain form of rational unity, a unity that must be knowingly achieved and sustained. This means that the group is sensitive to inconsistencies in group commitments, empirical facts inconsistent with shared beliefs, and a formation process for commitments and beliefs that is genuinely formative, not merely expressive of collected individual commitments and beliefs. In this sense some group agent, like "the polis" of ancient Thebes, may take itself to be such a rational unity, but in an enactment of its commitments discover that it is collectively committed to conceptions of familial obligation and to conceptions of political obligations that are not practically compatible. Geist can appear to have, be collectively taken to have, the required rational unity, but come to discover that it does not have it. Tragedy ensues. A revision of the commitments is necessary.

The community can be said to have learned, and acted on such learning, perhaps, to invoke another play, in the establishment of the homicide courts at the Aeropagus, as in Aeschylus's <u>Eumenides</u>.

3

Admittedly, the institutions and issues that Petit is concerned with are multiple in a society and need have no particular relation to one another. That is he takes no position on the question on whether various group agents, like corporations, universities, hospitals, armies, states, churches, could also be said to be, must be understood to be, themselves elements of one "common mind," to borrow the title of one of Petit's books, much like the way individuals are determinate individuals at all only within purposive groups. But it is not much of a leap to claim that this would be a necessary extension of the account. For one thing, many individuals are often members of several such groups and they would be subject to conflicting or incompatible commitments. The awareness of such conflicts would be unavoidable and so practically incoherent, were there no way of thinking of such several group agents as at least compatible. "Compatible," though, would still not get us to the more ambitious status of *Geist*. To reach that, we need a common like-mindedness in which institutional commitments are also not indifferent to one another even if logically compatible. Rather, they must genuinely cohere, or make some sense as enterprises that <u>belong</u> together. <u>These</u> art practices, for example, would be the art practices engaged in by persons engaged in <u>those</u> religious practices, that civil society, those sorts of universities, that conception of the purposes of an army, that political constitution and so forth. That overall unity would be yet another name for "Geist." Universities must take account of the religious preferences of their students. Religions must take account of the needs of an army, and so on. We can consider Geist the highest level, self-unifying rational form of unity in a community at a time.

There is little doubt that Hegel thinks of such a super-structural subject as such a substantial unity. In the passage where he introduces the notion in the PhG, he calls Geist,)

> ...this absolute substance which constitutes the unity of its oppositions in their complete freedom and self-sufficiency, namely, in the oppositions of the various self-consciousnesses existing for themselves: The *I* that is *we* and the *we* that is I. (Hegel 2013, § 174)

It is at this level of abstraction that Hegel wants to portray one such collective subject, Western *Geist*, the distinct inheritor of its *Greek* beginnings, as engaged in a practical, purposive project, a struggle for full self-understanding across historical time, propelled forward in that attempt by a series of breakdowns in the coherence of its self-consciousness. These breakdowns reflect the practical contradictions that we have discussed. We are now at such a high level of abstraction that nothing interesting in any overall defense of this suggestion can be said. But there is a smaller, more manageable topic left.

4

The Platonic Socrates long ago introduced the idea that there is a revealing analogy between the parts of, and the inter-relation between the parts of, the soul and the corresponding parts and inter-relations of the polis. But just how far can we go in extending the categories of assessment and analysis at home with individuals in understanding Geist? Psychic and political unity (and so health) is the main issue in the Politeia, and Hegel certainly focuses on that issue too. But he seems to go much farther.

One phenomenon (one that Petit has also devoted attention to) is collective *akrasia*, weakness of the will. It is easily conceivable that at the requisite level of abstraction, a community might express its allegiances to various courses of action; equality before the law, for example. Each person accused should have exactly the same status, entitlements and other freedoms as anyone else. The commitment is formally enshrined in a basic law and is implicitly and explicitly affirmed in various rituals and pronouncements. In practice however, wealthy people turn out to have an enormous advantage, and rates of conviction for persons above a certain income level are strikingly lower. Everyone knows this, and knows of, even affirms, the collective commitment, but no one does anything. The irrationality occurs, we could plausibly suggest, because while the commitment may be sincere (or at least not held hypocritically or in cynical fraudulence), the costs and efforts of realizing it are so high that when occasions emerge to address the problem, it is easier to hedge, dissemble, plead unavoidable constraints, one-time exceptions, etc. If we conceive of both individuals and Geist as some sort of unity among multiple motivational voices clamoring for attention and allegiance, it is not difficult to imagine incentives to attend to one or another voice at the expense of others, the one that provides the easiest or most self-interested path forward. How this exactly happens in either case might not be easy to understand, especially since this contradiction is available to consciousness or public explicitness. In various contexts in the Phenomenology, like Virtue and the Way of the World (*die Tugend und der Weltlauf*), or the Beautiful Soul (*die schöne Seele*) that cannot bring itself to act, Hegel appears to be thinking of something like this. The standpoint of *Tugend* demands that the agent "sacrifice" everything of his individuality, his role in the *Weltlauf*, but when it comes to acting on such a complete self-denial, it cannot. It cannot live up to its principles without practical incoherence. (Here we have to say as well that what might look like "weakness" might actually be the result of an incomplete and distorted practical self-knowledge.) And Hegel uses the language of strength or force to explain the dilemma that *die schöne Seele* is caught up in. (2)

> Inasmuch as the self-certain spirit as a beautiful soul does not now possess the strength to empty itself of the self-knowledge which it keeps to itself in itself, it cannot achieve a parity with the consciousness it has repulsed, and thus it cannot achieve the intuited unity of itself in an other, and it cannot attain existence. Hence, the parity comes about merely negatively, as a spirit-less being. (Hegel 2013, § 670)

But how could one be "pulled" in one way by one of the possible motives at hand, and not be just as aware of the demands of coherent rationality just as clearly as if one were not so "pulled"? But whatever problem there is, it does not appear greater in the group than in the individual case, and it seems equally familiar in both.

At one point in the <u>Phenomenology</u>, Hegel also begins to discuss what he calls "the world of self-alienated Spirit" [*die Welt des sich entfremdeten Geistes*] (Hegel 2013, § 793) and he returns to that characterization in accounting for several phenomena. These are cases of collectively held ideals, like state power and wealth [*Staatsmacht und Reichtum*], or the availability and inevitably of a perspective on every action of both the valet's lower, unmasking, deflationary perspective, what Hegel calls baseness or *Niederträchtigkeit* (seeing corrupt motives and weakness and hypocrisy everywhere) and yet also a more generous or magnanimous perspective, what he calls noble-mindedness, *Edelmütigkeit* (something like an ability to see the genuineness with which the ideal is held, despite the failures). Both are equally possible reactions to the lack of fit between professed ideal and what is actually done, a drearily familiar and frequent phenomenon is ordinary life. He wants to raise a question that is difficult address in traditional philosophical terms: what accounts for the attraction of one attitude as opposed to the other? This is similar to the situation described when Hegel assesses the philosophical significance of tragedy, but in a state of greater *Bildung*, or cultural maturation, the conflicting commitments do not force a tragic choice, one whereby acting well must also be acting wrongly. In effect they can be "hidden" more successfully, something that requires a more complicated psychology than available to the ancients. Such a state of alienation is a state of irrationality, but at the self-reflective level, in which, given the level of self-knowledge attained by some community, reflective coherence is not possible and a certain kind of dissemblance is needed and is possible. (It is this dissemblance that has replaced tragedy in the modern world.) It is also important that Hegel describes this situation as <u>self</u>-alienated *Geist*. This means that it is not a contingent manifestation that just happens at some moment in time. The situation has not happened to *Geist*; *Geist* has done something to bring it about, alienated <u>itself</u>. The phenomenon can thus be rendered philosophically intelligible, along the lines of practical necessity and contradiction discussed before. The situation also means that not only is Geist alienated from itself in this reflective sense, but individuals can not be said to be able experience as coherently satisfiable the claims made on them by their membership in the group unity. They are thus alienated from their own collective identity, bound to it but repelled by it at the same time. Moreover, the processes by which the mutual interdependence of individual and collective identity come to be formed are certainly not necessarily fixed, can be as much in dispute as any result of this formation process. One might well find oneself confronted by possibilities of work, or options among ideal general commitments, or political choices, none of which are experienced as possible expressions of one's own commitments and talents. They are the only ones available but they can appear "strange," foreign, merely positive, and so forth, even though one might voluntarily and effectively affirm them by what one says or does. As with *akrasia*, though, none of this need be evidence that the group identity or agency is really not what it presents itself as, all because of this alienation. The experience itself suggests rather that something is going wrong, some necessary unity is lacking, something essential to one's practical identity and the realization of that identity is not possible.

But if that phenomenon can be borne only by a kind of dissemblance, there is a natural link with the next phenomenon. For he says such things as the following. In his initial discussion of "True Spirit, Ethical Life" [*der wahre Geist, die Sittlichkeit*], Hegel first points out that the commonly shared ethical substance of the polis in the classical period

> ... breaks itself up into a differentiated ethical essence, into a human and a divine law. Likewise, in terms of its essence, self-consciousness, in confronting substance, assigns itself to one of these powers, and, as knowledge, it divides itself into both an ignorance of what it is doing and a knowledge of what it is doing, and it is thus a deceived knowledge. (Hegel 2013, § 444)

He is talking here, ultimately, about the way Creon and Antigone argue with each other, as if wholly ignorant of the credibility of counter-claims expressed by the other, but not really ignorant. This is an aspect of Hegel's account that is strikingly modern and not much attended to. Each knows what he or she is doing in defending the position, but in pretending not to understand such a claim's relation to credible counter-claims, he or she does not know what he or she is actually doing with its absolutism, and is, in a remarkable phrase, not making a false claim to know, but expressing a deceived knowledge (*betrogenes Wissen*). He thus introduces all the classic problems of self-deceit. How is it possible for some individual manifestation of *Geist* both to know what it knows and be ignorant, in some way, make itself ignorant, of what it knows?

This expression is hardly a *hapax legomenon* in Hegel. He had introduced the general topic of decet in the section in Reason called, "The Spiritual Animal Kingdom and deceit, or the Heart of the Matter"[1] (Das geistige Tierreich, und der Betrug, oder die Sache selbst." It is in this section that he insists on the social – that is the public and performative, and thus socially dependent – character of actions. At one point he notes,

> Since within this alternation consciousness has one moment for itself as
> essential in its reflection, while it has another merely externally in consciousness, or for others, what thus comes on the scene is a game individualities play with each other; in this game, each finds himself to be
> deceiving himself as much he finds each to be mutually deceiving each other. (Hegel 2013, § 415)

This seems like a kind of riot of deception and self-deception. And it is important to note again that Hegel is not talking here about individual pathologies. As with collective *akrasia*, there is some general disconnect between a collective self-representation, and what such a group or super-group agent actually does. In all three cases we have seen, the problem is the achievement of the rational unity necessary for rational action. In fact, these appeals to self-deception appear to be much more important or inclusive than *akrasia*. Our case of an expressed commitment to equality before the law, matched by no effective action, is much more likely an indication that there is no such commitment. In this sense, there can clearly be collectively self-deceit. Accounted for this way, it means that the interesting originality of Hegel's account of self-deception in this and many other cases is that it is not exclusively psychological, not a matter of a subject "hiding" something from, and inside, itself, prompting a hunt for deeper and real motives. The actuality of a motive is apparent only in action, in what one is willing to do. It is in this enactment that self-deception, that this disconnect, manifests itself. If we think of both individual and group agents as multitudes of possible voices for different motives, we will then look to how

---

[1] Pinkard translates *die Sache selbst* as "the salient thing."

any agent might avow one intention that is possible but not manifest in deeds, and then dissemble. This might involve a plausible but still false description of the act content itself. At any rate, such appears to be the central claim in the *die Sache selbst* section. The Beautiful Soul could just as easily be said not to be committed to his view of action, because he does not act on it. He is self-deceived, not weak.

In discussing Diderot's Rameau's Nephew and what is the height of self and social alienation in the Phenomenology, Hegel again invokes the concept of deception. In discussing "the musician," he means to say that the nephew's claim to be identity-less, and so capable of theatrically enacting any role, that there is no difference between such theatricality and the real social functions, is not only false, and not only deceives others, but is a case of self-deceit. (5)

> The content of spirit's speech about itself and its speech concerning itself is thus the inversion of all concepts and realities. It is thus the universal deception of itself and others, and, for that very reason, the greatest truth is the shamelessness in stating this deceit. (Hegel 2013, § 521)

Finally, there is Hegel's most pointed example, that of modern moralism. This occurs when some agent, or group agent, or super-structural group agent, Geist, assumes the role of moral judge and subjects everyone to a rigorous moral accounting, one in which they are always found wanting, never truly acting dutifully but always self-interestedly. (Again to say that Geist can assume the role of moral judge is just to say that there is a means of collective self-representation that is not a mere summative result, and avows adherence to such ideals.) Such rigoristic condemnation is, Hegel thinks he can show, irrational, self-contradictory even, and Hegel suggests that no one can be presumed to have adopted such a stance *without also being aware that it is so*. It demands that individuals not be the individuals they are, that morality is asking for some conformity to strict standards that are impossible to fulfill. He suggests also that this realization will eventually win out, that there will be something equivalent to the Christian confession that "we are all sinners," and this confession will occasion some mutual forgiveness. This is a strange moment in the Phenomenology, as if he thinks that the burden of this rigoristic moralism and the self-deception it requires, is impossible to bear. Whereas many of the other transitions in the book seem to follow some intellectual or conceptual realization of a practical contradiction, this one seems more existential and dramatic. But no matter for our purposes, he was obviously wrong in any sense about this. Such self-deception can clearly be borne quite well. Indeed, self deceived moralism has reached something like epidemic proportions in the post-Hegelian world, our world, something that is not merely the "fault" of the self-deceived, but also of their audience. Gullibility is also a form of self-deceit ("hearing what one wants to hear") and is as culpable. As Bernard Williams pointed out, in such cases deceiver and deceived are actually "conspiring" with one another.

5

This leaves us with many questions. For one thing, while Hegel invokes the concept of self-deception in an ancient context, it is not an ancient notion, does not it seem to have any resonance in that literature. Hence the question: when did it first become an important analytic tool, and might this show us some characteristic of the modern condition itself?

There is also the question of its possibility, or how one might dispel the aura of complete paradox that surrounds it. I have already suggested one way in which that might go, given Hegel's unusual understanding of the inner-outer relation in action. But the larger question involves a return to our earlier reflections on the bearing of Hegel's treatment of historical *Geist*

In fact, there is, from Hegel's point of view, reason to believe that the complexity of our situation has created something quite unprecedented that only his philosophy, with its ability to explain the "positive" role of the negative, and the reality of group agency and collective subjectivity, can account for. Life in modern societies seems to have created the need for uniquely dissociated collective doxastic states, a repetition of the various characters in the drama of self-deceit narrated by the Phenomenology. This is one wherein we sincerely believe ourselves committed to fundamental principles and maxims we are actually in no real sense committed to, given what we do. (This would be the sense in which Kierkegaard thought most modern people were (that is, were not) "Christians." This is not an idle reference. How else might we explain something like some "association of wealthy robber baron Christians" (which must exist somewhere), or billionaire Communists?[2] The principles can be consciously and sincerely ac-

---

[2] For all of Kierkegaard's explicit and contemptuous anti-Hegelianism, this situation is perfectly Hegelian, given that Hegel claims that determinate negation is equally also positive. In Kierkegaard's terms, those who take themselves to be Christian are really not Christians, where this does not mean they are Muslims or Jews or atheists; they are Christian non-Christians. And conversely, there is also a principled way of not-being a Christian (realizing its enormous difficulty, perhaps its impossibility) which is the only way one can be a Christian. (This touches on a well known objection to Hegel: that he confuses contrariety with contradiction.) I use Kierkegaard as

knowledged and avowed, but, given the principles they are, cannot be integrated into a livable, coherent form of life. (The social conditions for self-deceit in this sort of context can help show that the problem is not rightly described as one where many individuals happen to fall into self-deceit. The analysis is not a moral one, not focused on individuals. It has to be understood as a matter of historical *Geist*, in the sense in which it is the point of this paper to make plausible. Or we are committed to various policies that, nevertheless, we would, again in all sincerity and by means of the various representative practices available to *Geist* at a time, disavow, even though our actions again betray us.³ In his early works, Hegel claimed that the need for modern philosophy itself arises as an attempt at a reconciliation of what modern philosophy had left in "disunity." [*Entzweiung*] (Hegel 1968, p. 9), and a striking sort of disunity is this dissociated relation to ourselves. This seems especially to be the case in the political world.

Of course, it is also the case that there is in modern politics, as perhaps there has always been, massive outright, deliberate deception and fraud. This is sometimes even praised, not just admitted as necessary. I mean Machiavelli's famous case that the needs and interests of government are sufficiently different from those of individuals as to justify, even to regard as virtuous, practices of deception (Williams 2005, p. 607). So the NSA claimed not to be doing what Snowden's documents showed they were doing, and they certainly knew that. No doubt there was some self-deceit involved in the justification, but they knew they were lying through their teeth. There are also many other examples and they are not limited to politics. Cigarette companies discounted the risks of smoking, even as they knew otherwise. One could go on almost infinitely.

But collective self-deceit of the kind explored – and I would say, for the first time explored – by Hegel is a different and arguably an even more widespread phenomenon. As Williams pointed out, the entire political world now seems inconceivable without it, with politics understood as the field on which what plays out is an externalization of a particular sort of group agent, government. Political actors are presented, and present themselves, Williams suggests, like actors in a soap opera, playing roles in which they neither cynically pretend to represent positions they know to be false (not always or mostly, anyway), nor, given the theatricality, exaggeration, "posing," and the "protest too much" rhet-

---

a dramatic example, but there any number of ordinary ones. "We all believe" that global warming is precipitating an unprecedented catastrophe. Do we?

3 In (Pippin 2008) I try to show what conception of subjective mindedness and objective, public deed we need, according to Hegel, in order to account for such states, and suggest why they should not be seen as exceptional, or isolated puzzle case. See Chapter Six of that book.

oric, do they comfortably and authentically inhabit those roles. Williams's description is memorable.

> They are called by their first names or have the same kind of jokey nicknames as soap opera characters, the same broadly sketched personalities, the same dispositions to triumph and humiliations which are schematically related to the doings of other characters. One believes in them as one believes in characters in a soap opera: one accepts the invitation to half believe them. (Williams 2005, p. 615)

He goes on to say that

> ...politicians, the media, and the audience conspire to pretend that important realities are being considered, that the actual word is being responsibly addressed. (Williams 2005, p.615)

And of course it is not being addressed. The whole strategy is an attempt to avoid doing so.

Despite everything that has been said here, I realize that it may still strain credibility, even plausibility, to say that this is all best accounted for by saying that *Geist*, in this case, the communal *Geist* of a nation, is, in its self-representations, engaging in collective self-deceit. But if it is initially plausible, it means that there is perhaps a different and better way to assess the contemporary relevance (what is in German the "*Aktualität*") of Hegel's social and political philosophy than the "remaining points of contact," institutional approach. In point of fact, this issue of contemporeneity is tightly connected with the general issue of collective self-deceit. As presented here, such a phenomenon is a means for avoiding the acknowledgment of what one nonetheless knows to be true: that there is a disconnect between consciously held principles of action, and the actual actions that result. The need for such a strategy can be understood by understanding that the basic claim of the GPR, about the practical irrationality that would result were not the institutions of Abstract Right and Morality understood as moments within an over-arching, common ethical life or *Sittlichkeit*. If it is true that without such an ethical commonality, and, crucially, its distinguishability from civil society, various collective principles would appear insufficient, irrational, subject to practical contradictions, then understandably, the temptation to collective self-deceit would be great; greater and greater even.

I would suggest that this is exactly the situation we find ourselves in, in anonymous mass societies, in which the absence of what, according to Hegel, amounts to genuine commonality, Sittlichkeit, is a felt absence, not merely an indeterminate absence. Understanding such a situation as something essential to understanding the prevalence of collective self-deceit is preferable, I suggest in conclusion, to pointing to some sort of moral decay in individuals, inauthenticity or moral cowardice, something that would itself be an instance of the self-deceit Hegel detects in the institution of morality.

Bibliography

Hegel, G.W.F. (1968): "Differenz des Fichte'schen und Schelling'schen Systems der Philosophie". In: *Gesammelte Werke.* Vol. 4. Hamburg: Meiner.

Hegel, G.W.F. (1971): "Die Wissenschaft der Logik. Erster Teil, Enzyklopadie der philosophischen Wissenschaften". In: *Werke.* Vol. 8. Frankfurt am Main: Suhrkamp.

Hegel, G.W.F. (1971): "Vorlesungen über die Philosophie der Geschichte". In: *Werke*, Vol. 12. Frankfurt am Main: Suhrkamp.

Hegel, G.W.F. (1978): *Hegel's Philosophy of Subjective Spirit.* Dordrecht/Boston: D. Reidel Publishing Company.

Hegel, G.W.F. (2013): "Phänomenologie des Geistes/Phenomenology of Spirit". http://terrypinkard.weebly.com/phenomenology-of-spirit-page.html, visited on 15 September 2016.

Pippin, Robert (2008): *Hegel's Practical Philosophy: Rational Agency as Ethical Life.* Cambridge: Cambridge University Press.

Williams, Bernard (2005): *In the Beginning Was the Deed*, Princeton: Princeton University Press.

Sebastian Rödl
The Science of Logic as the Self-Constitution of the Power of Knowledge

I wish to inquire into the idea that the concept determines itself. As Hegel intends *the Science of Logic* to be the self-determination of the concept, this is an inquiry into what the *Science of Logic* is.

The concept that determines itself can only be the pure concept. This means that the self-determining concept is the self-consciousness of thought. As Kant says, the pure concept is contained in the *I think*. Moreover, the pure concept, as it determines itself, constitutes itself as knowledge; being contained in the *I think*, it is contained in the *I know*. My presentation falls into two parts: I first develop the idea that the pure concept is knowledge, which constitutes itself in this concept. Then I consider how we might comprehend the pure concept as determining itself, thereby constituting itself as knowledge.

1

Knowledge is judgment. Thus we develop the self-constitution of knowledge in the pure concept through a reflection on judgment.

And when we reflect on the nature of judgment, we note that a judgment is conscious of itself as a judgment. When I say that a judgment is conscious of itself, I mean that a judgment and the consciousness of it are one act of the mind. It is not that I judge, this being one act, and in a separate act, a second order representation, I am conscious of judging. Judging *is* being conscious of judging. We may call this consciousness of judgment, which is internal to judgment, the self-consciousness of judgment, as it is the judgment's consciousness of itself.

A judgment, as such, applies the concept of judgment; it constitutes itself as a judgment in this application of its concept. The concept of judgment, therefore, does not comprehend a reality that exists independently of it. The concept, here, is the ground of the possibility of what is thought through it. Hence, this concept does not depend on affection; it is a spontaneous representation; it springs from the representational power itself.

I said that the concept of judgment is a spontaneous representation; it springs from the power of judgment. More precisely, the concept of judgment, which is contained in any judgment, *is* the power of judgment. This concept is not an act of the power of judgment; it is this power. (Compare Kant, who identifies the synthetic unity of apperception with the understanding.) For, any act that springs from the power of judgment as such refers itself to this power in conceiving itself as a judgment. (The power of judgment returns to itself completely in its acts, says St. Thomas Aquinas.) So being an act of the power of judgement is nothing other than being a consciousness of being an act of this power. The power, present in all of its acts, is nothing other than the consciousness of the power, present in all of its acts.

The power of judgment, then, is self-constituting: it constitutes itself as the power it is in its concept. And this defines a spontaneous representation. A spontaneous representation is not one that springs from a psychic machine that spits it out irrespective of any input from the senses. (We set aside the question of whether this is an intelligible idea.) A spontaneous representation springs from a power that constitutes itself in this very representation; a spontaneous representation is the self-constitution of that power.

As we begin to articulate the consciousness of judgment contained in judgment, we note that a judgment represents itself as true. A judgment refers itself to the truth; it does not await appraisal from the outside. A judgment and its representation as true are one act of the mind. As a judgment represents itself as true, it represents itself as non-accidentally true. If its truth were an accident that befalls it on account of circumstances in which it finds itself, then it could not itself be a consciousness of its truth. For, a consciousness of an accident is not contained in the consciousness of that of which it is an accident. A judgment, representing itself as true, represents itself as non-accidentally true; it represents itself as knowledge. The power of judgment is conscious of itself as a power of knowledge; and as its self-consciousness is its self-constitution, we can say that it constitutes itself as a power of knowledge.

As a judgment's conception of itself as knowledge is internal to it, constituting it as a judgment, the power of judgment cannot ascertain its character as a power of knowledge after the fact, by considering its performance and comparing it with the facts. It must reveal its character as knowledge from the inside, that is, by articulating the self-consciousness that constitutes it. (This is to say, we must reject the quest for a criterion of knowledge as unintelligible. Knowledge is its own criterion.)

(The power of judgment constitutes itself as a power of knowledge. Is that not too quick a way with skepticism? It is true that we may ask, how is it possible for the power of judgment to constitute itself as a power of knowledge? This is a fine question. It requires us to articulate the self-knowledge of the power of knowledge. The reflections of the second part of the essay respond to this question. However, even if we do not manage to say how it is possible – even if what we shall say in the second part proves unsound – we cannot on this basis give in to skepticism. We cannot, from our inability to comprehend how something is possible, infer that it is impossible. It is true that the *that*, which the self-consciousness of judgment gives us, is finally secured only in the *why*, which must be found in self-consciousness, as well. But the *that* is not refuted by our inability, which must be judged to be accidental, to give the *why*.)

The concept of judgment, which is the power of judgment, is nothing other than the pure concept of an object of judgment, the category. We can see this as follows. For each power of the soul, specifically for each representational power, we can frame the formal concept of its object. This concept represents the object of the power solely insofar as it is an object of this power. Evidently, the formal concept of the object of a power and the concept of that power are the same.

Now, the power of judgment is represented in each of its acts; consequently, so is the formal concept of its object. The power of judgment, being a spontaneous, self-constituting power, represents its object through the formal concept of its object, the category. And as the power of judgment is a power of knowledge, the category is knowledge. It is the first and primary act of knowledge, the act in which the power of knowledge constitutes itself.

We thus realize that the power of knowledge, constituting itself, constitutes itself as the source of the form of its object. In general, the formal concept of the object of a power and the concept of that power are the same. If the concept of the power is spontaneous, so is the formal concept of its object, the category. The category cannot conceive itself as derived from the object known through it. Hence, the power of knowledge must conceive itself as the source of the form of its object, the form thought in the category. The Copernican revolution is a recognition of the power of knowledge as spontaneous, or self-constituting.

According to Kant, the power of judgment constitutes itself as a power of knowledge through its relation to another representational power, the power of sensory representation, sensibility. The first act of knowledge is knowledge of the object's form, and this knowledge is the category; and the category constitutes itself as knowledge of the object as it applies itself to sensibility, a priori determining sensibility. In this application the category acquires a content. For example, the category of causality acquires a content in the concept of one thing acting on another according to a law. The category, considered independently of this application, has no content; its has neither sense nor meaning, Kant says. Outside its a priori application to sensibility, the category is not knowledge.

Kant thus distinguishes a metaphysical deduction of the category, which reveals it to be contained in the self-consciousness of thought, from the transcendental deduction, which reveals it to be knowledge in its a priori application to sensibility. Another way to put this, which we find in Kant, is to say that the self-consciousness of thought is not as such knowledge. It is the mere form of knowledge. It is knowledge as it a priori determines sensibility. After the transcendental deduction, the principles of the understanding articulate the content that the category acquires in this application to sensibility, that is, the pure knowledge comprehended in the category so applied.

This is the self-constitution of the category as knowledge as Kant understands it; it involves the category's being applied to, and therein limited by, sensibility. That the self-constitution is limited in this way shows itself in the transcendental dialectic. In the transcendental dialectic, we recognize that the category is not exhausted by the content it acquires in the application to sensibility, an application, however, to which the deployment of the category in knowledge is limited.

We can convey an abstract idea of the *Science of Logic* by reference to this representation of Kant's conception of knowledge and the category. The *Science of Logic* is the self-constitution of the category as knowledge. The self-constitution of the category as knowledge in the *Logic* does not involve its relation to anything other; specifically, it does not involve its application to another representational power. So in the *Science of Logic*, the metaphysical deduction of the category, its representation as contained in self-consciousness, is as such its transcendental deduction, its vindication as knowledge. Equivalently, the category does not acquire content through its application to sensibility, but through itself, through self-consciousness alone. This metaphysical derivation of the category, which as such is its vindication as knowledge, Hegel appears to think, is a dialectic. I wish to consider the thought that this dialectic bears the form of the transcendental dialectic of the Critique of Pure Reason.

2

Let us consider this form. In the Third Antinomy, Kant observes that we fall into contradiction when we take the schema of causality – the category as applied to our sensibility – to exhaust the concept of causality. "The statement, as if all causality were possible only according to laws of nature, contradicts itself it its unlimited perfect generality." ("Der Satz, als wenn alle Kausalität nur nach Naturgesetzen möglich sei, [widerspricht] sich selbst in seiner unbeschränkten Allgemeinheit.") The assertion that causality in general is mechanical causality contradicts itself. Reflection on the concept of mechanical causality reveals that it does not exhaust the concept of causality; it reveals that mechanical causality is only one species of causality, alongside another species. Here then is a manner of progressing from concept to concept that does not owe anything to the relation of the concept to something other. It involves three concepts related as species to genus: there is causality, the genus, its species mechanical causality, and an unnamed other species, which is a causality that is not mechanical and that resolves the contradiction in which mechanical causality, taken to be simply causality, is entangled.

Such triads of concepts structure the Science of Logic. The genus *cause*, or causality, or sufficient ground of existence, divides into mechanism and teleology. The genus *end*, or teleology, divides into external teleology and internal teleology, or life. The genus *life* divides into immediate life and rational life, or knowledge. Knowledge divides into finite knowledge and absolute knowledge. In each case, one species is higher than the other. The higher is higher as it resolves a contradiction afflicting the lower; and it is higher in that it gives rise to a further specification, being the genus of the next triad. It is a notorious fact that, in philosophy, we are often drawn to designate a species by the same name as the genus, qualified by "mere": an action is an event, but no mere event, or a reason is a cause, but no mere cause. This manner of speaking suggests itself here. One species of life is mere life; rational life, we want to say, is life all right, but not mere life.

In the transcendental dialectic, the concept of mechanical cause falls into contradiction as it presumes to be the concept of cause simpliciter. I want to suggest that the concept of mechanical cause thus reveals itself to be what I want to call an imperfect species of the genus cause. Let me explain this way of speaking.

Anton Ford, in a recent essay, distinguishes various ways in which a species may relate to its genus.

Among these, I wish to focus on what he calls the essential species. The essential species is the concept of a perfect exemplar of its genus. Species that are contrary to it under a given genus are defined by various imperfections, various forms of, as Aristotle says, negation and subtraction from the genus. While the essential species is in perfect agreement with its genus, its contrary, an imperfect species, disagrees with its genus and in this way with itself; it contradicts its genus and thus itself. Ford's example is the healthy horse, distinguished from all manner of species of sickly horses, and pure gold, distinguished from all manner of species of impure gold. We might add as further essential species the just law and the knowledgeable judgment.

Let us suppose, for the sake of argument, that we think, thinking purely, a concept of what is in fact an imperfect species of a given genus. In a first step, a study of this species will reveal it to be in disagreement with itself, with what it is; it will reveal it to be in disagreement with its genus.

The inquiry into the species will distinguish the species from itself, distinguish it as imperfect from its genus: the concept breaks up into species and genus; it is now the contradiction of an imperfect species and its genus. Therefore, lower species and genus in such a triad *bear the same name:* life – mere life, conscious life – mere conscious life, rational life – mere rational life. They bear the same name because the lower species and its genus first appear as one; they separate as the inquiry reveals the concept to be in contradiction with itself. To articulate the contradiction is to distinguish the lower species from its genus.

Moreover, it explains why the lower species bears the name of the genus *qualified by "mere"* ("bloß"). It may be thought that this suggests that the genus is divided into a species that is merely what is signified by the genus concept, and one that is not merely this, but in addition something else; the genus "life" would then be divided into a species of what merely lives and a species of what lives and does something in addition, namely, perceives. However, the word "mere" may be used to indicate privation in relation to the concept to which it is attached, and this is how it is used here. A (perhaps silly) illustration: A private TV-station in Germany markets certain films it shows as "Film Film". This is like "Action Film", "Cowboy Film", etc; the kind of film is said to be the film kind of film. The suggestion is that it is a real film or true film (in fact, it is one that has not been shot for TV, but for the movie screen). In contrast, other films could be designated mere films: there is enough there for it to be a film, but this is it. In this language, the genus "life" could be said to be divided into mere life and life life.

To distinguish the lower species from its genus is at the same time to show that the genus does not exhaust itself in this species, but has a species in which the contradiction is resolved, a species that agrees with the genus that was distinguished from its lower species. The genus turns out to be, in truth, its higher species. We may put this by saying that the higher species is the truth of the lower species.

The Third Antinomy exhibits this structure. We think the concept of cause, and as we first think it, this concept exhausts itself in the concept of mechanical cause. Reflection reveals that this concept is in contradiction with itself: it conceives itself as the concept of sufficient ground of existence, while, as it locates the ground in something other, it can never represent anything's existence as having a sufficient ground. This reflection breaks up the concept, divides it from itself, distinguishing the genus from its imperfect species, a species found deficient as measured by its genus. Reflection on the deficiency of the species yields a concept of what supplies the deficiency; reflection on the contradiction within the concept of mechanical cause, on the contradiction of this concept with the generic concept of cause, yields a concept of what resolves the contradiction. This is not the—unintelligible—concept of a first member of a series of mechanical causes, but rather the concept of a unity of such a series that has causality in relation to each of its members. And this is the concept of an end, which thus stands revealed as the truth of the concept of mechanical cause, as the perfection of the genus of which mechanical cause is an imperfect species.

Once we think a concept that is in fact the concept of the lower, imperfect species of a triad of our form, the exposition of the entire triad develops from reflection of this concept alone; we do not need to revert to anything not provided by that concept in order to expound the triad of which it is the lower species. In this way, the manner of determination is pure self-determination. Thus we understand how the pure concept may be self-determining if and only if we understand how an imperfect species can figure in pure thought. We began by supposing that it does. But how can imperfection enter pure thought?

An imperfect species may figure in pure thought if a pure concept can arise through a division of the form we just described. The perfect species at which we arrived, following the self-determination of its genus through the contradiction within its imperfect species, may in turn, upon reflection, reveal itself to be in contradiction with itself. It will then distinguish itself as an imperfect species from its genus, giving rise to the concept of a species that resolves the contradiction and is the truth of that genus and thereby of the latter's imperfect species. So the manner of self-determination that is dialectical is possible only as a complete sequence of determinations. The Science of Logic is this sequence.

The general character of the contradiction in a dialectic is such that its resolution invites the use of "self": teleology is self-cause, inner teleology is self-end, absolute knowledge is self-knowledge. The contradiction is resolved as the relation to something other is turned into a self-relation. Consider mechanical causality: it is causation by something other; thus there is a series of causes, which admits of no end. The solution is not, absurdly, to posit a member of the chain that nevertheless is exempt from the question after its cause. Rather, the resolution of the contradiction is the concept of their unity as itself a cause, as a cause of every member of the series and their relation. This cause is an end, its causality, teleology.

Consider external teleology, or technai: the making of a thing is subordinate to the using of it. The using of it may however be subordinate to the production of something else. (Aristotle describes a sequence of technai in the beginning of the Nicomachean Ethics.) So there is series of making and using: the using of one is the making of another, using which is again making another, and so on. Resolving this contradiction, we do not postulate, absurdly, something that is made, but not the making of anything: a first mover in this series. Rather, we frame the concept of an act that is a making because it is a using, and a using because it is a making, and where this is one, and not per accidens, but where the unity itself underlies these moments of itself; the unity itself is the end, which now is an end in itself. This is life.

The animal is the cause of its off-spring, but not as individual. Reproduction is the self-teleology of the form, the species. The causality of the general form, the concept, in the animal is mediated by the relation of individuals to individuals. The concept has reality only in this relation of individuals.

It is not real as general. At the same time, the individuals are only possible through the general, the concept. Again, the resolution of the contradiction is not to posit an animal that has no ancestor. It is to think the general, which unifies the real individuals, as itself real, real as general, and real through itself. And thinking this, we think knowledge. For recall our description: judgment is constituted through its concept. The concept now is real as the judger, the power of judgment; its reality is as general as the concept.

In knowledge, as we now think it, there is a manifold of acts of knowledge, each depending on other knowledge as their ground. The resolution of this contradiction is not to dream up an act of knowledge which is exempt from the requirement of being grounded, but to think the totality of acts of knowledge, the power of knowledge, as itself an act of knowledge, which underlies all acts of knowledge and their relation. This is the concept of the self-constituting power of knowledge, which constitutes itself as knowledge in a primary act of knowledge, which is nothing other than this power. This act is nothing other than the Science of Logic, which thus achieves self-consciousness in and through its own development.

Jens Rometsch
Why there is no "recognition-theory" in Hegel's "struggle of recognition": Towards an epistemological reading of the Lord-Servant-relationship

1 Introduction: The Lord-Servant-relationship does not aim at a "theory of recognition"

Many important trends in recent scholarship seem to agree that Hegel's concept of "recognition" (*Anerkennung*) is in fact a "master-concept", since it provides the single most important clue even to his mature social philosophy or even to understanding the overall notion of "spirit" (*Geist*).[1] In these readings, Hegel's thoughts on the subjectivity and intersubjective relations of social agents, on social and ethical life (*Sittlichkeit*) are to be reformulated as a "theory of recognition".[2] Proponents of this reading tend to admit that it requires significant interpretational conjectures. They sometimes claim a covert continuity between Hegel's early Jena writings and his later works in order to justify their assumption that a fundamental role is played by recognition in Hegel's mature philos-

---

1 I am grateful to Luca Corti and Alex Englander for their very helpful comments.
2 "My thesis is that recognition (*Anerkennung*) is not only the existential phenomenological shape (*Gestalt*) of the concept of freedom but also the general intersubjective structure and pattern of Hegel's concept of spirit. As such it provides the ontological deep structure of his philosophy of spirit, practical philosophy, and account of ethical life (*Sittlichkeit*)" (Williams 1998, p. xi). To Robert B. Brandom, two "features of his master-concept of *recognition*" supposedly already account for what Hegel calls *Geist:* "First is his view that both self-conscious individual selves and the communities they inhabit (a kind of universal characterizing them) are synthesized by reciprocal recognition among particular participants in the practices of such a recognitive community. Self-consciousness is essentially, and not just accidentally, a *social* achievement. Second, recognition is a normative attitude. To recognize someone is to take her to be the subject of *normative* statuses, that is, of commitments and entitlements, as capable of undertaking responsibilities and exercising authority. This is what it means to say that as reciprocally recognized and recognizing, the creatures in question are *geistig*, spiritual, beings, and no longer merely natural ones." (Brandom 2011, p. 35). If, according to Hegel, things were generally that simple, one might wonder why he even bothered to write the second half of the 1807-*Phenomenology* or elaborated Philosophies of *Subjective, Objective and Absolute Spirit* in the *Encyclopaedia*. Other readings are more dubious about the significance of recognition, but nonetheless situate the Lord-Servant-Relationship as a chapter of social philosophy (e.g. (Sticker 2015)).

ophy.³ Quite clearly, in the *Philosophy of Right*, Hegel's most extensive, explicit and systematic treatment of topics of social philosophy, "recognition" is not a key term; the same applies to the *Philosophy of Right's* shorter presentation in the *Encylopaedia of Philosophical Sciences*, the *Philosophy of Objective Spirit*.⁴ Moreover, it remains questionable to what extent the standard passage about "recognition", the chapter on self-consciousness with its Lord-Servant-relationship in the *Phenomenology of Spirit* of 1807 is meant to provide a discussion of issues in social philosophy. It remains even more questionable with respect to the later and shorter version of this chapter in the *Encyclopaedia of Philosophical Sciences*, upon which the following reading will focus.⁵

Readings of "recognition" as a key concept in Hegel's mature social philosophy seem to be popular for at least two reasons, in spite of the mentioned difficulties. *Firstly*, thinkers with a primary interest in questions of social philosophy find that Hegel's presumptive "theory of recognition" proposes an interesting systematic stance. Quite independently of whether it proves to be an accurate reading of Hegel's early or mature works, a "theory of recognition" might still prove to be an important systematic tool for understanding the normative dimensions of contemporary social and political life. And in addition to his early Jena writings and his *Philosophy of Right*, Hegel's account of the

---

3 Cf. Robert B. Pippin's suggestion to treat Hegel's "mature theory of ethical life or the ethical community (*Sittlichkeit*) ... as an extension of the original, or Jena-period theory of recognition, not its abandonment" (Pippin 2014, p. 155). Cf. also Ludwig Siep, who claims relevant continuities with respect to Hegel's concept of recognition from Hegel's early Frankfurt years to his latest works (Siep 2014, p. 13).
4 Paradoxically, to J. Lawrenz, this fact seems even to *support* his reading according to which "recognition" provides the unmentioned but decisive clue behind Hegel's *Philosophy of Right*: "Although the *locus classicus* of the concept of recognition is the master/slave episode of the *Phenomenology*, it is readily portable into the *Philosophy of Right*. However, the fact that the term occurs only six times in the 400 pages of the *Philosophy of Right* has obscured its structural role, and accordingly scholarly effort is scant on the concept as it might pertain to this work. It is the argument of this paper that despite its 'invisibility' it governs foreground proceedings as if from behind a curtain, for it cannot be gainsaid that the conceptual foundation of the Rights *presupposes* the principle of recognition. The suspicion has been voiced that Hegel deliberately suppressed reminders of the presence of *Anerkennung* in his philosophy of rights in order to distance himself from the perceived limitations of the Fichtean exposition of the concept." (Lawrenz 2007, p. 153).
5 On the aforementioned and other difficulties pertaining to such an emphasis on "recognition", cf. (Krijnen 2013). Some recent readings strongly maintain that the respective paragraphs in the Encyclopaedia's Phenomenology are basically about intersubjectivity (interpersonal relations) and social philosophy (cf. e.g. (Bykova 2013) and (Ikäheimo 2011)).

Lord-Servant-relationship might still give some valuable insights into aspects that a "theory of recognition" would have to take into account.

Secondly, at a first and even at a second or third glance, it might seem hard to see how the Lord-Servant-relationship is not supposed to describe a fundamental dynamic structure of social life, a structural conflict between social agents. One might be inclined to think that the terminology of "Lord", "Servant" and of the "struggle" between them in a "process of recognition" makes for a sufficiently obvious case. And Hegel explicitly mentions issues of social and political philosophy in the relevant paragraphs (Cf. § 433). Both reasons draw on observations that seem to be confirmed by long and dominant traditions of Hegel interpretation.[6]

There is nothing wrong with the first reason for such a reading – on the contrary, it is legitimate to draw inspiration from classical authors for one's own systematic purposes without any concern for their original intentions. Hegel himself

---

6 The general tendency to read "recognition" in Hegel's treatment of the Lordship-Servitude-relationship as a key term for *social* philosophy has its decisive historical precedent in the long tradition of Marxist readings of Hegel (even though not all recognition-theorists are Marxists). Marx himself inaugurated this tradition; it was then further elaborated in the 20th century by authors such as Lukacs and Bloch; through Kojève's famous lectures, this tradition was the decisive spark for most readings of Hegel in French philosophy. There are close systematic ties between Marxism and Axel Honneth's famous theory of recognition, which operates in the tradition of Critical Theory and thus of a specific brand of Marxism; according to Honneth, the "bourgeois-capitalist form of society is to be interpreted as an institutionalised order of recognition" ("… der Versuch.. die bürgerlich-kapitalistische Gesellschaftsform als eine institutionalisierte Anerkennungsordnung zu interpretieren" Cf. (Honneth 2003, p. 162). Similarly, in a tone that reminds us of Hegel's ideas about a struggle for life and death in the process of recognition, Marx himself stresses that the mutual relationship between social agents acting as producers and consumers of objects is one of mutual *recognition:* "The measure for the power that I concede to my object over your object needs your *recognition* in order to become a real power. Our mutual recognition of the mutual power of our objects is a struggle won by those with more energy, force, insight or skill" ("Das Maß der Macht, welche ich meinem Gegenstand über deinen einräume, bedarf allerdings, um zu einer wirklichen Macht zu werden, deiner *Anerkennung*. Unsere wechselseitige Anerkennung über die wechselseitige Macht unserer Gegenstände ist aber ein Kampf, und im Kampf siegt, wer mehr Energie, Kraft, Einsicht oder Gewandtheit besitzt"; MEW Vol. 40, p. 460). Contrary to what Hans-Christoph Schmidt am Busch proposes (Schmidt am Busch 2011, p. 9), this passage does not seem primarily concerned with the (ethically important) mutual recognition between actual members of capitalist societies, but only with the mutual recognition of their product's desirability: Recognition only extends to our fellow citizens inasmuch as they count as owners (of property that others recognize as attractive). It might be worth mentioning that not only authors with Marxist inclinations succumb to the idea of reading the chapter as dealing with issues of social philosophy (cf. e.g. H.-G. Gadamer's reading in (Gadamer 1973)).

has frequently been found guilty of such insouciant and innovative borrowings in his numerous references to classical authors. The second reason, however, despite its apparent obviousness, usually fails to make fully plausible why Hegel should be dealing with topics of ethics and social philosophy in precisely those chapters of the *Phenomenology of Spirit* (1807) or in the middle section of his encyclopaedic *Philosophy of Subjective Spirit* (§§ 387–482) which also bears the title of *Phenomenology of Spirit* (§§ 413–439).[7] As aforementioned, I only aim to demonstrate this point with exclusive regard to the later work (however, the problems in the early *Phenomenology* are sufficiently similar). In the *Encyclopaedia's Phenomenology*, the paragraphs on self-consciousness, in which "recognition" is introduced as a key term (§§ 424–439) are immediately preceded by sections on perception (*Wahrnehmung*) and understanding (*Verstand*); their result is a concept of universal self-consciousness (*allgemeines Selbstbewußtseyn*, cf. §§ 436–437), which prepares the way for reason (*Vernunft*, cf. §§ 438–439), the last conceptual item in the *Encyclopaedia's Phenomenology*. The *Philosophy of Subjective Spirit* is to deal with "Spirit inasmuch as it is *cognising*" (§ 387)[8], whereas the *Philosophy of Objective Spirit* (or *Philosophy of Right*) is to deal with objectivations of the Spirit – namely with agents in the general context of legal institutions and their significance for shaping world history (§§ 483–552).

Hence, one would naturally expect to find topics of ethics and social philosophy in the paragraphs on *Objective Spirit*, not in those on *Subjective Spirit*, which deal with "Spirit inasmuch as it is *cognising*" (cf. above), and thus with cognition. Hegel, especially in his later years, was particularly concerned with questions of philosophical methodology and systematicity. As the full title of the book indicates, the *Encyclopaedia's* aim is to provide a foundational sketch (*Grundriß*) of all philosophical sciences (*philosophische Wissenschaften*). Given this general aim of Hegel's project and his methodological concerns, we would have to make sense of a blatant thematic misplacement if the relevant paragraphs on the Lord-Servant-relationship were meant to deal exclusively with a topic that one would otherwise expect to find in the *Philosophy of Objective Spirit*. It would be just as remarkable as if, analogously, the paragraphs on matter

---

[7] I will not conceal that my earlier reading of the Lord-Servant-relationship as an abstract interpersonal relation is guilty of this omission, even though it points out that the paragraphs are essentially about self-knowledge and does not partake of any enthusiasm for interpreting "recognition" as a "master-concept", cf. (Rometsch 2007, pp. 130–137). The reading I propose in the present text is, so I hope, a substantial revision of my first reading.

[8] "...der Geist als e r k e n n e n d." All translations are mine, all texts by Hegel are quoted in the original German in order to warrant full transparency of my translations.

and movement (§§ 262–268) in the *Philosophy of Nature* (§§ 245–376) were actually meant to secretly deal with the elements (§§ 281–285), cohesion, sound and warmth (§§ 295–307) or the particularisation of individual bodies (§ 316–325). Any reading which tries to explain the Lord-Servant-relationship and the explicit mention of the term "recognition" in the self-consciousness paragraphs of the *Encyclopaedia* as intended to introduce and establish perhaps the most central concept of Hegel's mature social philosophy, would have to find good reasons for thereby insinuating such an obvious misplacement of topics.[9]

However, such a misplacement might still seem plausible given Hegel's contention that fully fledged self-conscious individuals exist only in the social sphere.[10] Any structural analysis of self-consciousness might therefore find a valuable task in considering how self-consciousness owes elements of its constitution to its own involvement with a social sphere. But such a reading would still fall prey to a confusion of central aspects. If the *Philosophy of Subjective Spirit* is about the *cognising* subject, the social affiliation of self-consciousness would have to be one of its topics *only inasmuch as it accounts for certain forms of cognition*; but not necessarily inasmuch as it accounts for providing actual structural patterns for the social agency attributed to individuals. Given Hegel's division of labour in the *Philosophy of Spirit*, it is hard to see why Hegel should be concerned with patterns of social agency while explaining elements and aspects of cognition.

There are other contemporary readings that shed doubt on the recognition-theoretical mainstream. Adriaan Peperzak has already pointed out that the whole "struggle of recognition" is about a process of self-identification, not

---

9 This obvious misplacement is hardly ever a topic for authors who prefer to read the Lord-Servant-Relationship as a "recognition theory". H. Ikäheimo asks himself why the *Encyclopaedia's Phenomenology* only discusses horizontal recognition between individuals and leaves out vertical recognition (between institutions and individuals) (Ikäheimo 2014, p. 78–83). Under the premises of a recognition-theoretical reading, this would have to be an important question. However, for Ikäheimo, these apparent deficiencies of Hegel's "recognition theory" don't raise the follow-up question of why the text should or should not be read as a recognition theory at all. Ikäheimo seems content with the answer that the terminology of "Lord" and "Servant" provide a "welcome concretisation" in an otherwise "very abstract read" (Ikäheimo 2014, p. 70).
10 This follows plainly from what Hegel considers to be generally characteristic of *Geist:* "The determinations and levels of the spirit essentially are only as moments, states, determinations of higher levels of development" ("Die Bestimmungen und Stufen des Geistes dagegen sind wesentlich nur als Momente, Zustände, Bestimmungen an den höhern Entwicklungsstufen."; GW 20 § 380). Hence, the determinations of cognition, as spelled out in the *Philosophy of Subjective Spirit*, are being realised and brought to existence by social agents (the features of which the *Philosophy of Objective Spirit* spells out).

about intersubjectivity (i.e. interpersonal relations).[11] Pirmin Stekeler-Weithofer claims that the "struggle of recognition" in Hegel's *Encyclopaedia Phenomenology* stands for a conflict between two aspects of self-consciousness, namely an immediate self-certitude and its reflected control. There is substantial common ground between Stekeler-Weithofer's meticulous analysis and my reading, even though I do not see how and why the whole arsenal of explicit scepticism and critical self-reflexion ought to be motivated at this point of the *Phenomenology*.[12] In this volume, Markus Gabriel reads the respective chapter in the 1807-*Phenomenology* as an elaborate theory of intentionality that explores "how we can have a unified account of self-consciousness that explains how we can be both self-conscious of being conscious of any other object and self-conscious of being self-conscious." Again, there is substantial common ground between this reading and mine, even though I don't see why the synchronisation of several contents of awareness ("other objects", "being conscious of other objects", "being self-conscious") should be a central concern for Hegel.

In what follows, I would like to examine Hegel's concept of "recognition" in the *Philosophy of Subjective Spirit* as a primarily *epistemological concept*. For Hegel, "Spirit inasmuch as it is *cognising*" (cf. above) is meant to describe a sub-

---

[11] "The whole idea of the 'struggle for recognition' as contained in the *Encyclopaedia's Phenomenology* (§§ 424–37) is *in no way* about *intersubjectivity* (Discourse, Thought, Volition, Action, Right and Exchange are not yet topics), but only about the process through which the immediate or abstract Self-Consciousness has to become another (Self-)consciousness for itself, in order to self-identify." ("Der ganze Sinn des ‚Kampfes um Anerkennung' wie er in der *Phänomenologie der Enzyklopädie* (§§ 424–437) enthalten ist, liegt ganz und gar *nicht* in einer Thematisierung der *Intersubjektivität* (von Sprechen, Denken, Wollen, Handeln, Recht und Tausch ist noch keineswegs die Rede), sondern nur im Prozeß, durch den das unmittelbare oder abstrakte Selbstbewußtsein für sich selbst ein anderes (Selbst-)bewußtsein werden muß, um sich mit sich identifizieren zu können." Peperzak 1987, p. 40).

[12] "The struggle of recognition asks whether an initial certitude or sceptical doubt ends up victorious in cases where, out of self-control, an initially immediate certitude is questioned about the validity conditions of its content and about whether self-certitude isn't merely expressed as an uncontrolled feeling of satisfaction. Each aspect of a critical self-reflection puts, metaphorically speaking, ›the life‹ or the validity claims of the other side ›in danger‹: Critical self-knowledge can prove self-certitude wrong " ("Im Kampf des Anerkennens geht es nun um die Frage, ob in der Selbstkontrolle einer zunächst unmittelbaren Gewissheit, die daraufhin befragt wird, ob denn die Bedingungen der Geltung des Inhalts wirklich erfüllt sind und sich die Selbstgewissheit nicht bloß in einem unkontrollierten Befriedigungsgefühl äußert, die ursprüngliche Gewissheit oder der skeptische Zweifel den Sieg davonträgt. Jedes der Momente einer kritischen Selbstreflexion bringt, metaphorisch gesagt ›das Leben‹ bzw. die Geltungsansprüche der anderen Seite ›in Gefahr‹: Ein kritisches Selbstwissen kann die Selbstgewissheit als falsch ausweisen." Stekeler-Weithofer 2014, Vol. 2, p. 92).

ject as if the scope and range of its activities were limited to those that directly lead to cognition – i.e. those activities that some might choose to call "mental" activities (even though that label raises notoriously difficult questions of dualism that Hegel himself refutes as mistaken in § 389 of the *Philosophy of Subjective Spirit*). For Hegel, these activities – e.g. sensing and feeling in the *Anthropology* (§§ 388–412); perception, understanding and recognition in the *Phenomenology* (§§ 413–439), intuition, representation, thought and will in the *Psychology* (§§ 440–482) – allow us to become aware of things; and these activities shape the character of our respective forms of awareness. These specific forms of awareness allow for specific forms of cognition that in their turn may account for different types of knowledge claims. These activities constitute what Descartes (with a different classification) labels as *cogitatio*.[13] And they are in the focus of Kant's three *Critiques*, in which Kant examines how it is possible that we execute them in a way that enables us to claim knowledge about theoretical and practical (moral) matters. Their undeniable common factor is their indispensible contribution to the formation of knowledge by shaping forms of awareness (which is why I prefer to label them as *epistemic* activities instead of "mental" activities). We can only ever know about something by becoming aware of it through one of these activities – e.g. by sensing, perceiving it, or by thinking about it. The *Philosophy of Subjective Spirit* offers a systematisation of epistemic activities – it is in this context that "recognition" is introduced and should be examined. I will start by examining Hegel's line of thought in the *Anthropology* and the paragraphs leading immediately to the chapter on self-consciousness (2.). That will allow me to sketch Hegel's concept of self-consciousness and why the antagonism of a "struggle of recognition" (*Kampf des Anerkennens* § 432) does not involve any interpersonal or social realm, but is in fact about overcoming the inadequate attempt to acquire self-knowledge by means of self-representation (3). I will then sketch how "universal self-consciousness" provides the presupposition for self-knowledge that the "struggle" lacks (4.). Finally, I want to explore why Hegel might have chosen the vocabulary of "Lord" and "Servant", thereby seemingly hinting at a topic belonging to political or social philosophy, even though he was discussing the epistemological problem of self-knowledge (5.).

---

13 Cf. René Descartes, *Œuvres*, AT II 36; AT VII 34; AT VII 160; AT VIII 7; AT VIII 17.

2 From Self-Feeling to Self-Consciousness

The paragraphs about self-consciousness are situated at the end of the *Encyclopaedia's Phenomenology of Spirit*, which is the second section in the *Philosophy of Subjective Spirit*. The first section is labelled "Anthropology" – a short glance at some of the most important motives of this first section will help us to understand relevant features of self-consciousness and recognition.

Hegel's *Anthropology* discusses epistemic activities such as *sensing* (*Empfinden*) and feeling (*Fühlen*); it ends with reflections on self-feeling (*Selbstgefühl*) and habit (*Gewohnheit*). All of these activities are meant to be constitutive for consciousness. It is not the fact that we are conscious that is to account for the fact that we are sensing and feeling, but inversely: Through processes of habituation (§§ 409–411) the fact that we are sensing and feeling allows us to develop and discover forms of consciousness. Consequently, not every form of awareness is necessarily to count as a form of consciousness: On Hegel's account, consciousness is *a specific and advanced form of awareness*. Consciousness is fundamentally characterised by its capacity to notice that it doesn't merge with whatever it is conscious of. It is a self-distinguishing form of awareness. Other forms of awareness take place without being self-distinguishing. In the first moment of sensing a sudden and fierce pain, the sensation, the state of affairs the sensation hints at, and I myself as a subject of this specific sensation tend to indistinguishably conglomerate into one nasty experience. However, in an event of *conscious* awareness, I myself, the way I am aware of something and the objects and states of affairs I am aware of can be experienced as neatly separated. Therefore, being conscious of something (no matter what) requires some implicit but self-distinguishing awareness of the fact that one might just as well be conscious of something else. This kind of awareness is the backdrop of our being conscious of this or that. Whatever we are conscious of might be replaced by something else, and we would still be conscious. Other, more basic forms of awareness (e.g. sensing and feeling as discussed in the *Anthropology*) don't require such a backdrop awareness of the replaceability of whatever it is that we are aware of. Hence, consciousness constitutes a specific form of awareness, characterised by its self-distinguishing relative independence from whatever it is that it might be concretely aware of.

In the *Anthropology*, Hegel seems to argue that a specific and structured form of awareness such as consciousness can't just fall out of nowhere. Instead, it requires certain *natural* conditions. One of these basic conditions is our immersion in natural processes. Living means to live with..., to psychophysically resorb environmental processes. Hegel holds that there are "natural qualities" of how we live in and with nature. This "co-living" or "living with..." (*Mitleben* cf. § 392–

395) is but one very basic example of our manifold substantial and natural immersions with contents of sentience and emotion. To have an experience of sentience and emotion doesn't *require* one to consciously distinguish oneself from the experienced content (although we might be conscious of that distinction while we are sensing and feeling). Familiar experiences of feeling exhilarated, ecstatic, aghast, panicked, etc., might count as evidence for Hegel's account of a natural substratum of indistinguishable forms of awareness for our conscious relations to the world: In these experiences, our absorption in the experienced content happens to be so intense that we fail to establish a reliable contemplative or observational distance to whatever it is that we are confronted with. In these and other sentient and emotional states, our awareness doesn't necessarily distinguish between ourselves and other contents. Experiences of exhilaration, ecstasy or panic can make it hard to individuate ourselves from the overwhelming contents of these experiences. To simply sense something doesn't necessarily render us capable of sufficiently distinguishing what we are sensing. Consequently, to simply sense something doesn't necessarily render us capable of distinguishing ourselves from what we are sensing. I might sense or feel pain, unease, relief, excitement; I might feel strongly about religion or justice – the relevant psychophysical states of sentience or emotion in these examples don't require or provide a clear-cut representation or concept of what they are about. Giddy with excitement, I can forget myself and wholeheartedly indulge in my current feelings without any hidden recourse to opting out into other feelings; but I cannot forget myself and indulge in a content to which I am consciously paying attention without my undeniable awareness of the fact that I might replace it with another content. Especially clear-cut propositional contents are hard to get giddy with.

For Hegel, sentience and emotion count as forms of awareness that don't necessarily allow us to distinguish (1) ourselves (as that which is sensing or feeling), (2) what we sense or feel (the contents these states relate to) and (3) how we sense or feel about it. However, our capacities to consciously make those distinctions have a sentient and emotional basis. Hegel designates the most primary and most basic awareness of oneself (as opposed to everything that one is not) as self-feeling (*Selbstgefühl*). Self-feeling is not only about this or that specific content, but primarily about the sentient and emotional being whose emotion it is. However, Hegel thinks that we feel ourselves *only by feeling something else*, i.e. only in the course of having specific emotions about various contents: "In this way it [the subject] is *self-feeling* – but only so in (the course of) a *specific emotion*" (§ 407).[14] In simply feeling ourselves, there is not yet any conscious relation to a "self" from which we can distance ourselves while trying to consciously examine it. But in feeling this or that, we gain an accompanying *emotional* awareness of the fact that *we* are the ones who are feeling this or that.

An important factor for further developing self-feeling is habit (*Gewohnheit*). By habituating ourselves to certain emotional experiences we liberate ourselves from being absorbed or overwhelmed by them (Cf. § 410). As a consequence, habituation is essential for the structural composition of consciousness. As mentioned, in Hegel's understanding consciousness is not just content-awareness. It includes the awareness of the replaceability of any content we might be aware of: By a change of perspective or a failure to remember, etc., we might stop being conscious of *B*, but we would still be conscious of…. It is obvious why such an understanding of consciousness denies that we can be conscious of something while being fully absorbed or overwhelmed by it: A state of full absorption implies an incapacity to consider the affect-driven relation to what is absorbing us. In such a state, our awareness is restricted to what is absorbing us, without any additional awareness of this very absorption's restrictive character. Hegel's account of habituation stresses the liberating effects of acquiring and managing dull routines: They allow us to escape absorptions, especially when they take place on an as yet sub-conscious level out of which consciousness is to result. Hegel points out, that at the basic level of liberating oneself from being absorbed by one's feelings, the repetition of routine practice works in two different psychophysical directions: Our self-feeling soul develops its individuality only by a growing awareness of its own corporeal individuation; and it is in this very same process of habituation that our body gains its individual shape, by becoming the soul's most immediate and visible expression, the "sign" of the soul (Cf. § 411).

Consciousness is the structural result of processes of habituation that take place on the level of self-feeling:

> Pure abstract freedom for itself releases its determinacy, namely the natural life of the soul, as something equally free, as an *independent object*; and it is of this object as one that is *external to me*, that I know of first, thereby becoming consciousness. (§ 413).[15]

---

14 "Es ist auf diese Weise Selbstgefühl – und ist diß zugleich nur im besondern Gefühl."
15 "Die reine abstracte Freiheit für sich entläßt ihre Bestimmtheit, das Naturleben der Seele, als eben so frei als selbständiges Object, aus sich, und von diesem als ihm äußern ist es, daß Ich zunächst weiß, und ist so Bewußtseyn."

Whatever I am conscious of, the fact that it could be replaced by some other content proves that no single experienced content of my consciousness is intrinsic to it: In that sense, the object of which I am conscious of is an "independent object" and "external to me". I can only be conscious of something by implicitly presupposing it to maintain some form of existence independently of the fact that I am conscious of it. This would apply even for fictitious or hallucinated contents (even if they were hallucinated by a hardcore solipsist): Being conscious of them implies a consciousness of the fact that they could also be invented or hallucinated otherwise or by another consciousness. Their specific character doesn't restrict them to being current fabrications of my own making. In the same way that my consciousness does not depend on any particular content, no particular content I might be conscious of depends on my particular consciousness. Whereas the contents of my self-feeling are restricted to being individuated by my incorporated feeling self, the objects of my consciousness are under no such restriction. My sensations and feelings are private – having *them* (instead of other sensations and feelings) is what individuates my self-feeling. And my sensations and feelings are individuated by the fact that they are *mine*. In contrast, consciousness is a form of awareness characterised by an independence of whatever it is that we are conscious of. Conversely, whatever it is that we are conscious of retains some independence of our being conscious of it – even a solipsist could not fail to notice this.

Our feelings might be personal and thus irreplaceable; objects of consciousness are more general in the sense that they are not essentially private. This applies already to the most basic forms of consciousness discussed by Hegel, sensory certitude (*sinnliche Gewißheit*) and perception (*Wahrnehmung*). We could not develop the conscious attitude of being certain of any specific sense-induced content without the background idea of *objective* circumstances that we can be certain of – circumstances that essentially remain as they are independently of how our senses or our perception tackle them. We cannot avoid the claim that our *conscious* awareness of things and states of affairs is potentially objective. Only this unavoidable background claim allows us to discover that our conscious awareness of things and states of affairs can be threatened by perspectival restrictions – e.g. by our sensory or perceptive sampling of objective reality into segments that as such might be deceptive or even delusional. Hegel's *Encyclopaedia Phenomenology* tries to demonstrate how our consciousness proceeds at getting rid of perspectival restrictions. The forms of emotional awareness discussed in the *Anthropology* are absorbed by their content without any sufficient awareness of the distinctions between themselves (i.e. that which is aware) and their contents (i.e. that of which they are aware). As a structural result of the liberating processes of habituation, consciousness always already has an awareness of its perspectivally restricted confrontation with independent contents. Since Hegel's *Philosophy of Subjective Spirit* deals with cognition, the forms of consciousness are scrutinised under one key aspect: Namely to find out how consciousness manages to warrant a liberation from perspectival distortions of its contents.

3 The "struggle of recognition"

It is important to take this general orientation into account in order to understand Hegel's definition of *self*-consciousness:

> *Self-consciousness* is the truth of consciousness, of which it is also the reason, so much that in existence, every consciousness of another object is self-consciousness; I know of the object as of something my own (it is my representation), in it I therefore know of myself. (§ 424).[16]

Full awareness of one's own perspectival limitations requires awareness of the fact that they are *one's own* perspectival limitations: Therefore, Hegel considers self-consciousness to be the "reason" or basis (*Grund*) of consciousness. If I remained unaware of my perspectival limitations and of the replaceability of every content and object that I am consciously aware of, I couldn't juxtapose myself to these contents and objects – there simply wouldn't be any way to gain awareness of the difference between myself (or my "self") and that of which I am consciously aware. It is easy to see why self-consciousness on this account has to replace and integrate (*aufheben*) self-feeling in order to describe what a fully-fledged cognising subject would have to be. A juxtaposition of the self and the objects and contents we are aware of proves to be essential for any process of self-identification – knowing of the "object as of mine" is required for self-knowledge. An interesting aspect of this definition concerns a characterisation of the object that seems to go along with its status as an object which I know to be mine – namely its status as a *representation*. It is mainly this aspect, so I will argue, that helps to explain the general aim of Hegel's treatment of recognition in the "Lordship and Servitude"-paragraphs.

---

16 "Die Wahrheit des Bewußtseyns ist das S e l b s t b e w u ß t s e y n, und dieses der Grund von jenem, so daß in der Existenz alles Bewußtseyn eines andern Gegenstandes Selbstbewußtseyn ist; Ich weiß von dem Gegenstande als dem Meinigen (er ist meine Vorstellung), ich weiß daher darin von mir."

Hegel introduces self-consciousness as a form of awareness of oneself and other contents. On the account given in § 424, being self-consciously aware of contents is to *represent* them. And all we cognise *of ourselves* inasmuch as we are limited to self-conscious awareness, is a representation of ourselves. In an "abstract" sense, self-consciousness is

> the *impulse* directed against the object to posit what it [i.e. self-consciousness] inherently is, – that is to give content and objectivity to the abstract knowledge of itself and inversely to liberate itself from its own sensuality, to sublate the given objectivity and posit it as identical with itself; … (§ 425)[17]

Strikingly, and contrary to what the following paragraphs seem to suggest to many readers, according to this introductory characterisation, self-consciousness is not at all about (self-preservation-related) desires and life-or-death social struggles. The text points out that an "abstract" self-knowledge is to be replaced and to receive "content and objectivity"; this process is supposed to change self-consciousness, namely by liberating it from its sensuality (*Sinnlichkeit*) and by surpassing the conscious awareness of the difference between self-consciousness and that of which it is conscious (i.e. "the given objectivity", which can refer to a characteristic trait of both our conscious *self*-awareness and the relational awareness *of other things*). Quite clearly these requirements only concern the formation of conscious self-awareness. It is not clear from the text why these requirements should concern the question of how a self-conscious *agent* is to behave with regard to desirable objects and her competitive relation to other self-conscious agents in the social sphere. I take § 424 and 425 as a first obvious piece of textual evidence in favour of my reading according to which recognition-theoretical interpretations of the chapters on self-consciousness might be somewhat off-topic.

The immediately following paragraphs (§§ 426 – 429) about desire or appetite (*Begierde*) do not imply any recognition-theoretical reading either. The term "Begierde" is used by Hegel in the context of his *Philosophy of Nature* to describe the impulse that leads animals to devour things (cf. § 362). However, in the context of the *Phenomenology* the term is supposed to mean something else, in spite of the obvious analogies that seem to suggest otherwise. Hegel construes desire or appetite (both translations are possible) as a first version of the very "impulse" (*Trieb*) that § 425 introduces (cf. above) and that resurfaces throughout all of the

---

17 "… der Trieb das zu setzen, was es an sich ist, – d. i. dem abstracten Wissen von sich Inhalt und Objectivität zu geben, und umgekehrt sich von seiner Sinnlichkeit zu befreien, die gegebene Objectivität aufzuheben und mit sich identisch zu setzen; …"

stages of self-consciousness in the chapter. This impulse is directed against representations. Because self-consciousness manages only to be aware of things by means of representing them, even its own self-awareness retains the character of an "abstract knowledge of itself", self-opposing to a "given objectivity" (cf. above). As pointed out, every content that consciousness is aware of is experienced as replaceable. This general rule also applies to the conscious self-awareness that self-consciousness is to exemplify at this stage. Therefore, self-consciousness remains "abstract" in the sense of "impersonal" and "without foundation": All I know of myself inasmuch as I am reduced to being an individual self-consciousness, reduces me to a set of replaceable representations (narratives, stereotypes, clichés, etc.). All my self-images could be replaced by others. But what I *irreplaceably am to myself* (as opposed to what I only represent myself to be) remains fully embedded in the forms of sentient and emotional self-awareness that Hegel's *Anthropology* deals with (cf. above). By giving accounts and telling stories of who I am, I never quite manage to express what I am to myself, to actually show what it is like to be me. Inasmuch as my self-consciousness only manages to *represent* itself, any attempt to become aware of myself only ever throws me back to my unreflected sensuality (cf. § 425). Therefore, as § 425 points out, the impulse *to get rid of* replaceable self-representations in turn promotes a liberation from one's own sensuality.

Desire/Appetite (*Begierde*) is the first step this impulse has to take. First of all, the representational character of what we are consciously aware of is to be discovered as controllable. The *givenness* of "given objectivity" (§ 425) needs to be tackled. This happens of its own accord when self-consciousness becomes aware of the fact that it has some power to replace and control its own representations. Obviously, when everything self-consciousness can become aware of is experienced as replaceable by other representations, it is important to discover that the passage between representations is (at least to some degree) subject to control. In my reading, the paragraphs on Desire/Appetite (§§ 426–429) report *this* discovery (and not about how self-conscious agents are introduced into the social sphere by their basic material needs). Leibniz's *Monadology* contains a doctrine about how particular perceptions change through appetite without appetite being able to change "the whole of perception", i.e. the fact that there are constant passages from one perception to another.[18] In a striking anal-

---

[18] "The action of the inner principle that accounts for the change or passage from one perception to another, can be called *appetition*; it is true that appetite can't always arrive at the whole of perception towards which it is directed, but it always gets something of it and arrives at new perceptions" ("L'action du principe interne qui fait le changement ou le passage d'une perception à une autre, peut être appellé Appetition: il est vrai que l'appetit ne sçauroit toûjours par-

ogy, Hegel describes Desire/Appetite as an internal impulse to change from one representation to another one. The "given object is posited as subjective and subjectivity divests itself from its one-sidedness and becomes objective" (§ 427)[19] – in other words: Only inasmuch as our representations (i.e. the given objects) are discovered as controllable (as something that we can posit), are we able to *consciously* relate ourselves to our private forms of sentient self-awareness and to objectively consider what our feelings and emotions are about. If we remained forever stuck with any given particular representation about ourselves, our attempts to consciously represent our irreplaceable sentient self-awareness would be futile from the get-go. Thanks to the work of Desire/Appetite, the contents we are aware of have the character of a *"free* object, in which the I has knowledge of itself as an I, but an object that remains outside the I" (§ 429).[20] We know ourselves to be fundamentally unrestricted by whatever *particular* representation we might have of ourselves; to some extent, we are free to replace each particular self-representation with other representations, since each self-representation is a *"free* object" that remains "outside the I".

Just as Leibniz's *appetition* will not arrive at the whole of perception, *Begierde* won't free self-consciousness from only ever becoming aware of itself by means of representations. This is where the self-differentiation of self-consciousness sets in: The "recognising self-consciousness", its "struggle for life and death" (§ 432) and the subsequent dialectic of "Lordship and Servitude" (§ 433). The aforementioned self-representing consciousness of a *"free* object" is characterised as

> ... Self-consciousness for a self-consciousness, at first *immediately* as another one for *another one*. In this other self-consciousness, I immediately look at myself as an I, but also at an immediately present object that is absolutely independent of me inasmuch as it is an I. (§ 430)[21]

It is this constellation that finally initiates the "process of *recognition*" ("Proceß des *Anerkennens*"; ibid.) described in §§ 431–435. This process is to result in a

---

venir entiérement à toute la perception, où il tend, mais il en obtient toûjours quelque chose, et parvient à des perceptions nouvelles"; *Monadologie* § 15 ; Leibniz 2014).

[19] "Das gegebene Object wird hierin eben so subjectiv gesetzt, als die Subjektivität sich ihrer Einseitigkeit entäußert und sich objectiv wird."

[20] "eines freien Objects, in welchem Ich das Wissen seiner als Ich hat, das aber auch noch außer ihm ist."

[21] "... Selbstbewußtseyn für ein Selbstbewußtseyn, zunächst unmittelbar als ein Anderes für ein Anderes. Ich schaue in ihm als Ich unmittelbar mich selbst an, aber auch darin ein unmittelbar daseyendes, als Ich absolut gegen mich selbständiges anderes Object;"

"universal self-consciousness" (§ 436). The point of departure is a self-consciousness that can only consciously relate to itself and to other things by representing them and has an awareness of its own ability to freely replace its representations (i.e. the "free object") with other representations. If my conscious awareness of myself is reduced to representations that I have of myself and that I could replace by other representations, I am in a state where the self I am consciously aware of cannot coincide with my sentient self. My sentient forms of self-awareness cannot match my representation of myself: To myself, I am never quite the person that my arbitrarily replaceable self-descriptions represent. Even representing myself as trying to come to a representation of myself doesn't help – unavoidably, my representation of myself representing myself makes me someone else. Whatever self-conscious relation I entertain with respect to myself, I, inasmuch as I am sentiently aware of myself, remain the other one, *ein Anderer*. I cannot recognise (*anerkennen*) any self-description as a fully adequate description of what I am to myself.

The immediacy of my own sentient self-awareness defies representation. § 431 therefore introduces the idea of a "struggle" (*Kampf*) that § 432 famously defines as one of "life and death". If my immediate sentient self-awareness is only to be represented as "another one for *another one*", I cannot know of myself by means of conscious self-representation – every possible attempt at self-representation will fail with respect to the task of fully and adequately expressing what I am to myself. As a sentient self, I cannot live in a way that is ever to be captured by any single self-representation; I can only feign the hope of a full and adequate self-representation by pretending to be (quite literally) dead. Consequently, if the task of self-knowledge is to *represent* my immediate forms of sentient self-awareness, I cannot even hope to have any knowledge of myself – not my particular self-representations, but the very task of establishing valid self-knowledge by means of representation might prove a failure:

> I cannot know myself in the other one as myself, inasmuch as to me, the other one is an immediate other existence; therefore, I am directed at the sublation of this immediacy. But just as well, I cannot be recognised as an immediate existence unless I sublate the immediacy about me, thereby giving existence to my freedom. But this immediacy is also the corporeality of my self-consciousness, its sign and tool, in which it has its own *self-feeling* and its being *for others* and its relation that mediates it to others. (§ 431)[22]

---

[22] "... denn Ich kann mich im Andern nicht als mich selbst wissen, in sofern das Andere ein unmittelbares anderes Daseyn für mich ist; Ich bin daher auf die Aufhebung dieser seiner Unmittelbarkeit gerichtet. Eben so sehr kann Ich nicht als unmittelbares anerkannt werden, sondern nur in sofern ich an mir selbst die Unmittelbarkeit aufhebe und dadurch meiner Freiheit Daseyn gebe. Aber diese Unmittelbarkeit ist zugleich die Leiblichkeit des Selbstbewußtseyns,

Our self-representations and our sentient self-awareness ("self-feeling") don't match. Any attempt at representing myself will entail an implicit denial of my sentient self-awareness; but any such denial is an attempt at obliterating the very content it tries to represent. From its very beginning, the attempt to produce self-knowledge by means of self-representation proves to be absurd. The "struggle of recognition" highlights and spells out this absurdity. Self-consciousness trapped in this constellation can shift to either of two modes:

Lordship: *Self-consciousness insists on self-representation.* Since self-consciousness at this stage is bound to relate to itself by means of self-representation, this insistence will seemingly warrant full recognition or acknowledgement ("Anerkanntseyn", cf. § 433). After all, self-representations don't necessarily have to be wrong; even though they may not be suitable for adequately spelling out what sentient beings are to themselves, their descriptions might contain true propositions. We are therefore entitled to cleave to the basic justifiability of our self-representations.

Servitude: *Self-consciousness insists on its own sentient self-awareness*, even though it is as such not to be represented:

> Instead of the raw destruction of the immediate object, there is attainment, preservation and formation of it inasmuch as it serves as a medium in which the extremes of self-dependence and dependence consolidate – the form of universality in the satisfaction of needs is a *constant* measure and a precaution that considers and secures the future. (§ 434).[23]

The "immediate object" in this passage is our immediate sentient self-awareness, our "self-feeling" (§ 431) or "sensuality" (§ 425). Instead of denying this "immediate object", self-consciousness in this second mode grows an awareness of the fact that it has to take its underlying sentience into account, even though it is as such not to be represented. Whatever I represent (about myself or about other things), depends on what I am to myself, depends on how I live and prosper. Self-consciousness in the "Servitude"-mode gives in to this more basic, unreflected and corporeal other side of itself. Whereas the self-representing consciousness of the Lord insists on the acknowledgeable entitlement to its own self-represen-

---

in welcher es als in seinem Zeichen und Werkzeug, sein eignes S e l b s t g e f ü h l und sein Seyn für A n d e r e, und seine es mit ihnen vermittelnde Beziehung hat."

23 "An die Stelle der rohen Zerstörung des unmittelbaren Objects tritt die Erwerbung, Erhaltung und Formiren desselben als des Vermittelnden, worin die beiden Extreme der Selbstständigkeit und Unselbstständigkeit sich zusammenschließen; – die Form der Allgemeinheit in Befriedigung des Bedürfnisses ist ein d a u r e n d e s Mittel und eine die Zukunft berücksichtigende und sichernde Vorsorge."

tations, the consciousness of the Servant surrenders to not being restrictable to its representations of itself. The self-consciousness of the Servant "preserves itself as an individual self-consciousness, but forgoes its own recognition" (§ 433)[24] – the insistence on acknowledgeable self-representations is given up in order to maintain self-sentience. The Servant's priority shifts from an insistence on the entitlement to self-representations to the "satisfaction of needs" (cf. above, § 434). These "needs" (*Bedürfnisse*) are not the ones of Desire/Appetite (they are not about controlling our self-representations). They are the impulsive needs of the "immediate object", the needs we have in virtue of what we are to ourselves in our sentient self-awareness. Inasmuch as the Servant mode provides a "*constant* measure" (due to its catering for what we irreplaceably and unavoidably are to ourselves, namely for our "self-feeling"), it reaches a "form of universality" that our arbitrarily manageable self-representations can never have. As mentioned, our self-representations might sometimes be accurate (as the Lordship-strategy insists), but they lack all constancy and intrinsic objectivity because they fail to fully express or grasp what we are to ourselves. Their inaptitude for fully adequate self-description is highlighted by the fact that our self-representations essentially lack corrigibility: In principle, each of us is able to maintain *almost any particular self-image*, even though it may not provide a clue about our sentient self-awareness and even though our behaviour and how the whole world views us might speak against the adequacy of our self-images. There is no way to be sure when our self-representations effectively serve the aim of self-knowledge and when they serve the aim of self-denial.

To make it as clear as possible: In my reading, Lordship and Servitude are the titles of two modes that one and the same self-consciousness can assume with respect to the epistemological conflicts that arise from the task of self-representation. There is no convincing reason for reading the "relationship of *lordship* and *servitude*" (§ 433) as a schematic and ahistorical model constellation of genuinely conflicting intersubjective relationships between agents. Introducing such a constellation at this point in his *Philosophy of Subjective Spirit* would be a breach against basically all of Hegel's major insights about the irreducible historicity of social conditions, about their diverse and complex relations to law, religion and thought. And yet it is understandable (not only in the light of the aforementioned traditions) that intersubjectivity readings of the "Lord and Servant Relationship" have come to overwhelming prominence. Not only the 1807 version, but also the *Encyclopaedia's Phenomenology*, contains passages like the following:

---

[24] "... sich als ein einzelnes Selbstbewußtseyn erhält, sein Anerkanntseyn aber aufgiebt, ..."

> The struggle for recognition and the submission under a Lord is the *appearance* in which the coexistence of humans, as a beginning of *states*, has emerged. [...] It is the external or *appearing beginning* of states, not their *substantial principle*. (§ 433, annotation)[25]

This passage seems to make explicit (against my proposed reading) that Hegel is in fact talking about an intersubjective and political constellation, about a fundamental conflict between individual social agents. But the decisive hint, so I take it, is the italicised "appearance" (*Erscheinung*) and the reference to an "*appearing beginning* of states". Life-and-death-struggles between individual social agents (and their resolution by means of establishing a forceful and generally accepted political authority) are nothing but an appearance – an appearance that proponents of a political contract-theory, authors like Hobbes, Locke, Rousseau and to a certain extent Kant, might have taken as a fundamental reality, as a "*substantial principle*". But, as the cited passage unmistakably claims, no such "struggle for recognition" is in fact a "*substantial principle*". It doesn't tell us anything about what a state or, more generally, what political and public order is about. As a consequence, for Hegel, no recognition theory attempting to propose a model of mutual and peaceful recognition between individuals in order to resolve a "struggle of recognition" (understood as a state of nature between mutually hostile individuals) could be suitable for providing a relevant conceptual foundation for a social or political philosophy. The opening paragraphs of the *Encyclopaedia's Philosophy of Objective Spirit* point in a similar direction. § 483 admits "external material for the existence of free will"; part of this material is "the relationship of individual wills with individual wills, wills that are a self-consciousness of themselves and each other as different and particular" (§ 483).[26] But even though Hegel thereby concedes that latently antagonistic relationships between individuals exist, he doesn't consider them as essential for the formation of objective spirit:

> Freedom, shaped as the reality of a world, acquires the *form of necessity*. The substantial context of this freedom is the system of the determinations of freedom. Its appearing con-

---

[25] "Der Kampf des Anerkennens und die Unterwerfung unter einen Herrn ist die Erscheinung, in welcher das Zusammenleben der Menschen als ein Beginnen der Staaten hervorgegangen ist. [...] Es ist der äußerliche oder erscheinende Anfang der Staaten, nicht ihr substantielles Princip."
[26] "das äußerliche Material für das Daseyn des Willens"; "das Verhältniß von einzelnen zu einzelnen Willen, welche ein Selbstbewußtseyn ihrer als verschiedener und partikulärer sind;"

text in the form of *power*, is the *state of being recognised*, i.e. freedom's validity for consciousness. (§ 484)[27]

Again, recognition is part of the appearance; it exists, but it doesn't account for the "substantial context" of the socio-historic sphere (that Hegel takes to be a realisation of freedom). This matches precisely with Hegel's comment about how the "struggle for recognition" only concerns appearances (cf. above).[28]

Self-consciousness in the mode of servitude is about serving the needs of one's own sentient self-awareness, about the "attainment, preservation and formation" (§ 434, cf. above) of those very needs. Sentient self-awareness is a prerequisite to self-representation. By serving it and by giving up self-representation, self-consciousness loses its Desire/Appetite (its internal impulse to change from one representation to another one):

> This one, the servant, works off his particular self-will, sublates the inner immediacy of Desire/Appetite and, by means of this externalisation and the fear of the lord, makes for the beginning of wisdom, – the transition to *universal self-consciousness*. (§ 435)[29]

It is precisely by keeping in mind our sentient self-awareness that we are able to understand that our self-conscious impulse to represent ourselves does not do us justice as individuals. The desire or appetite (*Begierde*) to do so is replaced and integrated (*aufgehoben*) when self-consciousness shifts from the two conflicting

---

[27] "Die Freiheit, zur Wirklichkeit einer Welt gestaltet, erhält die Form von Nothwendigkeit, deren substantieller Zusammenhang das System der Freiheits-Bestimmungen, und der erscheinende Zusammenhang als die Macht, das Anerkanntseyn, d. i. ihr Gelten im Bewußtseyn ist."

[28] S. Buck-Morss book *Hegel, Haiti and Universal History* explores the possibility that Hegel's 1807-treatment of the Lord-Servant-relationship might have been a direct philosophical comment of historical events in Saint-Domingue between 1791 and 1805, when a successful slave revolt lead to the legal abolition of slavery and finally to the independence of the former slave colony under the name of Haiti. As inspiring and insightful as Buck-Morss' observations are, they fail to address the unavoidable exegetic questions raised at the beginning of the article (Why would Hegel introduce a section on the abolition of slavery in a chapter on the constitution of self-consciousness? Why should *this* chapter follow Hegel's reflection on "force and the understanding"? Why would the slavery concept lead into observations on stoicism, scepticism and the unhappy consciousness?).

[29] "Dieser, der Knecht, aber arbeitet sich im Dienste des Herrn seinen Einzel- und Eigenwillen ab, hebt die innere Unmittelbarkeit der Begierde auf, und macht in dieser Entäußerung und der Furcht des Herrn den Anfang der Weisheit, – den Uebergang zum allgemeinen Selbstbewußtseyn."

modes of Lordship and Servitude into what Hegel calls universal self-consciousness.

4 Universal Self-Consciousness

As it turns out, both modes of self-consciousness – Lordship and Servitude – are in a sense independent and dependent (§ 434, cf. above). To actually insist on the entitlement to one's own self-representations requires a complementary mode of insisting on the irreplaceability of one's own sentient self-awareness, and vice versa. The replacement and integration of Desire/Appetite into a *universal self-consciousness* brings about the sought-after reconciliation of these two conflicting modes of self-consciousness: With universal self-consciousness, self-representation turns into an "affirmative knowledge of oneself in another self" (cf. § 436). This knowledge allows *"absolute independence"* (*absolute Selbstständigkeit*) to self-consciousness in both the (former Lordship-mode of a) representing self and the (former Servitude-mode of a) represented self. My impulse to find an image or representation of myself that portrays the dynamic particularities of my sentient self disappears. Correspondingly, the constancy of my sentience, discovered only by my catering to it in the servant's mode, becomes the universal feature of both modes. As a universal self-consciousness, I can know of myself without my sentient self-awareness resisting representation. The resistance ceases inasmuch as the complementary urge to represent the particularities of my sentient self disappear. With my self-consciousness in the self-sentient servitude mode focussing on my immediate needs, I lose the Desire/Appetite of my self-representing lordship's mode to come to adequate representations of my particular self. The attaining, preserving and forming activities of self-sentient awareness account for a "form of universality" (cf. § 434). That is why servitude liberates self-consciousness from the task of grasping itself through particular representations. In universal self-consciousness, I can manage to reconcile the two formerly struggling modes of myself:

I (former Lord) know that not even the correct self-representations to which I am entitled can fully represent what I am to myself or what it is like to be me.

I (former Servant) cater for my sentient self-awareness to the sole end of maintaining the aforementioned knowledge that I (former Lord) can have:

> *Universal self-consciousness* is the affirmative knowledge of oneself in the other self, each of which, as a free singularity, has *absolute independence*, but, due to the negation of its immediacy or Desire/Appetite, does not differ from the other, being universal and objective and having a real universality qua mutuality, inasmuch as it knows itself to be recognised

in the other and inasmuch as it knows this by recognising the other and knowing it to be free. (§ 436)[30]

Self-consciousness so defined is universal in the sense that it knows of itself neither by self-sentience nor by any particular self-representation, but merely *by being known by itself* in a certain way that Hegel labels as recognition (*Anerkennen*). The desire or appetite to represent ourselves is modified to a universal form of self-recognition by which we no longer treat ourselves as an "immediate object" (§ 434), i.e. as a sentient self-awareness anticipating and resisting its self-representation. Generally, by giving up on the "immediacy or Desire/Appetite", i.e. on the attempt to directly represent ourselves, we are aware of the fact that our self-representations cannot fully and adequately match up to what we are to ourselves. This awareness grows out of the fact that we (in the Servant mode) cater for the needs of our self-sentience. But it is also the case that this universal self-recognition is absolutely independent: As a case of knowledge, it remains true and valid independently of how we gain it. The mutuality of our two modes of self-consciousness (Lord and Servant) only describes the genesis of a universal case of knowledge from our individual self-consciousness. But this case of knowledge might also be claimed without reference to its genesis: I only ever know of myself not by representing my particular self-sentience (which, as such, defies representation), but as someone *defined* by being known about by myself. This principle is implied by a structural presupposition of self-knowledge – namely the presupposition that the knowing subject and the content of its knowledge are to be one and the same. The subject of affirmative self-knowledge (my knowing about myself) and the content of this knowledge (i.e. my being known by myself) can obviously be considered the same only if this particular case of a knowledge-relation is of "real universality qua mutuality" – that is, if the attempt to represent one's individual self succumbs to self-consciousness' original impulse (cf. above, cf. § 425) *to get rid of* replaceable self-representations.

Affirmative self-*knowledge* cannot restrict itself to particular representations of our individual self-feeling's particularities. Since, by definition (cf. § 424), self-consciousness can only acquire knowledge by representation, its original im-

---

[30] "Das allgemeine Selbstbewußtseyn ist das affirmative Wissen seiner selbst im andern Selbst, deren jedes als freie Einzelnheit absolute Selbstständigkeit hat, aber, vermöge der Negation seiner Unmittelbarkeit oder Begierde, sich nicht vom andern unterscheidet, allgemeines und objectiv ist und die reele Allgemeinheit als Gegenseitigkeit so hat, als es im freien Andern sich anerkannt weiß und diß weiß in sofern es das andere anerkennt und es frei weiß."

pulse to get rid of self-representations proves to be originally self-destructive. Instead of just another form of self-representing consciousness, universal self-consciousness turns out to be "this universal reverberation of self-consciousness, the concept that in its objectivity knows itself to be (a form of) subjectivity identical with itself and therefore universal" (§ 436, Annotation).[31] The term "concept" (*Begriff*) indicates what the following paragraphs confirm – namely that this self-consciousness turns out to be a form of reason (*Vernunft*, cf. § 438). Universal self-consciousness qua reason is a case of "affirmative knowledge" and as such to be equally and unequivocally shared by each individual self-consciousness capable of grasping it: Inasmuch as your particular self-consciousness shifts into the mode of universal self-consciousness, it is aware of nothing that my or anybody else's self-consciousness in that same mode would not be aware of. This shift can only work if we gain an awareness of the fact that we are not just made up of individual stories of how we have been feeling and trying to image ourselves. What is required is an awareness of the fact that we are defined in a universal way by the fact that we can know of ourselves as subjects that are exclusively definable by the fact that they know of themselves as being known by themselves.

This universal self-consciousness implies a new knowledge of the mutuality or interdependence of the modes we differentiate within ourselves when trying to represent ourselves: The difference between the representing self (Lord) and the represented self (Servant) turns out to be without content, a "wholly undetermined disparity, or, more exactly, a difference that isn't a difference" (§ 437).[32] Hegel calls this knowledge "recognition". Recognition allows us to experience ourselves as instantiating reason. Inasmuch as we consider ourselves to be reasonable, we care neither for the particularities of our individual modes of self-consciousness nor about our personal individuality in contrast to other individuals.

5 Is this reading allegorical?

Even though we can discard the idea that Hegel's explicit mention of historical phenomena such as the "the coexistence of humans, as a beginning of *states*" (cf. above) justifies a recognition-theoretical reading, some doubts concerning

---

[31] "Diß allgemeine Wiederscheinen des Selbstbewußtseyns, der Begriff, der sich in seiner Objectivität als mit sich identische Subjectivität und darum allgemein weiß..."
[32] "...die ganz unbestimmte Verschiedenheit, oder vielmehr ein Unterschied der keiner ist. "

the proposed reading might remain. Why would Hegel employ this remarkable vocabulary of "Lord" and "Servant" and their "struggle for life and death" if he did not intend to stage some kind of natural or in other ways foundational social conflict to be resolved by "recognition"? This is a serious concern, but I believe it can be allayed. Robert Pippin resists the "allegorical or figurative interpretations in both Brandom's and McDowell's accounts" of the self-consciousness chapter in the *Phenomenology* of 1807.[33] But this critique and the general concern it stands for are not to be directed against every interpretation that doesn't take the "struggle of life and death" and the talk of "Lord" and "Servant" to aim at a recognition-theory in the contemporary sense. Otherwise, recognition-theoretical readings might face the same reproach. In my reading, "Lord" and "Servant" are not literally to be understood as social agents acting out some proto-feudal hierarchical order. By contrast, self-consciousness is *quite literally* to be understood as self-consciousness and the "struggle of life and death" is about the complicated discovery that one cannot make an image of oneself without noticing that being alive quite literally defies being matched by any particular representation. Every recognition-theoretical reading that takes "Lord" and "Servant" as more or less literal descriptions of specific social roles distributed among agents must explain why its reading of Hegel's notion of *self-consciousness* is not in turn allegorical or figurative: After all, my self-consciousness is not reducible to my existence as a social agent acting out a certain social role, and vice-versa.

Even though readers have always taken note of the biblical reference in § 435, there is a generally overlooked but fairly straight-forward explanation for Hegel's choice of vocabulary at hand, if we look at a theological tradition that Hegel was very familiar with.[34] In spite of its author, Martin Luther's pamphlet "On the Liberty of A Christian" helped to trigger the German Peasants' War of 1525. Drawing on St. Paul, Luther's text comments on the important question of how a good Christian is to consider herself as free. According to Luther, a Christian self-consciousness instantiates an immediate paradox:

> A Christian is a free Lord of all things and subject to nobody.
> A Christian is a subservient Servant to all things and subject to everybody.[35]

---

33 Cf. (Pippin 2011, p. 15).
34 The reference is Psalm 111, 10: "The fear of the LORD is the beginning of wisdom; a good understanding have all they that do thereafter; his praise endureth forever."
35 "Eyn Christenmensch ist eyn freyer herr ueber alle ding und niemande unterthan.
   Eyn Christenmensch ist eyn dienstpar knecht aller ding und jederman unterthan." (Luther 1961).

This Christian self-representation repeats the doctrinal role model of Jesus Christ, who, being the Lord of all things, turned himself into a servant in order to save our souls.[36] Christian Self-Consciousness is to encapsulate both the freedom of the Lord (which consists in being subject to nobody) and the voluntary Servant's renunciation of all freedom (which implies being subject to everyone) – the two sides turn out to be mutual. Even though Hegel's Lord-Servant-Relationship is not an exact repetition of the Lutheran theme, the latter might still provide a terminological model, sanctioned by a long Christian tradition of thinking about conscience and consciousness. This conjecture seems plausible in the light of the reading I propose: Self-consciousness operates under the paradoxical self-description of "Lord" and "Servant", both of which describe opposed modes of self-consciousness that turn out to be mutual.

Hegel's adoption of this vocabulary engenders an amusing twist, if we consider that it helps to reveal the initial failure of self-representation. According to Hegel, Christian Religion counts as the sole *representation* of the *Absolute Spirit* (cf. §§ 564–571). But it doesn't provide a *concept* of the *Absolute Spirit* (which is why there can be a philosophy of religion, but inversely no such thing as a "religion of philosophy"; cf. § 572). In analogy to the self-conscious attempt to acquire self-knowledge by means of representation, Religion stands for the failure of representation to grasp and manifest *Absolute Spirit* (In other words: Just as self-consciousness does not acquire self-knowledge by means of self-representation, there is no adequate description of the Absolute Spirit by means of representation, but only by means of conceptualisation). Representations to Hegel are mere "*metaphors* of thoughts and concepts."[37] This premise makes it highly appropriate to deploy the representational and figurative vocabulary of "Lord" and "Servant" and their "struggle" in order to demonstrate how and why any form of self-consciousness trying to acquire self-knowledge by representing itself is

---

36 "Adopt the mindset you see in Christ. Who, even though he was full of divine form, self-sufficient and without needing his life, work and suffering to become godly and blessed, still gave all of this away and behaved like a servant, did all kinds of things and suffered, with nothing in mind but our best, and therefore became a servant for our sake despite being free." ("Seyt also gesynnet wie yhrs seht yn Christo. Wilcher ob er wol voll gottlicher form ware und fur sich selb gnug hatte und yhm sein leben, wircken und leydenn nicht nott ware, das er da mit frum odder seligk wurd. Dennoch hatt er sich des alles geeußert und geperdet wie ein knecht allerley gethan und gelidenn, nichts angesehen, denn unßer beßtis, und also ob er wol frey ware, doch umb unßer willenn ein knecht wordenn.", Id.)

37 "In general, representations may be viewed as *metaphors* of thoughts and concepts." ("Vorstellungen überhaupt können als M e t a p h e r n der Gedanken und Begriffe angesehen werden." § 3, Annotation).

bound to fail. To borrow this vocabulary from a religious understanding of self-consciousness displays the unavoidable cunning of reason.

Bibliography

Brandom, Robert B. (2011): "The Structure of Desire and Recognition: Self-Consciousness and Self-Constitution." In: Heikki Ikäheimo/Arto Laitinen (Eds.): *Recognition and Social Ontology*. Leiden/Boston: Brill, pp. 25–51.
Buck-Morss, Susan (2009): *Hegel, Haiti and Universal History*. Pittsburgh: University of Pittsburgh Press.
Bykova, Marina F. (2013): "The 'Struggle for Recognition' and the Thematization of Intersubjectivity." In: David S. Stern (Ed.), *Essays on Hegel's Philosophy of Subjective Spirit*. New York: SUNY Press.
Descartes, René (1996): *Œuvres de Descartes*. Ed. by C. Adam and P. Tannery (= AT). 11 Vol., Paris.
Gabriel, Markus (2017): "A Very Heterodox Reading of the Lord-Servant-Allegory in Hegel's Phenomenology of Spirit." In: Markus Gabriel/Anders Moe Rasmussen: *German Idealism Today* pp. 95–119.
Gadamer, Hans-Georg (1973): "Hegels Dialektik des Selbstbewußtseins." In: *Materialien zu Hegels ›Phänomenologie des Geistes‹*. Ed. By H. F. Fulda and D. Henrich. Frankfurt/M: Suhrkamp, pp. 217–242.
Hegel, Georg Wilhelm Friedrich (1992): *Enzyklopädie der philosophischen Wissenschaften im Grundrisse*. Historisch-Kritische Edition Bd. 20 (ed. by U. Rameil, W. Bonsiepen, H. C. Lucas). Hamburg: Meiner.
Honneth, Axel (2003): "Umverteilung als Anerkennung. Eine Erwiderung auf Nancy Fraser." In: N. Fraser & A. Honneth, *Umverteilung oder Anerkennung? Eine politisch-philosophische Kontroverse*. Frankfurt/M.: Suhrkamp, pp. 129–224.
Ikäheimo, Heikki (2011): "Holism and Normative Essentialism in Hegel's Social Ontology." In: Heikki Ikäheimo/Arto Laitinen (Eds.): *Recognition and Social Ontology*. Leiden/Boston, pp. 145–209.
Ikäheimo, Heikki (2014): *Anerkennung*. Berlin/Boston: DeGruyter 2014.
Krijnen, Christian (2013): "Recognition – Future Hegelian Challenges for a Contemporary Philosophical Paradigm." In: Christian Krijnen (Ed.): *German Idealism as an Ongoing Challenge*. Leiden: Brill, pp. 99–127.
Lawrenz, Jürgen (2007): "Hegel, Recognition and Rights: ‚Anerkennung' as a gridline of the philosophy of rights." In: *Cosmos and History: The Journal of Natural and Social Philosophy* 3, pp. 153–169.
Leibniz, Gottfried Wilhelm (2014): *Monadologie und andere metaphysische Schriften*. Ed. by U. J. Schneider. Hamburg: Meiner.
Luther, Martin (1961): *Von der Freyheyt eynisz Christenmenschen*. Wittenberg 1520 [Facsimile-reproduction ed. by B. Wendt, Munich 1961].
Marx, Karl (1956 ff.): *Marx-Engels-Werke* (= MEW). Berlin: Dietz 1956 ff.
Peperzak, Adriaan (1987): *Selbsterkenntnis des Absoluten: Grundlinien der Hegelschen Philosophie des Geistes*. Stuttgart-Bad Cannstatt: frommann-holzbog.

Pippin, Robert B. (2000) : "What is the question for which Hegel's Theory of Recognition is the Answer?" In: *European Journal of Philosophy* 8. No. 2, pp. 155–172.
Pippin, Robert B. (2011): *Hegel on Self-Consciousness. Desire and Death in the Phenomenology of Spirit.* Princeton/Oxford: Princeton University Press.
Rometsch, Jens (2007): *Hegels Theorie des erkennenden Subjekts. Systematische Untersuchungen zur enzyklopädischen Philosophie des subjektiven Geistes.* Würzburg: Königshausen & Neumann.
Schmidt am Busch, Hans-Christoph (2011): *"Anerkennung" als Prinzip der Kritischen Theorie.* Berlin/Boston: DeGruyter.
Siep, Ludwig (2014): *Anerkennung als Prinzip der praktischen Philosophie. Untersuchungen zu Hegels Jenaer Philosophie des Geistes.* Hamburg: Meiner.
Stekeler-Weithofer, Pirmin (2014), *Hegels Phänomenologie des Geistes. Ein dialogischer Kommentar.* Hamburg: Meiner.
Sticker, Martin (2015): "Hegels Kritik der Anerkennungsphilosophie. Die Aufhebung verwirklichter Anerkennung in der *Phänomenologie des Geistes*" In: Hegel-Studien Bd. 49. Hamburg: Meiner, pp. 89–122.
Williams, Robert R. (1998): *Hegel's Ethics of Recognition.* Berkeley/Los Angeles: University of California Press.

III Themes from the Post-Hegelian Tradition

Catherine Malabou
"Idealism": a new name for metaphysics
Hegel and Heidegger on *a priori* synthesis

I intend to demonstrate that "idealism", in the generic expression " German Idealism ", is a new name for metaphysics. It defines the identity of metaphysics after its transformation and renewal accomplished by Kantian criticism. Hegel is the main author of this change of identity of metaphysics into Idealism, that not only consists in a switching of names, but in a radicalization of both the form and the content of the field. Such a radical mutation is rooted in Hegel's understanding of synthetic *a priori* judgments and *a priori* synthesis in general. Hegel is very clear: after Kant, metaphysics has to achieve the unification of ontology and theology. Such a unification is precisely what appears as the "ideal". In that sense, "idealism" designates the unity of general metaphysics – ontology – and the branch of special metaphysics that contains and speculatively dominates the two others – theology. The reunification of these two dimensions of metaphysics is not an artificial one that would be imposed upon it from the outside. It is a result of the immanent deduction that the *Science of Logic* constitutes. As we know, for Hegel, the "logic" is the very development of metaphysics itself.

Commenting on this philosophical turn, Heidegger affirms that Hegel's supposed accomplishment of metaphysics *as* and *in* idealism is in reality a closure: it just brings to light and radicalizes the onto-theo-logical tendency that has inhabited metaphysics since its beginning. A tendency that Kant had, for the first and unique time in this tradition, precisely started to challenge. If "idealism" only means onto-theo-logy, then its metaphysical content is congealed, and it certainly does not represent any progress toward the "*Destruktion*" of metaphysics and the breakthrough of "transcendence" initiated by Kant. It is striking to notice that Heidegger's claim also relies on an interpretation of *a priori* synthesis, but this time to prove that Kant's concept of metaphysics is not reducible to "idealism". So what exactly is at stake in the opposition between Hegel and Heidegger on their reading of *a priori* synthetic judgments?

1 Synthetic a priori judgments and the possibility of metaphysics

Hegel's and Heidegger's insistence on the metaphysical value of *a priori* synthesis is of course not surprising. In the introduction of the *Critique of Pure Reason*, Kant precisely identifies the possibility of synthetic *a priori* judgments with the possibility of metaphysics itself. He declares: "The real problem of pure reason is now contained in the question: How are synthetic judgments *a priori* possible?" (Kant 1998, p. 146) Further: "(…) Th[e] (…) question, which flows from the general problem above, would rightly be this: **How is metaphysics possible as science?**" (Kant 1998, p. 148) Nevertheless, if the ontological dimension of the *a priori* synthesis forms the core of both Hegel's and Heidegger's approaches to Kant, it constitutes also their major point of controversy.

Hegel immediately sees the metaphysical potential and meaning of *a priori* synthesis as the opening of a new alliance, as I just said, between ontology and theology. Ontology first. If metaphysics has to be regrounded as a science, it has to provide a firm basis to its own "questions", which means that it has to first critically determine what being is. The possibility of *a priori* synthesis precisely coincides with this fundamental determination. As early as in *Faith and Knowledge* (1802), Hegel presents the *a priori* synthesis as the expression of the absolute identity between thought and being. "How are synthetic judgments *a priori* possible? This problem expresses nothing but the Idea that subject and predicate of the synthetic judgment are identical *a priori:* "The subject which is the particular and in the form of being, and the predicate, which is the universal and in the form of thought, are at the same time absolutely identical." (Hegel 1977, p. 79) The elementary core of ontology is the speculative unity of two modalities of the "form", namely the form of the form, that of being (the substantial), and that of logos (the judgment). The "Idea" is constituted by the dialectical merging of the subject and the predicate in both the judgment and objective reality (*Realität*) – a merging that determines the Idea as the actuality (*Wirklichkeit*) of being itself.

Second, theology. In *Faith and Knowledge,* Hegel that *a priori* synthesis is nothing but the speculative form of God. This explains Hegel's surprising affirmation according to which *a priori* synthesis is assimilable, as we will see, to the intuitive, divine understanding.

In his lectures on the *Phenomenology of Spirit, (Hegel's Phenomenology of Spirit)* Heidegger declares: In Hegel, "we find speculative theology in an originary unity with ontology. This unity of speculative theology and ontology is the proper concept of Hegelian logic."*(Heidegger 1988, p. 3)* Of course, the divisions of the *Encyclopædia* into Logic, Nature, Spirit, and, within Spirit, those between

Objective Spirit (cosmology), Subjective Spirit (Psychology) and Absolute Spirit (Theology), respect, even if reelaborated, the traditional twofold structure of metaphysics: *metaphysica generalis* (ontology), and *metaphysica specialis* (psychology, cosmology and theology). The unity of ontology and theology does not amputate metaphysics from any of its parts, but it realizes a strong change in its conception and orientation. Hegel's ontologization of theology, and theologization of ontology, can be said to be the salient signification of the substitution of idealism for metaphysics.

Hegel's gesture is for Heidegger nothing surprising or new, as it just renders obvious the inherent structure of metaphysics as "onto-theo-logy". "Onto-theology" refers to the fact that metaphysics asks two different questions – even if indissolubly linked – at the same time: 1. A "horizontal" one: What are beings (*ta onta*) in general, as a whole, and what do they have in common? 2. A "vertical one": What is the highest being that overhangs the others, and precisely appears as their common essence? The "highest being" can of course only be God: "the highest and thus divine being". (Heidegger 1999, p. 275) In the section of *Identity and Difference* that is precisely called "The Onto-Theological Constitution of Metaphysics" (Heidegger 2002), a text which originally served as a conclusion to a seminar conducted in 1956/57, Heidegger deals more specifically with Hegel's achievement and radicalization of onto-theo-logy. Heidegger explains that Hegel's god is the overall structure of beings, and not an individual being. Therefore, "if science [i.e. ontology] must begin with God, then it is the science of God: theology" (Heidegger 2002, p. 54), Heidegger writes. Hegelian metaphysics is thus inseparable from "statements of representational thinking about God." (Heidegger 2002, p. 54)

Through his reading of Kant, and his assimilation between ontology, speculative theology and religion, Hegel brings the fundamental tendency of the whole Western metaphysical tradition to its accomplishment. If, according to Heidegger, Kantian philosophy does not escape this structure, it at least attempts at destroying it – contrarily to Hegelian philosophy – and cannot, for that very reason, be purely and simply assimilated with it.

Heidegger also interprets the metaphysical meaning of a priori synthesis as a fundamentally ontological one. In § 3 of *Kant and the Problem of Metaphysics*, he affirms: "Kant reduces the problem of the possibility of ontology to the question: 'How are *synthetic a priori judgments* possible'?" (Heidegger 1990, p. 9) Further: "In the problem of synthetic judgments *a priori* a type of synthesis is concerned which must bring something forth about the being not first derived from experience. This bringing forth of the determination of the Being of the being is a precursory act of reference to the being. This pure "reference to" (synthesis) first constitutes the direction and the horizon within which the being is first capable of being experienced in the empirical synthesis." (Heidegger 1990, p. 10) The fundamental difference with Hegel is that Heidegger, for his part, radically disentangles the *a priori* synthesis from any theological meaning, and defines it as "transcendence". Contrary to what it might induce, transcendence is not all the transcendence of god, but the very structure of finitude, which requires a pre-orientation of the human mind toward the given. Transcendence, in that sense, is a "horizon" against which the objects can "stand". (Heidegger 1990, § 25, p. 87) Such a structure Heidegger considers as Kant's fundamental redefinition of ontology – an ontology that resists onto-theo-logy, and already points toward the destruction-deconstruction of traditional metaphysics.

2 Common points

Before developing on this point, it is necessary to notice that the confrontation between Hegel and Heidegger is all the more interesting given that the two philosophers share a strong common point: they both acknowledge the ontological meaning of transcendental imagination, and assign the ontological value of *a priori* synthesis to the part played by imagination in the production of the pure synthetic binding of concept and experience. As we will see though, this common point is also the locus of the utmost division between the two philosophers. Transcendental imagination, then, appears as both a bound and a sword.

If insistence upon the role of transcendental imagination constitutes such a striking common view between Hegel and Heidegger, it is to the extent that for both of them the fundamental ontological meaning of *a priori* synthesis rests entirely upon it. The originary co-implication of subject and the predicate (Hegel), or of Being and beings (Heidegger), is made possible in and as a pure image. The production of pure images is what makes synthesis possible. It provides an anticipatory view or aspect of the co-implication. Both Hegel and Heidegger thus interpret Kant's *a priori* synthesis as a specific economy and regime of visibility. Such an economy is nothing but ontology itself.

We have to go back for a moment to the distinction between analytic and synthetic judgments in order to understand this point. As we know, in the introduction of *Critique of Pure Reason*, Kant distinguishes between analytic judgments, in which the predicate is contained in the subject, meaning that it is not necessary to leave the concept to determine it, and synthetic ones, whose predicates are not contained in their subjects or concepts, thus rendering an excursion into experience necessary. The example Kant gives of the first kind of judgment is: "If I say 'All bodies are extended', then this is an analytic judgment." (Kant 1998, p. 130, [A7/B11]) In such a judgment, the concept "body" contains the predicate "extended"; the concept "extended" is part of the definition of the concept "body", and is "analytically" comprised in it: it appears as a part of the concept that can be obtained by division (analysis) of this same concept. Likewise, for "triangle" and "has three sides", and so on.

The example of the second kind of judgment is: "'All bodies are heavy'." (Kant 1998, p. 130, [A7/B11]) Such a judgment, on the contrary, makes it necessary to get out of the concept "body" to characterize it as "heavy" as this predicate is not comprised in the concept. This time, the detour via experience is necessary. Such a synthetic judgment, though, is an *a posteriori* one.

Kant explains how we can obtain knowledge of synthetic a posteriori propositions. That leaves only the question of how knowledge of synthetic *a priori* propositions is possible. And at that point, the decisive question appears: how are synthetic *a priori* judgments possible if they do not request the detour of experience? And if we consider that all metaphysical statements are precisely made of synthetic *a priori* propositions, we understand why the very possibility of metaphysics is suspended to that of *a priori* synthesis. "But in synthetic *a priori* judgments this help [of experience], Kant declares, is entirely lacking." (Kant 1998, p. 131, [A9/B13]) Upon what, then, am I to rely, when I seek to go beyond the concept A, and to know that another concept B is connected with it? Through what is the synthesis made possible? "Take the proposition: 'Everything that happens has its cause'. In the concept of something that happens", I think, to be sure, of an existence which was preceded by a time, etc., and from that analytic judgments can be drawn. But the concept of a cause indicates something different from the concept of something that happens, and is not contained in the latter representation at all. How then do I come to say something quite different about that which happens in general and to cognize the concept of cause as belonging to it even though not contained in it? What is the *X* there on which the understanding depends when it believes itself to discover beyond the concept *A* a predicate that is foreign to it and that is yet connected with it?" (Kant 1998, p. 133, [A12/B26]) If it cannot be experience, what is it?

The answer can only be transcendental imagination. It provides us with pure determinations of time and space, that is, pure "images" given before any empirical phenomena.

Both Hegel and Heidegger immediately understand and acknowledge the ontological value of creative imagination. Transcendental imagination determines *a priori* synthesis as a structure of visibility anterior to the visible itself. The synthesis is a threefold process: it unites the concept, the predicate (the sensuous), and their in-between – the medium of their encounter by providing an outside without externality for their encounter. The pure images form a spatial and temporal scene for the synthesis that goes beyond the analytic closure of the concept without transgressing experience.

For Hegel, pure images as brought to light by Kant determine the true nature of ideas. In *Faith and Knowledge,* he declares: We must "reckon it to Kant's credit that ...he assigned the idea of authentic a priority to the form of transcendental imagination and in so doing also established a beginning of the Idea of reason within the understanding itself." (Hegel 1977, 89) Further: Imagination is a "truly speculative idea." The speculative meaning of *a priori* synthesis pertains to the fact that it expresses and actualizes the identity of the opposites, and thus appears as the absolute concept. In the *Science of Logic* – Doctrine of the Notion –, Hegel affirms: "Kant has introduced this consideration by the extremely important thought that there are synthetic *a priori* judgments. This original synthesis of apperception is one of the most profound principles for speculative development; it contains the beginning of a true apprehension of the nature of the Concept and is completely opposed to that empty identity or abstract universality which is not within itself a synthesis." (Hegel 1991, § 587)

Heidegger in his turn insists upon the in-between situation of imagination, that "forms the essential unity of pure intuition (...) and pure thought (...)". (Heidegger 1990, § 26, p. 90) Productive imagination accomplishes the synthesis of the sensuous and the conceptual, as expressed in § 23, a synthesis that is "authentic concept-formation as such". (Heidegger 1990, § 23, p. 78) Such a unity, again, is said to be "the foundation on which the intrinsic possibility of ontological knowledge, and hence of metaphysica generalis, is constructed". (Heidegger 1990, § 26, p. 90, trans. modified) Why? Because this unity – that of pure synthesis – is determined as an opening, outside any outside. The originary unity of pure intuition and pure thinking forms the primordial horizon of all possible presence. Imagination is thus, in a sense, the arche-visibility of the visible. "The imagination forms in advance, and before all experience of beings, the aspect (Anblick) of the horizon of objectivity as such." (Heidegger 1990, § 26, p. 92, trans. modified) The capacity of bringing something in the form of an image (etwas in den Blick bringen) has to do with the "inmost essence of ontological knowledge." (Heidegger 1990, § 26, p. 92)

We could, then, consider that Hegel and Heidegger share the same approach to *a priori* synthesis. This seems all the more true given that they also have another important view in common: according to both of them, Kant has, in a way, covered and occulted his own discovery in repressing the role of transcendental imagination at the same time as he brings it to light.

Hegel notices that the types of judgments that Kant characterizes as synthetic are in reality analytic: "[A *priori* synthesis] is the genuine expression of the identity of identity and difference. Nevertheless, the examples that Kant takes remain inadequate to this dialectical identity: "All bodies are," or worse, mathematical examples like "7+5 equal twelve". Kant substitutes addition for the authentic synthesis, and formal juxtaposition for the essential connexion (*Verbindung*)." (Hegel 1991, § 587) Moreover, the idea of "synthetic judgment", Hegel notices, is in itself contradictory. The form of judgments is that of separation, dislocation, division – not that of synthetic unity. Only syllogisms, never simple and isolated propositions, can achieve an authentic synthetic unity. In other words, Kant does not come to terms with his own discovery, which remains silenced by these empty and meaningless examples that are paradoxically supposed to express it.

The fundamental metaphysical propositions are also said to be synthetic *a priori* judgments, but we have difficulties figuring out what the genuine synthetic dimension of these propositions may be, to the extent that the arithmetic model Kant brings forward constantly fails to give us access to ontological statements. Ontology is, in a way, deprived of any ontological content. In the Doctrine of the Notion, Hegel writes: "The further development, however, does not fulfill the promise of the beginning. The very expression *synthesis easily* recalls the conception of an *external* unity and a *mere combination* of entities that are *intrinsically separate.*" (Hegel 1991, § 587) *Kantian synthesis remains analytic.*

In order to do justice to Kant's own discovery, that is, to the utmost speculative value of *a priori* synthesis, one has to resituate and reelaborate its content and meaning, and to assign it its specific phenomenality – which cannot be provided by mathematical examples. It is as if one had to discover the genuine locus of Kantian ontology against Kant himself.

Let's now see how Heidegger insists upon the same problem, even if in a different way. Heidegger also affirms that Kant, as he says in Being and Time (§ 6), has "shrunk back" from his own discovery. (Heidegger 1996, p. 21) For Heidegger, it is not so much a matter of criticizing Kant's examples of synthetic judgments, rather than bringing to light a strong discrepancy between the two editions of the first *Critique*.

"In the 2nd edition of the *Critique of Pure Reason*, Heidegger writes in *Kant and the Problem of Metaphysics*, the transcendental imagination, as it was described in the vigorous language of the first edition, is thrust aside and transformed – to the benefit of the understanding. (...) The pure synthesis is [now] assigned to the pure understanding. The pure imagination is no longer indispensable as a faculty in its own right. (...) The substitution [of the understanding for the imagination] characterizes Kant's new position with regard to the transcendental imagination. It is no longer a "function" in the sense of an autonomous faculty, but is now a function only in the sense of an operation of the faculty of understanding. While in the first edition, all synthesis, ie synthesis as such, arises from the imagination as a faculty not reducible either to sensibility or understanding, in the second edition the understanding alone assumes the role of origin for all synthesis." (Heidegger 1990, § 31, p. 113, trans. modified)

So here again, the reader or interpreter has to unveil the genuine Kantian ontological question and put an end to its occulting or covering.

Now, how do both Hegel and Heidegger, with and against Kant, assign *a priori* synthesis its genuine visibility, and consequently also its authentic metaphysical value and meaning? They precisely both proceed to an analysis of *transcendental visibility* as a synonym to *a priori* synthesis.

What does this say? We are touching here the sensitive point. Born from the same concern, the question of transcendental imagination's and *a priori* synthesis' ontological value finds two different and incompatible answers. Hegel's and Heidegger's interpretations of transcendental visibility and its metaphysical meaning are profoundly irreducible to one another.

3 The conflict: visibility vs. visibility

For Hegel, transcendental visibility is just another name for revelation. Transcendental imagination is the revelatory condition of possibility for the unity between the concept and the sensuous for everything that is. The German term *Offenbarung* means both manifestation and revelation. These two terms phenomenologically describe the possibility of the visible and the modalities of its appearances. If transcendental imagination determines the *a priori* synthesis as the fundamental structure of revelation, it is because all phenomenal appearances (*Erscheinungen*) can only manifest themselves by the sake of an originary *Offenbarung*. *Offenbarung*, as the name indicates, is first of all an opening.

The opening Hegel is talking about is that of presence. *A priori* synthesis situates presencing in between the concept and the sensuous at their very crossing point. The pure image produced by creative transcendental imagination allows the concept to appear phenomenally, and the phenomenon to show itself as categorically structured by the concept. Such is the value of the double nature – sensuous and conceptual – of the transcendental image. This intrication determines the ontological economy of visibility. The concept does not exist without revealing itself, and the sensuous is never independent from its speculative form. Their difference exists in and as their *a priori* identity or synthesis.

Far from simply characterizing human finitude and its intuitive and phenomenal horizon, the problem of *a priori* synthesis in reality brings to light the speculative structure of absolute spirit, which implies the perfect coincidence between the concept and its manifestation in time and space. We remember that the task of the *Phenomenology of Spirit* is that of making the concept's phenomenon identical to its essence. The *Erscheinung*, the phenomenon, is always the *Erscheinung* of its own essence.

If Hegel makes use of the word "manifestation", it remains true that for him, every kind of manifestation has to be understood as a modality of revelation. Of course, we hear the theological determination of the word "revelation", which is absent from "manifestation". And we remember that in *Faith and Knowledge*, *a priori* synthesis is described as the structure of the intuitive understanding, that is, the structure of God's essence. God, for Hegel, is the name of the absolute coincidence between the concept and its phenomenological appearance. We can then understand why Hegel can assimilate *a priori* synthesis with God's nature or essence. In *Faith and Knowledge*, Hegel writes: "The idea of an archetypal, intuitive understanding is at bottom nothing else than this same idea of transcendental imagination." (Hegel 1977, p. 89) Kant is "driven toward this idea" (Hegel 1977, p. 89) and at the same time repelled by it. Kant could not accept the extreme consequence of his own insight, namely that the ontological dimension of *a priori* synthesis consists in the absolute identity between the concept and its manifestation, and thus seals the speculative identity between ontology and theology.

Speculative revelation has to be understood as absolute manifestation, without secret, without reserve. Revelation means absolute transparency: "God is out and out manifestation". The speculative absolute transparency also explains why God is said to be "not jealous".[1] He does not hide, or keep anything for himself. This total openness, which elevates the transcendental image into the clarity and power of the ideal, actualizes the transformation of metaphysics into idealism.

Hegel's notion of the "open", allowed by speculative revelation, is of course incompatible with Heidegger's own concept of the opening, *Entschlossenheit*, which also designates the disclosure of presence, but which remains definitely irreducible to any dialectical significance. For Heidegger, visibility is assimilable to an economy of manifestation, not of revelation.

Heidegger interprets the originary structure of manifestation as the very essence of time. The title of § 33 of *Kant and the Problem of Metaphysics* is explicit in this respect: "The Inner Temporal Character of the Transcendental Power of Imagination" (Heidegger 1990, p. 123). In this very important paragraph, Heidegger shows that the operation of transcendental imagination appears in all its force in transcendental schematism. The pure images that hold the concept and the sensuous together are schemas, and schemas derive from the three fun-

---

1 On this particular point, see (Malabou 2005, p. 91 et seqq.).

damental extases of time grounded in imagination: first the possibility of looking at (present), then of looking ahead (future), and finally of looking back (past). Therefore, Heidegger can write: "Transcendental imagination is primordial time." (Heidegger 1990, § 33, p. 131, trans. modified)

How are we to understand the dramatic difference between Hegel's and Heidegger's readings? Is such a difference reducible to a simple opposition between a theological understanding of *a priori* synthesis and a "human" one? Between infinity and finitude? Between absolute knowledge and transcendence? If such is the case, how can we explain at the same time that such diverging approaches derive from the same problem? The answer is more complex than it initially seems.

4 Identity and difference between theology and religion

In "The Onto-Theological Constitution of Metaphysics", Heidegger precisely develops a critique of Hegel's understanding of Kant and *a priori* synthesis. Heidegger asks a very profound question concerning the legitimacy of Hegel's assimilation between ontology and theology. This question is a twofold one. Hegel's assimilation between ontology and theology lays the ground on his understanding of phenomenality as revelation. The first level of the question is then: is such an understanding acceptable? This first question leads to a second one: is not the choice of the term "revelation" inducing another assimilation, namely that of theology with religion? Here is the nerve of Heidegger's critique of speculative "idealism": it transforms metaphysics, through the identification between ontology and theology, into a philosophy of religion. We know that for Hegel, the highest discourse on revelation is that of Christianity. Hegel's reading of Kant would then be an enterprise of Christianizing critical philosophy. We see the abyss that the apparently harmless question: "how are synthetic *a priori* judgments possible?" is opening!

On the one hand, Heidegger is cautious not to *reduce* purely and simply Hegel's onto-theo-logical metaphysical operation with a Christianization of philosophy. The identification of *a priori* synthesis with God's understanding is not originally a religious statement that would have anything to do with ecclesial power, but an ontological one. Heidegger goes on: "Speculative theology is not the same as philosophy of religion, nor is it identical with theology in the sense of dogmatics. Rather, speculative theology is the ontology of the *ens realissimum*, the highest actuality as such" (Heidegger 1988, p. 3)

At the same time, Heidegger underscores the ambiguity of the term Offenbarung, which can be translated, as we said, as both manifestation and revelation.

Manifestation designates any kind of appearing or *phainestai* (Greek, Roman, whatever) and is not attached to any divine gift, whereas revelation is always religious. Such a religiosity is restrained, in Hegel, to Christianity. There is only one authentic, revealed religion, namely Christianity. This explains why the theological part of the Absolute Spirit in the *Encyclopœdia* is called Revealed Religion and not Speculative or Rational theology. (Hegel 1971, § 564)

Defining "the true religion", in § 564, Hegel writes: "It lies essentially in the concept of religion – the religion whose content is absolute spirit – that it is revealed and, what is more, revealed by God." (Heidegger 1988, p. 3) Revelation, for Hegel, always means "self-revelation", and "self-revelation" is Christian in essence. *A priori* synthesis thus coincides with Trinity: Father/Concept, Sensuous/Christ, and Imagination/Spirit. As surprising as it may seem, a priori synthetic judgments express the nature and essence of Christianity. Ontology, Theology and Christianity then absolutely coincide.

This explains why Heidegger characterizes the Hegelian achievement of onto-theology as a Christianization: "My inaugural lecture *What is Metaphysics?* (1929) defines metaphysics as the question about beings as such *and* as a whole. (...) To those who can read, it means: metaphysics is onto-theo-logy – both the theology of the Christian faith and that of philosophy (...)." (Heidegger 2002, p. 31) How to explain this unity of philosophy and faith?

"(...) Metaphysics, Heidegger goes on, is theology, a statement about God, because the deity enters into philosophy. Thus the question about the onto-theological character of metaphysics is sharpened into the question: How does the deity enter into philosophy, not just modern philosophy, but philosophy as such?" (Heidegger 2002, p. 31) For him, the two questions: 1) why and how does God enter into philosophy ("How does the deity enter into philosophy?") and 2) why is the metaphysical God necessarily the Christian god? are necessarily interrelated. The "entrance" of God into philosophy can only be – at least such is the powerful Hegelian version of it – a "revelation".

Hegel, in his reading of Kant and his confusion between revelation and manifestation, simply achieves the traditional vision of metaphysics as onto-theology, and raises this traditional vision to its culminating point: its fundamental Christian structure. Therefore, Hegel's "idealism" both accomplishes and radically misses the authentic role and meaning of transcendental imagination.

The understanding of transcendental imagination as time, as the temporalization of time itself, totally changes the conception of transcendental visibility, which ceases to be identical with revelation and thus with presence. This change clearly appears in § 20 of *Kant and the Problem of Metaphysics*, called "Image and schema" (Heidegger 1990, § 20, p. 65). In this paragraph, Heidegger takes the example of a photograph – that of a death mask – in order to explain what an image is. He shows that there always two images in one, consequently also two levels of visibility in the visible. Looking at the photograph of the death mask, we see that it shows this particular mask, but it "is also capable of showing how something resembling a death mask appears in general." (Heidegger 1990, § 20, p. 66)

An image thus has both an ontic dimension: the manifestation or aspect of a particular being, and an ontological : the appearing of what appears, the visibility of the visible itself ("in general"). This second dimension would be,, in Kantian terms, condition of possibility for all empirical images.

Contrarily to what Hegel affirms, the pure image itself remains invisible. The appearing of what appears is the condition of manifestation, but does not itself come into presence. We see the general image of the mask through its non-appearing in this particular mask. Such is the profound difference between manifestation and revelation. In revelation, both the ontic image and the ontological structure of the image appear, or come into presence. Nothing remains hidden. For Heidegger, on the contrary, the general structure of appearing appears as non-appearing. Or it can be said to appear as difference; the difference between presence and withdrawal. We can seize here the link between image and time.

Time defined as the production of pure schemes in itself never appears. We see through it but never see it. It is not a being. It is always already there – such is the fundamental meaning of its *a priori* form – but it is never present. The essential difference between what is manifest and what withdraws in manifestation is the Kantian prefiguration of ontological difference, which is where Kant escapes onto-theology, and his Hegelian interpretation by the same token. By bringing onto-theology into question, Heidegger hopes to open up a different way of thinking about beings and a different way of relating to the divine. This does not mean, however, that God should remain hidden, or secret, or jealous. Difference, which opens manifestation, is not reducible to any kind of presence, including a hidden one. That is why, when Heidegger talks about the sacred, he always specifies the non-religious dimension of sacrality, to the extent that religion fundamentally belongs to traditional metaphysics. Destruction of traditional ontology fundamentally implies the dechristianization of being.

5 Conclusion

In conclusion, we can say that for Hegel, revelation and revealability are one and the same. Revealability reveals itself in the revealed, God is a *synthesis a priori*, and this appears everywhere and in everything. On the contrary, for Heidegger, there is a difference, in the strong sense of the term, between the visible and visibility. Hegel understands *a priori* synthesis as the systematic unity of concept and intuition in and as revelation. Such is the reason why, according to Heidegger, Hegel does not need time and eventually sublates temporality in absolute knowing. Heidegger understands *a priori* synthesis as the prior opening of being which at the same time suspends itself in the non-appearing of the image. Philosophical thinking starts with a trace, never with a present being or a perception. Therefore, if the "Idealism" of "German Idealism" tends, with Hegel, toward an assimilation of the " ideal " with the presentation (*Darstellung*) of noetic as well as phenomenal visibility, its pretention to substitute metaphysics is illegitimate. Heidegger's critique of German Idealism is not exhausted by his reading of Hegel, as his approach to Schelling is, let's say, much more generous! Nevertheless, Heidegger will constantly try to separate metaphysics from idealism in general, even in its Kantian sense of transcendental idealism. Idealism is another name for the onto-theo-logical structure of metaphysics, and after all, the name " onto-theo-logy " comes from Kant!

I would like to close with two questions. First: Is it certain that Hegel's assimilation between a priori synthesis and Christian Revelation exclude time? In reverse, second: Is it certain that Heidegger succeeds in dechristianizing philosophy? If Heidegger can declare, in *The Anaximander fragment*, that "Belief or Faith has no place in thought (*der Glaube hat im Denken keinen Platz*)" (Heidegger 1977, p. 372), his vocabulary is constantly borrowed from religion. "Destruktion", to start with is, as we know, a Lutheran term. We also know his constant insistence upon the sacred. Hegel, when assimilating the philosophical god with that of religion, does not only retrieve the onto-theo-logical character of metaphysics, he also shows that revelation, and consequently all determination of appearing in general, are always historical and linked with the specific event of monotheism through which we necessarily receive it. Revelation is the historical name for manifestation. It associates it with a datable event, a historical beginning, a determined tradition. In that sense, Hegel's onto-theo-logy is a philosophy of time.

Where does time appear in the most insistent way? In the anonymous mysticism of ontological sacrality, or in the irreducible historical dimension (revelation) of manifestation? In reading *a priori* synthesis as revelation, is not Hegel introducing history in the transcendental? Who then is thinking temporality more strongly? Heidegger when he declares that the visibility of the visible resists its own manifestation, or Hegel when he declares that everything appears, including the resistance of appearing itself, thus stating that resistance consists in the opening of all secrets? To what extent does this confrontation between Hegel and Heidegger, more precisely between Hegel, Heidegger and Kant, determine our current philosophical horizon? Can we consider that the destruction of metaphysics has succeeded in dismantling onto-theo-logy, or is God's presence still haunting the contemporary deconstructive reelaborations of transcendental imagination? The enigma of synthetic a priori judgments seems to reside in this alternative.

Bibliography

Hegel, G.W.F. (1971): *Encyclopaedia of Philosophical Science, Philosophy of Mind [Spirit]*, "Absolute Spirit". Oxford: Clarendon Press.
Hegel, G.W.F. (1977): *Faith and Knowledge: An English Translation of "Glauben und Wissen"*. Albany: SUNY Press.
Hegel, G.W.H (1991): *Doctrine of the Notion, Science of Logic, Encylopædia of the Philosophical Sciences*. Indianapolis: Hackett Publishing.
Heidegger, Martin (1977): *The Anaximander Fragment*. New York: Harper and Row.
Heidegger, Martin (1988): *Hegel's Phenomenology of Spirit*. Bloomington: Indiana University Press.
Heidegger, Martin (1990): *Kant and the Problem of Metaphysics*. Bloomington: Indiana University Press.
Heidegger, Martin (1996): *Being and Time*. New York: SUNY Press.
Heidegger, Martin (1999): *Pathmarks*. Cambridge: Cambridge University Press.
Heidegger, Martin (2002): "The Onto-Theological Constitution of Metaphysics". In: *Identity and Difference*. Chicago: Chicago University Press.
Kant, Immanuel (1998): *Critique of Pure Reason. The Cambridge Edition of the Works of Immanuel Kant*. Cambridge: Cambridge University Press.
Malabou, Catherine (2005): *The Future of Hegel. Plasticity, Temporality and Dialectic*. New York: Routledge.

Anders Moe Rasmussen
Self and Nihilism.
Kierkegaard on Inwardness,
Self and Negativity

Kierkegaard's thinking is of a radical, polemic, hyper critical and provocative kind, and this in combination with both an apodictic way of writing and a tendency for vagueness and ambiguity has presented, and still represents, a stumbling block to many readers of Kierkegaard's texts; especially those trained in philosophy. The topic of this paper, Kierkegaard's notion of inwardness, shares a number of the characteristics just mentioned: it is highly critical of and polemical against Hegelian philosophy as well as against a culture of commerce, it is apodictic in the sense of the absolute distinction Kierkegaard draws between the inner and the outer, and it is ambiguous in its content as it is open to a number of different interpretations. At least two different interpretations rather obviously present themselves, both of which witness Kierkegaard's infamous subjectivism and acosmism. The first way of interpreting the notion of inwardness is to read it autobiographically as an expression of Kierkegaard's own religious pietism, which is a pietism in a more radical and critical sense that is hostile to clerical dogmatism and orthodoxy while stressing individualism and making the inner experience the highest criterion of truth. The second way of understanding inwardness is to read it as an expression of some kind of mysticism. Such a reading could be based on the fact that Kierkegaard intimately connects his notion of inwardness to what is a constitutive element in all different versions of mysticism, namely the idea of something inexpressible or ineffable, the idea of an immediate inner experience beyond language; compare Kierkegaard's notion of "Inkommensurabilitet".

However, is it really the case that Kierkegaard's notion of inwardness exclusively refers to a specific inner domain or to a specific inner experience? That is the question I am going to discuss in the following, and I will begin with a quite different version of internalization or interiority, namely the epistemological internalization developed by Descartes. Kierkegaard's notion of interiority and inwardness scarcely has anything in common with Descartes', although his relation to Descartes is more complex than one might expect as it makes Hegel the real villain of modern rationalist thinking by turning doubt and skepticism into a purely scientific enterprise, thereby neglecting the personal and existential aspects of doubt still present in Descartes' philosophy. Nonetheless, interiority in Kierkegaard means something very different from Descartes' inner theatre of representations, just as his distinction between inner and outer does not refer to carving up the world into an inner world of representations and an outer world of a demystified mechanistic cosmos.

Despite all the differences, Descartes and Kierkegaard do agree with each other in one very important aspect in that they both connect interiority with the notion of reflection; for both Descartes and Kierkegaard, internalization refers to a reflexive turn. This claim implies the rejection of the idea that Kierkegaard's notion of inwardness is reducible to some sort of immediate inner experience; in fact, I think Kierkegaard is not a proponent of immediacy at all. Reflection in Kierkegaard obviously refers to something quite different from Descartes' idea of introspection or inner sight, so the task now is to give a positive account of Kierkegaard's notion of reflection. Undertaking this enterprise leads us directly to the very heart of Kierkegaard's thinking, which I would like to call a "Phenomenology of Spirit". Despite his ever present polemics against Hegel, it makes perfectly good sense to label Kierkegaard's philosophy a "Phenomenology of Spirit", thereby placing Kierkegaard not only in the neighborhood of Hegel, but in the neighborhood of German Idealism in general.

Here we are presented with a number of questions. In what way is the concept of reflection connected to the concept of spirit, as suggested, and is anything gained in clarifying the notoriously complex notion of reflection with the even more complex notion of spirit? For what is spirit? This latter question is one that Kierkegaard famously posed and answered: "A human being is spirit. But what is spirit? Spirit is the self. But what is the self? The self is a relation that relates itself to itself, or it is the relation's relating itself to itself in the relation. The Self is not the relation but it is the relation's relating itself to itself" (Kierkegaard 1980, p. 13). This passage from the beginning of The *Sickness unto Death* is probably the most famous and most cited of all in Kierkegaard's oeuvre and countless commentators have elaborated on it. Nevertheless, I will present yet another reading, but in a language somewhat different from Kierkegaard's.

In contrast to other beings, humans not only have mental states such as emotions, volitions and beliefs – mental states that we also ascribe to animals – but are conscious about having such states, and we express this awareness in sentences such as, "I know that I believe or want that p" or simply "I believe etc." This capacity for self-reflection or self-relation constitutes another characteristic specific to human beings, namely a certain plasticity or variability, as it makes other forms of self-reflection and self-relation possible. Self-consciousness does not involve the idea of immunity to error or the idea of privileged access, as promoted in a still influential philosophical tradition; rather, self-consciousness involves the idea of a lack of transparency and self-sufficiency. It is this lack of transparency that makes other forms of self-relation possible.

Firstly, knowing that I have this or that belief or this or that volition, I simultaneously know that I have these and other beliefs and volitions. In self-consciousness, the diversity of my mental states is gathered into a unity, thus implying that I am able to relate to a belief in the perspective of other beliefs. Secondly, in having beliefs that p, I am aware of the possibility of beliefs that are not p. As such, I find myself hovering between different possibilities. Thirdly, I am conscious of myself as being the same person now as the person I will be later, and I know that I will also have beliefs and volitions later. Fourthly, and in connection with the consciousness of identity, I am able to perform yet another form of self-relation, a form that could be labeled practical in the sense that it concerns my ability to pursue future goals willingly. Finally, this specific practical self-relation can be divided into two different forms: one centered on the question of whether I should pursue this activity rather than another and how I should pursue it in the best possible way, and another concerning my life as a whole or as a totality centered around the question "how I will and should live my life".

This map of different forms of self-relation is, in fact, neither a commentary on the quoted passages from *Sickness unto Death* nor a list of self-relations making up what could be called Kierkegaard's "Phenomenology of Spirit". The list just outlined is very much centered on the basic fact of self-consciousness, our ability to know about our states of mind, and the implications following from this fact in terms of other forms of self-relation; however, in contrast with many of his contemporaries, Kierkegaard was not concerned with theoretical problems about the structure and conditions of self-consciousness. Even the quoted passage, which very much has the appearance of a theory, should be carefully read so as not to interpret it as a general statement concerning the nature and structure of subjectivity. After all, the condensed remarks on the self at the beginning of The *Sickness unto Death* function as a way of exposing the conditions for the concept of despair as a sickness of the self. However, my remarks are not altogether beside the point.

Here I would like to draw attention to two things. The notion of self-relation. The concept of self-relation is Kierkegaard's interpretation of the notion of reflection and his interpretation of the concept of Spirit, and as such it plays an essential role in Kierkegaard's thinking. Secondly, the specific practical form of self-relation is divided in a narrow sense to concern deliberations about what activities and goals to undertake and how to pursue them in the best and most appropriate way, as well as a wider sense concerning my life as whole. Given that the notion of self-relation plays an essential role in Kierkegaard's thinking, self-relation is primarily discussed in its specific practical sense and that also holds for Kierkegaard's remarks on the self at the beginning of *Sickness unto Death*, in so far as these have the status of a general argument about subjectivity and the self. For Kierkegaard, self-relation is understood as a person's relation to his *life*, and he develops his "Phenomenology of Spirit" as a system of practical self-relations. In what follows, I will try to give an outline of this system and thereby situate the notion of inwardness within it as a specific form of practical self-relation. Inwardness in Kierkegaard is neither reducible to an inner immediate experience, nor to a theatre of introspection; it is rather a way of relating to oneself. However, before turning to what can only be an outline of Kierkegaard's phenomenology, I want to address the distinction between what I have called practical self-relation in the narrow sense and self-relation in a wider sense, and once again I will do it with a vocabulary somewhat distanced from Kierkegaard's own.

I will take my point of departure in the distinction between first and second order volitions introduced by Harry Frankfurt in his famous paper *Free Will and the Concept of a Person* from 1971. In a critique of contemporary theories of a person, especially the concept of a person as an entity ascribable by both physical and psychological predicates presented by Peter Strawson, Frankfurt points to the ability of distancing oneself from oneself in deliberating about and evaluating ones immediate wants. These immediate wants Frankfurt calls first order volitions, and consequently the evaluations of these wants are called second order volitions. According to Frankfurt, it is this ability to rise above and deliberate upon our immediate wants that constitutes a person as a person. Due to this ability, human beings are not only able to create an order of preferences and goals and consider how to obtain these goals, but also transform our wants into a goal of action. Frankfurt claims that this ability, which could be called practical self-distance, is how we should conceive freedom and morality. However, while freedom and morality are closely connected to practical self-distance, I will not go into these matters but rather point to yet another form of practical self-relation that is not even hinted at in Frankfurt's text. Although this other form of self-relation presupposes the ability to evaluate and deliberate, it has a specific form and is irreducible to second order evaluations. It thereby refers to a differentiation within second order evaluations and could therefore be called third order evaluation. What this third order evaluation concerns is my life as a whole or my life as a totality. Now what does that mean? Two things characterize third order evaluations: 1) In contrast to second order evaluations, which concern singular contents and goals, third order evaluations concern the way or the "how" of conducting one's life; 2) third order evaluations imply the act of retracting from the multiplicity of one's plans and goals in collecting one's life as whole. What is at stake in third order evaluations concerns how I understand myself and what is of ultimate importance to my life; or to put it more bluntly: third order evaluations concern the meaning of life.

Returning to Kierkegaard, I claim that the essential features of Kierkegaard's phenomenology of self-relation can be captured and interpreted by the system of different orders or steps just developed. While Kierkegaard's work contains types of self-relation not included in the system, it is possible to interpret Kierkegaard's description of aesthetical figures as representatives of first order volitions, with the figure of Don Juan as a borderline case and the so called reflective aesthete as a transitional figure. While Don Juan seems totally absorbed in his immediate wants and drives, the reflective aesthete is on the way to the second order volitions as he is able to detach himself from his immediate wants while still being unable to choose which he prefers, thereby creating an order of preferences. The ability to perform this kind of self-relation is the real change or progress from the so called aesthetical stage of existence to the ethical stage of existence. It is no coincidence that the representative of ethical existence, Judge William, is a judge as he is able to judge and evaluate his wants and drives, and in judging and evaluating he is also capable of transforming them. Accordingly, Judge William urgently emphasizes that judging and evaluating one drives does not imply rejecting or suppressing them, but rather integrating them into one's life by way of transformation. Very much could be said about the kind of self-relation characteristic of ethical existence; however, in the following I will focus on the specific kind of practical self-relation that I have termed third order evaluation concerning life in its totality. I do this in order to explicate the subject at hand, namely the notion of inwardness, and to qualify the claim that inwardness signifies a kind of self-relation. What I will try to show is that the self-relation involved in Kierkegaard's notion of inwardness signifies relating to oneself in terms of relating to one's life as a whole or as a totality. Explicating this also makes it possible to conceive of Kierkegaard's distinction between inner and outer in a new way. The decisive distinction in Kierkegaard's thinking is between first and second order volitions, which refer to a life engaged in and concerned about a multiplicity of activities and plans, and third order volitions, which are concerned with collecting and gathering oneself. What Kierkegaard calls "outer" is a mode of life committed to the sheer multiplicity of project and plans – a life led in what Kierkegaard would call "the differences" – and what he calls the "inner" is a life of collecting oneself and is conducted in the mode of seriousness.

What I have called third order evaluations concerning existence or life as a whole play a decisive role in Kierkegaard's work, and if Kierkegaard can be named the founder of existential philosophy, then the primary reason is that he introduced the thought about existence in its totality; recall that the key question in Heidegger's *Being and Time* concerns the question about the whole of existence, "die Ganzheit des Daseins". While it not only underlies all of his so called edifying discourses but also plays a major role in his philosophical works, it is rather difficult to locate passages where Kierkegaard explicitly addresses the question concerning existence as a whole. However, there are at least two texts in Kierkegaard's work that deal more thoroughly with the question. One is a passage from *The Concept of Anxiety* and the other is a separate text named *At a Graveside*, which is contained in the publication *Three discourses on imagined occasions*. These texts are equally important and supplement each other, but I will begin with the passage from *The Concept of Anxiety* because it is provides the main evidence for my claim about inwardness as a specific kind of self-relation.

The relevant passage is entitled *What is certitude and inwardness?*, which is a subsection of a part called *Freedom lost Pneumatically*, which in turn is a subsection of §2 called *Anxiety about the Good (The demonic)*, which forms the last of two paragraphs in Caput IV named *Anxiety of Sin*. Although located deep within this Chinese box, the section dealing with the notion of inwardness plays an essential role in Kierkegaard's famous analysis of the demonic, which is defined as the absence of inwardness. A lot of things are going on in Kierkegaard's interpretation of inwardness as he also explicitly turns the notion into a battle of how to understand subjectivity or self-consciousness. The opponents are German Idealists in general and specifically Fichte's philosophy of the I, and in this connection Kierkegaard says: "The most concrete content that consciousness can have is consciousness of itself, of the individual himself – not the pure self-consciousness... This self-consciousness is not contemplation, for he who believes this has not understood himself, because he sees that meanwhile he himself is in the process of becoming and consequently cannot be something completed for contemplation. This self-consciousness, therefore, is action, and this action is in turn inwardness.... (Kierkegaard 1980, p. 143). Here Kierkegaard opposes Fichte's philosophy of what could be called theoretical self-consciousness in terms of an analysis of its structure and constitution, while at the same time introducing another conception of subjectivity, namely that of a practical self-consciousness, explicitly called inwardness. Inwardness is practical self-consciousness or practical self-relation. It is concrete and it is active. What this means becomes clearer in Kierkegaard's specification of inwardness as seriousness or earnestness. Kierkegaard asks: "What is inwardness?" and answers: "It is no doubt difficult to give a definition of inwardness. In the meantime, I shall at this point say that it is earnestness" (Kierkegaard 1980, p. 146), and after having rejected any attempt at a definition, stating that definitions are inadequate in relation to existential concepts, Kierkegaard makes what he calls "a few remarks for orientation" (Kierkegaard 1980, p. 147) concerning earnestness. In this connection he refers to the work *Psychologie oder die Wissenschaft vom subjektiven Geist* (from 1837) by the German philosopher Johann Karl Rosenkranz (1805–1879). Rosenkranz was not only the first to write a biography of Hegel, he was also one of the most loyal proponents of Hegelian philosophy and defended it against attacks while applying Hegelian doctrines to different academic disciplines, such as studies of culture and literature, and theories of education and psychology. It seems that Kierkegaard was well acquainted with Rosenkranz's work, and in particular his psychology, as its plays an important role in Kierkegaard's effort to determine notions of inwardness and earnestness. In determining earnestness, Kierkegaard specifically refers to Rosenkranz's concept of "Gemüt" (mind) while also citing a longer passage from his psychology that deals with this concept. The essence of Rosenkranz's reflections of "Gemüt" is that it is a unity of feeling and self-consciousness. The feeling must open itself to self-consciousness and vice versa; the subject must feel the content of consciousness as its own. Without cognition and knowledge, feeling is nothing but natural compulsion, and without feeling there is nothing but an abstract concept detached from what is called "the final inwardness" ("die letzte Innigkeit"). So in Rosenkranz's definition of "Gemüt" there is both a passive and factual aspect, namely feeling, and an active and interpretational aspect, namely cognition and knowledge, and it is precisely this dialectic of passivity and activity that attracted Kierkegaard's attention as it seems to fit his project to determine a notion of concrete subjectivity that is equated with inwardness.

However, there is much more to say on Kierkegaard's reflections on inwardness and earnestness. Until now I haven't specifically addressed what I take to be one of the most important aspects of inwardness and what delivers the strongest evidence for calling inwardness a specific kind of practical self-relation, namely the totality aspect specifically connected to earnestness. Here an important quotation from Shakespeare's Macbeth comes in. The quotation, uttered by Macbeth in the second act, scene two where the murder of the king has been discovered and announced, reads as follows: "Had I but died an hour before this chance, I had lived a blessed time; for, from this moment there is nothing serious in mortality. All is but toys, renown and grace is dead. The wine of life is drawn and the lees is left this vault to brag of". There are three important aspects in this quotation: contingency (chance), totality (all, nothing) and negativity (dead, nothing, drawn) and Kierkegaard especially highlights totality and negativity. What is at stake is life or existence as a whole, the question of what is of worth and importance in life. I have called these sorts of questions third order evaluations, or a self-relation concerning one's life as a totality. Questions of this specific sort are anything but alien to the philosophical tradition, in fact it would not be far-fetched to claim that philosophy, at least western philosophy, begins with it if we recall Plato's question about the good life making up the very core of his philosophy. However, in contrast to Plato, where the question concerning the meaning of life is located in a dialogue where protagonists and antagonists exchange thoughts and reflections with each other in a civilized atmosphere, Kierkegaard locates the question in the midst of negativity.

As often reflected upon, negativity plays a decisive role in Kierkegaard's work. But when talking about negativity in Kierkegaard's thinking, one must be aware that negativity comes in different versions or flavors. One of the versions that have not been addressed very intensely in the literature on Kierkegaard is negativity in terms of what I would like to call "nihilism". By nihilism I mean a total lack of sense, an absolute loss or breakdown of meaning. It is not that this or that activity or this or that thing that loses its worth and importance, it is everything in the world. Everything loses its radiance and glory. The world becomes grey and cold. In Kierkegaard's work there are at least four types of nihilism and in what follows I will comment on each of them by initially dividing them into two categories, one which I would like to label "self-inflicted nihilism" and the other "contingent nihilism". The category "self-inflicted nihilism" refers to a self-destruction of the mind. Even the destruction of mind is an act of mind. For Kierkegaard the self-destruction of mind comes in two shapes, one pointing back to Friedrich Heinrich Jacobi's notion of nihilism, and the other anticipating what must be regarded as being currently the most influential version of nihilism, that is, naturalistic nihilism.

In his famous letter to Fichte from 1799, Jacobi introduces the term "nihilism" into the philosophical tradition. According to Jacobi, Fichte's philosophy of the "I" is just a reversion of Spinoza's philosophy, an idealistic transformation of Spinozist naturalism resulting in nihilism. According to Jacobi, Fichte's enterprise of a universal system of rational thought, the idea of grasping the universe from one single principle, inevitably leads to the destruction of reality and concrete living individuality. Reason is but a parasite and a destructive business as it can only sustain itself by destroying the living mind. So, in Jacobi's words, reason "comes from nothing, goes to nothing, for nothing, in nothing" (Jacobi 2004, p. 202 (my translation)). In Kierkegaard's work, we find numerous echoes of Jacobi's charge of nihilism, whether inspired by him or not. Kierkegaard does not miss a single opportunity to attack the philosophy of Hegel. His polemics against Hegel are simply omnipresent and he is able to model it in infinitely many ways. However, the substance of the polemic remains the same: Hegel's system of speculative reason rests on the idea of a detached point from nowhere, a point *sub specie aeterna*, transforming everything into an abstract totality and leaving the world uninhabitable for human beings. Representative of countless of attacks, I have chosen the following passage from *Concluding Unscientific Postscript* to illustrate the nihilistic consequences of a purely rational world-view: "And the same thing could easily repeat itself in the individual's relation to himself – namely that the ethical and the responsibility and the power to act and the strong-nerved sorting out of repentance evaporate in a brilliance of disintegration, in which the individual dreams about himself metaphysically or lets all existence dream about itself and confuses himself with Greece, Rome, China, world-history, our age and the century. The individual immanently comprehends the necessity of his own development, and then in turn objectively lets his own I become moldy like a fluff on the whole, forgetting that even though death changes a person's body to dust and mixes it with the elements, it is terrible in living to become mold on the immanental development of the infinite" (Kierkegaard 1992, p. 545). Worse than being dead, is being living dead.

Though seldomly explicitly addressed, there is yet another form of "self-inflicted nihilism" in Kierkegaard. Kierkegaard could not foresee the great advances and progress of modern science, especially within neuroscience, making grand theories of both man and the world possible; yet I think he anticipated the scientific nihilism that is currently virulent in many different fields and disciplines, including the arts. The very beginning of *Fear and Trembling* states: "If a human being did not have an eternal consciousness, if underlying everything there were only a wild, fermenting power that writhing in dark passions produced everything, be it significant or insignificant, if a vast, never appeased emptiness hid beneath everything, what would life be then but despair? If such were the situation, if there were no sacred bond that knit humankind together, if one generation emerged after another like forest foliage, if one generation succeeded another like the singing of the birds in the forest, if a generation passed through the world as a ship through the dessert, an unthinking and unproductive performance, if an eternal oblivion, perpetually hungry, lurked for its prey and there were no power strong enough to wrench that away from it – how empty and devoid of consolation life would be!" (Kierkegaard 1983, p. 15). Besides testifying that *Fear and Trembling* is just as much a defense of humanity as it is a defense of faith, the picture painted in the quotation corresponds to the views of current scientific naturalism and the nihilism inherent in it.

When it comes to what I have called "contingent nihilism", we need to return to the quotation in *The Concept of Anxiety* from Shakespeare's Macbeth and the nihilism contained within it. In contrast to the other forms of nihilism, which are pure products of the mind, the total loss of sense and meaning addressed in the quotation and in Kierkegaard's comments is an experience open to and possible for every human being. Kierkegaard writes: "Macbeth was a murderer; therefore the words in his mouth were a dreadful and shocking truth. Yet every individual who has lost inwardness can truly say. "The wine of life is drawn" and also "There is nothing serious in mortality, all is but toys" (Kierkegaard 1980, p. 146). Nowadays we would called such an experience a depression where there is the experience of a total breakdown of one's world, the experience of utter impossibility of living in a world without any color, devoid of any resonance. Human beings are susceptible to radical changes and transformations – this is part of the plasticity of human existence that I discussed at the beginning of this text, and if you haven't personally experienced everything crumbling into utter indifference, your neighbor probably has. Experiencing losing one's world is something that happens to you; some contingent event totally turns your world upside down. However, passivity and facticity is only one aspect of it. As in the case of my earlier discussion of inwardness, the radical change expressed by Macbeth also involves an activity in the sense that it implies an act of understanding or evaluation, an evaluation of life in its totality.

Turning to the fourth and last form of nihilism in Kierkegaard, it is one again about inwardness in terms of earnestness, facticity, negativity and the totality of life. What is at stake is ultimate negativity. And what is ultimate negativity? Death, of course. The exemplary text is *At a Graveside*, which belongs to Kierkegaard's so called edifying work. In general, Kierkegaard's edifying discourses are filled with philosophical reflections, but the discourse *At a Graveside* stands out in so far as it has the appearance of a philosophical treatise rather than an edifying discourse. It also breaks with the conventional view about edification as it is harsh, radically unsentimental and almost hyper realistic, repeating again and again the definite facticity of death and its devastating power. The discourse symptomatically opens with the frightening words: "Then all is over!" (Kierkegaard 1993, p. 71) and it is repeated again and again. All sentimental thoughts about death as a sleep and a flowering after-life are almost brutally swept away. Every door is closed, every possible way of sneaking out of the horrific facticity of death blocked and one sometimes gets the impression that the discourse is more of an ode to or praise of death than edifying words of consolation. In fact it is just the opposite. *At a Graveside* is an anti-death discourse, it is about death **and** life and in the end it is all about life. Closing all escape routes and destroying all our sentimental moods is not an expression of some morbid fancy, but rather a way of determining the right attitude or the right relation to death, and the right relation to death is earnestness. Earnestness has, in a very strict sense, nothing to do with sentiments or emotions as it has much more to do with thinking. Earnestness is a way of relating to death in terms of what Kierkegaard calls "considering death" ("at betænke døden"). Excavating that term not only leads to the heart of Kierkegaard's notions of inwardness and earnestness, but also to what I take to be Kierkegaard's original contribution to philosophy as well as theology, that is, his dialectics of existence. Considering death is forming a dialectical relation to death. In all its facticity, death is not mute but speaks to us as it tells us about life. Breaking with his iconoclastic principle of not speaking about death in pictures, Kierkegaard comments on the certainty and uncertainty of death as follows: "The certainty of death is earnestness; its uncertainty is the instruction, the practice of earnestness. The earnest person is the one who through uncertainty is brought up to earnestness by virtue of certainty" (Kierkegaard 1993, p. 94). So death is an instructor or a teacher, as Kierkegaard calls it, and an immensely powerful one as it is capable of changing and transforming life. Out of death a "retroactive power" springs. Kierkegaard writes: "What is decisive about explanation, what prevents the nothingness of death from annihilating the explanation, is that it acquires retroactive power and actuality in the life of the living person; then death becomes a teacher to him and does not traitorously assist him to a confession that denounces the explainer as a fool" (Kierkegaard 1993, p. 97). So death only has this retroactive power in virtue of a self-relation or self-understanding, and this is exactly what earnestness means – the retroactive power is the retroactive power of earnestness. As just mentioned, this retroactive power has the capacity to transform and to change the living person. In this connection Kierkegaard talks about the power to "transform life". Now this transformation has two aspects: Firstly it contains an incentive to make maximal use of the times of life. Secondly it gives our life on earth a worth and a dignity independent of time. I think these two aspects and the very essence of inwardness and earnestness is captured in the following passage with which I will conclude: "to think that all was over, that everything was lost along life, in order then to win everything in life –this is earnestness" (Kierkegaard 1993, p. 76)

Bibliography

Frankfurt, Harry (1988): "Freedom of Will and the Concept of a Person". In: *The Importance of What We Care About*. Cambridge: Cambridge University Press.
Jacobi, Friedrich Heinrich (2004): *Friedrich Heinrich Jacobi Werke*. Bd.2, 1. Klaus Hammacher/Walter Jaeschke (Eds.). Hamburg: Meiner Verlag.
Kierkegaard, Søren (1980): *The Sickness Unto Death*. Princeton, NJ: Princeton University Press.
Kierkegaard, Søren (1980): *The Concept of Anxiety*. Princeton, NJ: Princeton University Press.
Kierkegaard, Søren (1983): *Fear and Trembling*. Princeton, NJ: Princeton University Press.
Kierkegaard, Søren (1992): *Concluding Unscientific Postscript to Philosophical Fragments*. Princeton, NJ: Princeton University Press.
Kierkegaard, Søren (1993): *Three Discourses on Imagined Occasions*. Princeton; NJ: Princeton University Press.

Camilla Serck-Hanssen
Rediscovering the *Critique of Pure Reason* as a Propaedeutic to Metaphysics: What Heidegger Saw and McDowell Missed

1 Introduction

In 1994, John McDowell's Locke lectures appeared in *Mind and World*. The book was to become highly influential. It both set the agenda for a number of philosophical debates within contemporary philosophy and framed the reception of the philosophers that McDowell chose as his interlocutors. In our context his take on Kant is particularly interesting because of its distinctively Hegelian twist.[1] Indeed, I think it is safe to say that *Mind and World* is one of the central contributions to our understanding of German Idealism today.

In this paper I shall argue that although McDowell brings out some of the systematic philosophical potential in a reading of Kant's *Critique of Pure Reason* (*KrV*), his criticism of Kant's so-called transcendental story[2] shows that he misses important aspects of the *KrV* – aspects that would indeed be congenial to the way he attempts to draw on Kant in his own philosophical project.

Before I present to you what I take to be the crucial shortcomings of McDowell's Kant reading, a caveat is, however, in order. My point is not that McDowell fails to engage in a sufficiently careful exegesis of the first Critique. Such a criticism would not do justice to the way in which McDowell philosophizes. Indeed, his errand is not to interpret Kant, but to bring out, often in metaphorical lan-

---

[1] This much is recognized by McDowell himself, cf. (McDowell 1994, p. 44, p. 83).
[2] In *Having the World in View*, McDowell regrets his way of portraying the "transcendental story" as necessarily being from an external or sideways on perspective. He admits having equated "transcendental" with "transcendent" (cf. p. 18, n. 26) and also admits having imported an unwarranted two-worlds picture of what Kant is up to (p. 42, n 30). Nevertheless, also in the later work, McDowell argues that Kant's theory ultimately fails to establish robust empirical realism, mainly because of the faults of the *Transcendental Aesthetic* (cf. pp.76–80), which he still believes commits Kant to some notion of a transcendental or transcendent Given matter (cf. p. 81, p. 83). He also, however, fails to give any alternative account of the transcendental level. Hence, despite his regrets in *Having the World in View*, the fact is that McDowell not only continues to worry about the Given, but also finds no proper place for its correlate viz. the transcendental subject and its operations. As such, a criticism of his earlier claims (in *Mind and World*) of the "transcendental story" is still warranted.

guage, some rather deep ideas about the aims and pitfalls of philosophy. To succeed in presenting an interesting criticism of McDowell's Kant reception, one must therefore confront him with a reading that in a broad sense shares the aims of McDowell's own approach, while at the same time challenging it.

My aim in this paper is to show that Heidegger's reading of the *KrV* can take on such a role. I shall argue that this reading provides a perspective that is congenial to the way McDowell attempts to draw positive insights from Kant's position, and also that it avoids the pitfalls that McDowell believes accrues to it. In short, I shall suggest that McDowell's philosophical agenda would have been strengthened had he taken not only the Kant of German Idealism, but also that of Heidegger seriously.[3]

To set the stage for this alternative route, let me begin by reminding you of how McDowell reads his Kant, and where he takes him to fail.

2 McDowell's Kant

In *Mind and World*, McDowell's aim is twofold. He seeks to disclose how a powerful myth, the Myth of the Given,[4] has haunted and bewildered the minds of even some of his dearest philosophers, namely Davidson, Evans and Kant. McDowell also attempts to offer an alternative picture, which while responding to the philosophical worries and questions that gave rise to the Myth in the first place, does not itself fall prey to it.

In McDowell's view, the Myth of the Given is not just any old philosophical misconception. It is an idea that follows naturally from the Kantian insight that "rationality operates freely in its own sphere".[5] For if that is the correct understanding of reason, i.e. our ability to think and judge, one must indeed ask

---

[3] In *Mind and World* Heidegger is not mentioned at all. In the more recent collection of essays, *Having the World in View*, Heidegger is only mentioned as the one who claimed that the *KrV* is not at all a theory of knowledge, which is a view McDowell finds excessive, but in some sense correct. In addition to offering a take on Kant that would be congenial and fruitful for McDowell's project, I also think that a study of Heidegger along the lines presented in this paper would provide McDowell with strong arguments against the way Dreyfus attempts to use Heidegger against him. I will not, however, develop this point here.

[4] Here I will follow McDowell's notation in *Having the World in View* and write Given with a capital G when it is the given in the sense of the Myth, and given when it is not. Cf. e.g. (McDowell 2013, p. 264 f.).

[5] For this particular way of putting it, see (McDowell 1994, p. 85). Other places in *Mind and World* McDowell writes about the spontaneity of understanding being *sui generis*, e.g. p. 67. For more about spontaneity, see e.g. p. 5, pp. 7–13 and pp.29–34.

how we can ever successfully know anything outside this sphere. How can our thought adequately respond to the world and its objects? According to McDowell, this worry is not just that of (shallow) skepticism, which is why he does not rest content with Davidson's answer, i.e. that most of the time most of our thoughts are true (McDowell 1994, p. 17). The deeper question is how, if reason is spontaneous and operates freely, our thinking can be about the world and its objects at all (McDowell 1994, p. 17). In short, why isn't our rational activity a mere "spinning in the void" (McDowell 1994, p. 50)?

According to McDowell, this question expresses a legitimate worry because it follows from the insight, the Kantian insight as it were, into how reason ought to be conceived. Hence, the worry about a mere empty spinning cannot be seen as the conclusion of *a reductio*. In that case, the worry could be relieved simply by rejecting the autonomy of reason and opting for a strict or bald naturalism instead (McDowell 1994, p. 72ff, p. 85, p.108). What then is the alternative?

McDowell once again refers to Kant's first Critique and argues that an appropriate answer can at least partly be found here. In addition to the insight that reason is spontaneous, Kant realized that without a relation to intuitions, or to use McDowell's preferred locution: "bits of experiential intake", thoughts are not merely empty, but not thoughts at all. Moreover, and more importantly, McDowell also takes Kant to have realized (albeit not fully, which we shall return to below) that such intuitions cannot be devoid of conceptual structures. For if they were, they could not constrain thinking and judging in the required way. Once we realize that thinking might be a mere spinning in the void, intuitions or experiential intakes are called upon to function as justificatory grounds for our beliefs. And mere intuitive Givens can never justify anything. At best they can offer exculpation, but what we want and need is justification (McDowell 1994, p. 8). In other words, the Kantian insight, according to McDowell, is that we can only get the appropriate kind of friction for our spontaneity if the intuitions themselves are through and through conceptual (McDowell 1994, p. 66, p. 67). That is, intuitions must be placed within the space of rationality without thereby losing track of their intrinsically receptive or passive nature. Kantian intuitions are therefore experiential intakes not "as a bare getting of extra-conceptual Given, but as a kind of occurrence or state that already has conceptual content" (McDowell 1994, p. 9, see also p. 46). This means that somehow rationality must be operative already in receptivity or sensibility.

Despite his admiration and praise for Kant, McDowell argues that there are at least two shortcomings in Kant's way of thinking. First, Kant lacks the appropriate resources for fleshing out the idea that rationality must also be operative in sensibility. What Kant has to offer instead is a rather dubious story about the activity of certain so-called transcendental faculties. What he should have done is to recapture the Aristotelian idea of second nature (McDowell 1994, p. 99). That way we can supposedly understand how humans, *qua* rational animals, can even have our sensible nature permeated by rationality. Second, although Kant does resist the Myth of the Given at the empirical level of his theory since he understands intuitions as being permeated by concepts, he nevertheless falls prey to the Myth of the Given at the transcendental level. For from the transcendental perspective, "receptivity figures as a susceptibility to the impact of a supersensible reality, a reality that is supposed to be independent of our conceptual activity in a stronger sense than any that fits the ordinary empirical world." (McDowell 1994, p. 41) And "[o]nce the supersensible is in the picture, its radical independence of our thinking tends to present itself as no more than the independence any genuine reality must have. The empirical world's claim to independence comes to seem fraudulent by comparison." (McDowell 1994, p. 42). Hence, "[i]t is as though Kant were saying that although an exculpation cannot do duty for a justification, and although, empirically speaking, we can have justifications for empirical judgments, still the best we can have for empirical judgments, transcendentally speaking, is exculpations. This is a profoundly unsatisfactory aspect of Kant's philosophy" (McDowell 1994, p. 43).

As we have just seen, McDowell argues that when operating from the transcendental perspective Kant is still victim to this persistent Myth. The problem is allegedly that Kant's understanding of the possibility of representational content has as its foundation a transcendental story where the Given pops up again; this time in the guise of the impact of supersensible reality on our sensibility (McDowell 1994, p. 41). Moreover, because of this transcendental story, he fails to see that rational powers should be assigned to real human beings and not to transcendental minds and their operations. But is this really Kant's transcendental perspective or story?

As already announced, I will address this question, but not by diving into the scholarly debate as to whether the thing in itself should be understood in, e.g., epistemological, perspectival or ontological terms. Indeed, I think that at least some of those alternatives deserve to be included in the Myth of the Given, but I will not substantiate that view here. Instead I shall call your attention to the radically different reading of Kant's transcendental story provided by Heidegger.

3 Heidegger's Kant

Whereas McDowell's Kant begins with spontaneity and autonomy and the problem of justification, Heidegger's Kant begins with the problem of metaphysics.

That Heidegger downplays spontaneity and autonomy does not imply, however, that he takes Kant to be a "bald" naturalist.[6] Rather, for Heidegger, Kant's crucial insight is (i) the fundamental aim of philosophy is metaphysics and (ii) the quest for metaphysics comes hand in hand with a natural propensity to pursue metaphysics from God's point of view.

This implies that the role of the given is also quite different from that which McDowell assigns to it. As Heidegger reads it, the role of the given, on the transcendental level, is just a corollary to our finitude.[7] The point is simply that our spontaneity is not of a kind that can literally create the being of its own objects. What this rather trivial point is supposed to tell us is that the quest for metaphysics must be pursued while keeping our finitude in mind. Indeed, to lose track of this feature of our rationality in our philosophizing is to attempt to do metaphysics "from the view from nowhere" or from "sideways on", to borrow a phrase from McDowell (McDowell 1994, p. 34–5, p. 82).

Kant's reference to some kind of transcendental givenness or transcendental receptivity thus satisfies two quite different tasks in the two readings. Whereas according to McDowell's reading the *given* (*qua* Given) is invoked to function as a kind of deep level justificatory friction (and fails to do so) (McDowell 1994, p.41), on Heidegger's reading it is supposed to, and indeed succeeds in, giving us the only model or perspective within which the project of metaphysics can be carried out successfully. Secondly, what the *transcendental* level contributes, according to Heidegger, is not an extra story that is supposed to "suspend and tie" the empirical perspective from above and below, like a kind of rampant Platonism (McDowell 1994, pp. 77–78, pp. 83–85, pp. 92–93). It is not a duplication of the empirical mind and world story, as it were. Instead the transcendental level, or more correctly, the level of the critique (McDowell unfortunately equates the two) is the level where the very possibility of metaphysics (*qua* ontology) is inquired into in a quite special manner. The recognition of the finitude of our spontaneity, together with the question about being, is only the starting point for this project, a project that in a piecemeal manner sets the stage for metaphysics proper.

To see how, I shall focus my attention on three interrelated themes that I take to be particularly germane to my criticism of McDowell's Kant reception, namely: (i) Heidegger's understanding of the method of *KrV*; (ii) his reading of the tran-

---

[6] For the issue of bald naturalism see (McDowell 1994, 72ff and 108).

[7] In (McDowell 2013, p. 85 and p. 102), McDowell also calls the attention to this finitude and applauds it. Nevertheless, he does not utilize this point the way Heidegger does.

scendental aesthetic; and (iii) his reading of the Metaphysical Deduction of the Categories or the Guiding Thread.

4 Kant's method: The meaning of the Copernican Revolution

According to Kant, no investigation can have the hope to advance to the level of a science unless it has an idea of its own method. Not only has no metaphysics in the scientific sense ever existed, even its idea has been lacking. For human reason, albeit naturally disposed to metaphysics, has failed to see where to begin and how to proceed. Kant's own answer to this problem is well known: it is the Copernican Revolution. It is equally well known that the *Critique of Pure Reason* is the work of this revolution, but in what sense?

According to the traditional reading, the conclusions of the *KrV* count as conclusions of *metaphysica generalis* or ontology as long as one realizes that its domain consists not of things in themselves, but appearances. And appearances are objects that are somehow constituted by our a priori means of knowing them. This reading of Kant's transcendental turn can be seen as kind of an antirealistic salvation of metaphysics. It can, however, also be seen as an act of euthanasia. For if metaphysics concerns mind dependent, subjective objects, it is not much of a metaphysics!

On Heidegger's reading of the *KrV*, both these responses to the transcendental turn are, however, based on a misunderstanding of Kant's project. The aim of the *KrV* is not to bring forth a set of necessary truths about objects even when understood as appearances. For the *KrV* is not an *organon*, but a *canon*. This means that the *KrV* guards us against metaphysical miscarriage, but it does not by itself give us any substantive metaphysical insights. More specifically the work is first and foremost a contribution to the question of *method*, i.e. it tells us how *to do* philosophy.[8]

The view that the *KrV* is a work that centers on the question of philosophical method is not unique to Heidegger.[9] Nevertheless, his understanding of the level to which this method applies and how it applies surely is. According to Heideg-

---

[8] Notice that Heidegger rejects the view that the *KrV* is "a doctrine concerning the technique for proceeding" (KPM, p. 11). But this does not imply that he dismisses its importance as a piece of methodology where the method is one that shows itself rather than being the object of a doctrine. For the same understanding of the *KrV*, cf. also (Heidegger 1997, p. 45).

[9] Cf. e. g. Giorgio Tonelli (in particular Tonelli 1995), according to whom the *KrV* is a work on the method of metaphysics, and Henry Allison (in particular Allison 2005), who argues for a methodological reading where the *KrV* is understood as a contribution to meta-epistemology.

ger's reading, the *KrV* must be read as a methodological instruction to philosophy not *qua* metaphysics, but *qua* propaedeutic to *metaphysica generalis* or ontology.[10] In short, the KrV is a work in meta-metaphysics. Moreover, the *KrV* is not so much a work *on* method as a work *of* a certain method. That is, it is supposed to *show* us rather then *tell* us how to proceed in the philosophical pursuit that precedes and eventually grounds ontology. Or in Heidegger's own words: "The task [is to show] how this development of the possibility of ontology from its seeds is to be carried out" (KPM, p. 12).

In this way, Heidegger's reading also gives new meaning to the metaphor of the Copernican Revolution. The *KrV* is the work in which the revolution which needs to proceed metaphysics is carried out. It puts before our eyes – to use an expression from Kant – where to begin and how to proceed in order to arrive at the place where the questions of ontology can finally be addressed properly.[11]

5 Where to begin

Recall that for McDowell, Kant's philosophical project springs from the insight that reason is spontaneous and autonomous. Alas this insight also pushes Kant towards fraternizing with the Given – a pressure he only partially deals with in a successful manner. I believe, however, that Heidegger's understanding of Kant's philosophical starting point is closer to home.

According to Heidegger, Kant's starting point is to ask how "knowledge which unveils the being itself" is possible (KPM, p. 9). At first this might seem to go against Kant's claim in the introduction to the *KrV* where he sets the agenda for the Critique by asking his famous question about the possibility of the synthetic a priori. But in fact what Kant tells us there is that: "The real problem of pure reason is now *contained* in the key question: How are synthetic judgments a priori possible?"[12] What I want to draw attention to is precisely the point that, for Kant, the "real problem" and indeed the mystery[13] of (theoretical) philosophy is not identical to that of the synthetic a priori, but somehow contained in it. The "real problem" I surmise is rather what Kant draws our attention to in the transcendental deduction, viz. that the lack of attention to the question about the function and ground of the copula has given rise to many troublesome consequences in metaphysics (*KrV*, B 140–42). If so, Kant's real question can be

---

10 Cf. e.g. KPM pp. 28–29.
11 Cf. also KPM p. 29 about the meaning of "Analytic".
12 KrV B 19, my emphasis. Cf. also KrV A 10.
13 Cf. KrV A 10, last paragraph where Kant uses the term 'mystery' or better 'secret' (*Geheimnis*).

rephrased as follows: "How is it possible to judge that something *is* something at all?" And this is just another way of asking Heidegger's question how "knowledge which unveils the being itself" is possible.

If this reading is correct, the next question is why Kant would let the real problem of metaphysics be presented as a secret "contained in" another question? I believe that the answer is partly that the secret, i.e. the fundamental question of philosophy, is typically concealed because we simply take for granted that we do have access to the being of things. That logicians in a narrow sense typically overlook the significance of the question of being is acceptable for Kant. After all, analysis of mere logical relations (i.e. relations between concepts) does not bring in the domain of being at all. But the problem is that in the history of metaphysics the logical tools have been used surreptitiously over and over again to draw illusory metaphysical conclusions (*KrV*, B 141, footnote). This, I suggest, is why the fundamental question of being must be made visible to us through a question of a less familiar kind. And this certainly holds for that of the synthetic a priori. Never before has the challenge of metaphysics been posed like this!

This accords well with Heidegger's reading of the *KrV*. As he sees it, it is a work that provides a cure against the "forgetfulness of being" in two senses. Firstly, it manages to set up the real question of metaphysics in a way that does not immediately lend itself to surreptitious metaphysical reasoning. For the demand that the a priori feature of our judgments must be answerable to justification guards us against naïve empiricism, while the demand concerning the synthetic feature guards us against logicism. Secondly, the *KrV* guides us towards the place where the question of being can first be addressed properly. The Critique of Pure Reason is as such "laying the ground for metaphysics as unveiling the essence of ontology" (KPM, p. 10). To see more precisely how and it what sense the *KrV* serves as a such a special kind of propaedeutic to metaphysics, I will first turn to Heidegger's reading of the transcendental aesthetic. Here we shall find a very original reply to McDowell's worry that the Given is an unavoidable corollary of the transcendental aesthetic (McDowell 2013, pp. 76–81).

6 The Transcendental Aesthetic: We sense because we are finite

The first part of the *KrV* is the Transcendental Aesthetic. It concerns the receptive element in human cognition and its transcendental conditions, namely space and time. A common way to read the Transcendental Aesthetic is to see it as the first step in the attempt at restricting the proper domain of metaphysics to that of appearances. Nevertheless many or even most interpreters object that Kant's arguments do not suffice to rule out that mind independent "things in themselves" exist, and as such ought to be the objects of metaphysics proper. Indeed it seems that Kant himself admits this much since he talks about a transcendental kind of affection where the thing in itself appears to be posited as a kind of transcendental and yet material condition of the content of our sensibility. As we have already seen, this way of understanding Kant also causes McDowell a great deal of concern, for "[o]nce the supersensible is in the picture, its radical independence of our thinking tends to present itself as no more than the independence any genuine reality must have. The empirical world's claim to independence comes to seem fraudulent by comparison" (McDowell 1994, p. 42).

Heidegger's reading of the Transcendental Aesthetic is, however, quite different and offers an interesting reply to McDowell's worry. For Heidegger the Transcendental Aesthetic is the result of a starting point of outmost importance, a starting point Kant himself was only brought to through the whole process of the "most original self-knowing of Reason", i.e. the Critique (KPM, p. 13). I have already anticipated that this starting point is the perspective that we are finite intellects. But we can now see why this starting point is of "outmost importance" to metaphysics. Kant's crucial insight, according to Heidegger, is that only finite beings are confronted with being as a problem and hence only finite beings can engage in the question of being as well as in the question of how this question is to be answerable (KPM, pp. 15–18).

If we assume, or could assume, the standpoint of the infinite intellect, the problem of being would not in fact appear to us at all. The hallmark of the infinite intellect is its creativeness. That means that for the infinite intellect its representation of the object and the being of the object come down to the same thing. And where there is no gap between the representation and the object, the question of how the object can be available in its being cannot arise.

Kant's first important insight is therefore to place the problem of metaphysics firmly within the horizon of the finite intellect. His next insight, according to Heidegger, is to question what this starting point discloses. What it unveils is a new question, to wit: "How must the finite being that we call "human being" be according to its innermost nature so that in general it can be open to being that is already there independently of its own creation, and which therefore must be able to show itself from itself?" (KPM p. 30) The transcendental aesthetic is the preliminary or provisional answer to that question.

Notice that this way of reconstructing Kant's path towards the inquiry into the nature of space and time is quite different from the reading which causes McDowell's worry and discontent. To recall, that reading assumes that the transcendental aesthetic comes hand in hand with an assumption about the necessity of positing a transcendental level of the Given. And if this were the only way to read Kant, I do think McDowell's objection would be appropriate. It does indeed seem as if "[o]nce the supersensible is in the picture, its radical independence of our thinking tends to present itself as no more than the independence any genuine reality must have. The empirical world's claim to independence comes to seem fraudulent by comparison" (McDowell 1994, p. 42).

On Heidegger' reading, however, this problem does not arise. For the premise that we are finite intellects is not tantamount to a causal or quasi claim about transcendental affection.[14] Instead it follows from the arguably non-controversial and merely negative assumption that we are not creative intellects.[15] And this starting point, as we shall see, gives quite a different perspective on our sensibility than any causal readings supply.

The Kantian conception of sensibility is neither psychological nor neurological, and nor is it any dubious transcendental analogue of such empirical conceptions. As Heidegger says, Kant is the first philosopher who properly grasped the ontological concept of sensibility rather than the sensualistic one. On his account our sensible faculties are the result of our metaphysical status as finite intellects, rather than the other way around (KPM, p. 19). This must of course not be taken as a competing hypothesis to evolution, as far as the *causal origin* of sensible faculties go. The point is rather that the insight that we are finite intellects discloses that when having metaphysics as one's aim, sensibility must be investigated from a certain perspective.[16] This perspective is to be guided by the question of how, through the senses, a finite being "can be open to a being that it itself is not and that therefore must be able to show itself from itself" (KPM, p. 30).

Recall that since this is a problem belonging to a Critique, or in Heideggerian terminology, a fundamental ontology, this question must be situated within a framework that does not already presuppose a reified model of subjects, objects and their interaction. This restriction clearly gives quite a particular kind of perspective on our sense organs. They are not to be conceived as pre-given objects open to empirical investigation. Instead they are to be seen as functions that are analyzed from the point of view of their role as enabling the *transcendence of sensibility*, i.e. of letting that other being show itself from itself. And it is from

---

14 For the opposed view cf. (McDowell 1994, p.95).
15 Cf. also KPM pp. 50–51.
16 Notice the close affinity to McDowell, who argues that naturalism of the bald kind actually opts out of philosophy altogether. Cf. (McDowell 1994, p. 77ff.) and particularly his criticism of primitive metaphysics (McDowell 1994, p. 82).

this perspective that the peculiar status of space and time is first brought to light. For space and time are the sensible principles or horizons through which particulars are able to stand forth as fully saturated particulars. Space and time also constitute the framework within which the subject finds himself as being always already there with the particulars. Moreover, space and time are *pure a priori* intuitions in the sense of being *ways* of intuiting, i.e. as ways of taking in particulars directly in their wholeness. As finite beings we are open to being in its particularity by sensing temporally and spatially. This is what the Transcendental Aesthetic discloses, and arguably this insight does not depend on a transcendental framework, which "slight[s] the independence of the reality to which our senses give us access" (McDowell 1994, p. 44).

7 Transcendental logic and transcendence

As I have already shown, Heidegger reads the *KrV* as a propaedeutic to general metaphysics or ontology. He also understands this propaedeutic in a special methodological manner according to which each of the different parts of the *KrV* unveil how the previous conclusions were just provisional and require new steps so as to approach the question of being in the appropriate way. In this sense we can call the *KrV* a work in methodological meta-metaphysics. We have also seen how this reading yields a very different understanding from McDowell's of the role of the transcendentally given. For McDowell, it can only be read as the transcendentally Given, which deflates Kant's empirical realism and turns it into an unfortunate kind of idealism (McDowell 1994, p. 44).[17] For Heidegger, the given is instead the corollary of our finitude. And it is the recognition of this finitude that enables Kant to approach the question of being in the appropriate way, i.e. a way that eventually will also allow us to see how empirical realism is possible.[18]

As we just saw, one of the insights that followed from this starting point is that philosophy must address sensibility not in a sensualistic or quasi-sensualistic manner, but rather ontologically. And by assuming this perspective on sensibility, one in effect avoids precisely what McDowell believes belongs to the transcendental framework, namely the lofty idea of transcendental affection. What, then, about the transcendental logic? Does that part of the *KrV* require

---

[17] For a somewhat subtler exposition, see (McDowell 2013, pp. 78–80).
[18] I will not attempt to show how Heidegger understands empirical realism or how he takes it to be possible.

a transcendental framework of the kind that McDowell objects to? Does it imply "operations of an off-stage transcendental mind" (McDowell 1994, p. 159)? Heidegger's answer is once again negative. To see why, we need to turn to his understanding of the transcendental logic.

The understanding of space and time as manners through which being can announce itself in its particularity and wholeness is, for Heidegger, only a partial and indeed provisional answer to the problem of being or transcendence. For arguably the knowing of being is not made out by intuition alone. To know something is always to know it as such or such, which requires thinking and concepts (KPM, p. 36).

From the point of view of a Critique (or a fundamental ontology), the question that must be raised with respect to thinking at this point is therefore how thought must be like in order to enable a grasp of being. How can thought, as it were, reach out beyond itself and let that being, which it itself is not, be known in itself?[19] For Heidegger this is not simply an additional question alongside that of the nature of our sensibility. It is not as if Kant starts out with the premise that the human mind has two basic kinds of representational faculties: thought and sensibility that need to be analyzed. In accordance with Heidegger's special methodological reading of the *KrV*, the idea is instead the following: While the insight that we are finite intellects led us to investigate the function of sensibility from the point of view of its possibility *qua* transcendence, that manner of investigating also unveils to us how thinking must be approached. It is not as if we have thinking somehow in addition to intuition – that we both think and intuit. It is rather that Kant's question about being leads him to the insight that discursive thinking itself is the mark of finitude because this kind of thinking so to speak springs out of intuition: "Thinking is in the service only of that particular object or of the being itself in its immediacy, and it is [a necessary means for making the being itself] accessible to everyone" (KPM p. 16, for the points inserted in brackets cf. p. 19).

In other words, although knowledge of being is primarily and originally intuition, and intuition "always remains bound to specifically intuited particulars" (KPM, p. 19), a being is only known in the full sense if it is known as something at all times for everyone (KPM, p. 19). It is indeed this independence from the particular knower and situation that signifies genuine knowledge. Somewhat ironically, this character of knowledge also easily leads one towards the view

---

19 Cf. KPM, pp. 23–24. The locution "in itself" should not in this context be identified with "the thing in itself". The point is rather that of McDowell's project, i.e. to inquire into the possibility of realism

that the question of the being of objects, i.e. ontology, must be treated absolutely independently of any considerations about the knowing subject.

However, for Kant as well as for Heidegger, such an absolute separation of epistemology and ontology is a misguided starting point. The problem is precisely to understand how an object can stand against us at all, and how we as finite *cognizers* must be like in order to let it stand against us (KPM, p. 50). This is the horizon within which the problem of being must be placed and it leads to the part of Kant's critical investigation known as the transcendental logic. To believe that ontological questions must be treated in absolute separation from questions about knowing subjects is indeed to forget that ontology or metaphysics is a project only for finite intellects; it is to assume that philosophy can be based on a Theo-centric model; it is to attempt to do "philosophy from sideways on" (McDowell 1994, p. 34–5, p. 82).

As we have just seen, so far there is no appeal to an "off stage transcendental mind" in Heidegger's reading of Kant's transcendental logic. Just as in the Transcendental Aesthetic, the function of the reference to the subject is to keep the quest for metaphysics on the right track. It serves to remind us that metaphysics must be pursued within the constraints of the finite intellect and that the analysis of thinking must be grounded in intuition. But let us go into the transcendental logic in some more detail to see if McDowell's worry about Kant's transcendental story can be met a bit more precisely.

8 The Metaphysical Deduction of the Categories

The logic that Kant presents in his table of judgment has been met with suspicion. The reception of his move from this table to that of the categories in what is commonly referred to as the "metaphysical deduction of the categories" is, in general, even less charitable. Here Kant in some way or another infers the table of categories from the table of judgment. According to Kant, this "deduction" can take place because:

> The same function that gives unity to the different representations in a judgment also gives unity to the mere synthesis of different representations in an intuition, which, expressed generally, is called the pure concept of understanding. (*KrV*, A 79/B 104f.)

For most readers, this argument, if indeed it can be called an argument at all, is extremely cryptic. McDowell has, however, been surprisingly positive. To him these passages contain the essence of the insight that intuitions must be permeated by conceptual structures; that rationality must be operative in sensible nature as well as in thought.[20] McDowell's worry is, however, partly that Kant has no resources for explaining how this can be the case and partly that according to the transcendental story, the categories are representations that belong to a transcendental mind with its dubious transcendental operations.

Again, I believe Heidegger's reading provides valuable points against McDowell's reading. Heidegger too rejects the idea that these passages are obscure. But this does not mean that positive solutions or conclusions can be found in them the way McDowell suggests. Instead, Heidegger sees these passages as an expression of a certain phase in the metaphysical project in which the "laying of the ground for metaphysics comes to the point where the matter itself is deeply veiled" (KPM p. 46). Hence Kant's claim that the same function is involved in judgment, and intuition "cannot be the conclusion, but must instead be the correct *beginning* of the laying of the ground for ontological knowledge" (KPM, p. 46).

For Heidegger, Kant's idea about the same function in thought and sensibility can be rephrased like this: Since the question of being has revealed to us that thought must be in the service of intuition,[21] but must still transcend what is given immediately *from* intuition, the possibility of ontological knowledge would require that there is a way of comporting oneself towards being in its givenness, which at the same time enables reflective conceptualization to spring forth.

At this point in our meta-metaphysical inquiry, we have therefore reached a new insight. We have discovered a task, namely to look for something that can carry the weight of serving as one and the same function that is operative in sensibility and thought. As such the metaphysical deduction of the categories leads us towards a better grasp of our problem of being. For the question now reads: How can intuition and judgment spring forth in such a way that being itself can become available to us in its being through ontological predicates, i.e. categories? Nevertheless, this "deduction" is preliminary and conditional and only points us in the direction of where to look. In fact Kant's own title for the section suggests this much. Its official title is not "metaphysical deduction" (which suggests an attempt to disclose the *origin* of the categories), but a *Leitfaden*, i.e. a guiding thread that leads us towards the proper ontological approach (KPM p. 40).

---

[20] Cf. (McDowell 1994, bottom of page 46 and top of page 47). See also (McDowell 2013, pp. 30–35, p. 70, pp. 94–97, p. 260).
[21] See above, and KPM p. 40.

Heidegger's reading of the passages from *Leitfaden* helps us see the shortcomings of McDowell's. Because he suffers from a lack of awareness of the propaedeutical and methodological character of the Critique, McDowell takes the passages to attempt to offer conclusions of a kind they do not (yet) aim to deliver. In short, his first fault is that he looks for the answer in the wrong place. Hence, his objection that Kant fails to give the full answer falls to the ground. Although I will not expand on that point here, on Heidegger's reading Kant's answer as to how that same function must be conceived is first found in the *Transcendental Schematism* – a part of the *KrV* that McDowell does not refer to at all.

The second fault of McDowell's is that he believes that instead of drawing on the real and embodied human being, Kant invents a transcendental mind where the functions (of synthesis) mysteriously take place. On Heidegger's reading, however, no transcendental mind of the kind McDowell alludes to is needed. For just as sensibility in the Transcendental Aesthetic is not a curious kind of transcendental faculty but a particular understanding of human sensibility that springs forth from the question of being, the transcendental mind referred to in the Transcendental Logic is simply the human mind examined and disclosed from the ontological standpoint. Indeed, rather than drawing us away from the real human being, on Heidegger's view Kant's approach will eventually bring us to a proper understanding of it.[22]

9 Conclusion

I began this paper by reminding you of McDowell's objections to Kant. According to McDowell, despite Kant's philosophical ingenuity[23] he fell prey to the Myth of the Given, albeit only in his so called transcendental story. But this story is not innocent, for it seriously deflates the reality of the empirical world and displaces the mind or self. I have attempted to show how Heidegger's reading of the same Kantian text, i.e. the *Critique of Pure Reason*, conveys a quite different understanding of the transcendental story. My main concern has been to show firstly how for Heidegger Kant's concept of the transcendentally given is not a myth but a corollary to the concept of the infinite intellect. Moreover, what McDowell takes to be an indefensible "transcendental story" is, on Heidegger's reading, a crucial insight into the requirement of a methodological propaedeutic to metaphysics

---

[22] Just how Heidegger takes this to unfold in the Schematism of the *KrV* falls beyond the scope of this paper.
[23] For McDowell's praise of Kant, see e.g. (McDowell 1994, p. 98).

proper. Accordingly, for Heidegger's *Critique* there simply is no need to posit the level of reality that McDowell finds so troubling – be it the transcendentally Given or the "off stage self". Finally, although I cannot develop that point here, on Heidegger's reading Kant also provides a place for that "second nature" that McDowell scorns him for having overlooked. For by seeing the Critique as a propaedeutic to metaphysics, one is brought to the insight that eventually it is only by placing the subject in the world and analyzing it in light of its agency that the question of being can be addressed properly.

Bibliography

Allison, Henry A. (2004): *Kant's Transcendental Idealism. An Interpretation and Defense. Second Edition.* New Haven/London: Yale University Press.

Heidegger, Martin (1997), *Kant and the Problem of Metaphysics*, 5. Edition, Translated by R. Taft. Bloomington and Indianapolis: Indiana University Press. (= KPM)

Heidegger (1997): *Phenomenological Interpretations of Kant's Critique of Pure Reason.* Translated by P. Emad and K. Maly. Bloomington: Indiana University Press.

Kant, Immanuel (1998): *The Critique of Pure Reason.* Edited and translated by P.Guyer and A. Wood, Cambridge: Cambridge University Press. (= *KrV*)

McDowell, John (1994): *Mind and World.* Cambridge, Mass.: Harvard University Press.

McDowell, John (2013): *Having the World in View. Essays on Kant, Hegel and Sellars.* Cambridge, Mass.: Harvard University Press.

Tonelli, Giorgio: *Kant's Critique of Pure Reason Within the Tradition of Modern Logic.* Hildesheim/Zürich/New York: Olms.

Index

Adorno, Theodor W.   43
Aeschylus   140
Agrippa Menenius Lanatus   80
Allison, Henry   3, 8, 11–13, 18f., 220
Ameriks, Karl   3, 11, 18f., 50
Aristotle   45, 84, 90, 100, 137, 155, 157

Baumgarten, Alexander   19
Beck, Jakob Sigismund   29, 33, 42, 56–60, 63–65, 67
Berlin, Isaiah   67, 75
Brandom, Robert   95, 106, 126, 159, 182
Breazeale, Daniel   50
Buck-Morss, Susan   178
Bykova, Marina F.   160

Callender, Craig   4
Campbell, John   103
Chisholm, Roderick   5
Clarke, Randolph   3, 5
Coffman, E.J.   5
Copp, David   4

Deligiorgi, Katerina   3f., 9
Descartes, René   1f., 39, 165
Diderot, Denis   145
Düsing, Klaus   28

Eberhard, Johann August   47

Fichte, Johann Gottlieb   6, 8, 27–40, 42f., 49f., 53–56, 62–64, 66f., 73–78, 84–86, 88f., 100, 121
Foot, Philippa   4
Forberg, Friedrich Karl   31, 43, 46
Ford, Anton   155
Forster, Michael N.   97
Frank, Manfred   28, 50, 54
Frankfurt, Harry   4, 67, 160
Franks, Paul   28
Fries, Jakob Friedrich   29, 56, 60–62, 64–66

Gabriel, Markus   95–98, 106, 164
Gadamer, Hans-Georg   161
Gardner, Sebastian   27, 32, 39

Halfwassen, Jens   105
Hanna, Robert   3
Hegel, Georg Wilhelm Friedrich   1f., 7f., 27–29, 50, 53f., 56, 67, 73–78, 85–89, 95–115, 117f., 121–132, 135–138, 140–149, 151, 154, 159–173, 176–183, 189–201
Heidegger, Martin   6, 136, 189–201, 215f., 218–230
Henrich, Dieter   50, 66
Hobbes, Thomas   74, 76, 78–81, 177
Hölderlin, Friedrich   64
Honneth, Axel   161
Horstmann, Rolf-Peter   100
Hudson, Hud   3, 11

Ikäheimo, Heikki   160, 163
Irwin, Terence   11

Jacobi, Friedrich Heinrich   8, 40–44, 46–48, 51, 61, 64, 66
Jaeschke, Walter   28

Kane, Robert   3, 5, 14, 19
Kant, Immanuel   3–11, 13–23, 27–31, 33, 39–51, 54, 56–59, 61, 64–66, 73–78, 82–85, 89, 95f., 104, 121, 126, 137, 151–154, 165, 177, 189–201, 215–230
Kelly, George Armstrong   97
Kierkegaard, Søren   1–11, 146
Kneller, Jane   63
Koch, Anton Friedrich   95, 98
Korsgaard Christine   3, 10f.
Krijnen, Christian   160

Lawrenz, Jürgen   160
Leibniz, Gottfried Wilhelm   21, 96, 172f.
Livy (Titus Livius)   80, 87
Locke, John   73–75, 78–84, 177, 215

Lowe, E. J. 3
Luther, Martin 182

Machiavelli, Niccolò 147
Malabou, Catherine 189, 197
Marx, Karl 161
McCarthy, Richard 14
McDowell, John 95f., 182, 215–219, 221–230
Mele, Alfred R. 5, 14
Meyers, Diana T. 14
Mill, John Stuart 75, 102
Montesquieu 73, 78, 81

Neiman, Susan 43
Neuhouser, Frederick 128, 130
Novalis 29, 56, 62–65

O'Connor, Timothy 3
O'Neill, Onora 132

Peperzak, Adriaan 163f.
Pippin, Robert 95–97, 108, 135, 147, 160, 182
Plato 8, 41, 73f., 77, 87

Quine, Willard van Orman 113

Reinhold, Karl Leonhard 16, 28, 40
Rickert, Heinrich 18
Rödl, Sebastian 95, 151
Rometsch, Jens 97, 159, 162
Rosefeldt, Tobias 3
Rosenkranz, Johann Karl 7
Rousseau, Jean-Jacques 73f., 76, 78, 81–84, 177

Schelling, Friedrich Wilhelm Joseph 27–29, 36–39, 42f., 47, 49–56, 60, 63f., 66f., 73, 100, 201
Schmidt, Heinrich 45
Schmidt am Busch, Hans-Christoph 161
Searle, John 99
Sgarbi, Marco 19, 21
Shakespeare, William 7, 9
Siep, Ludwig 160
Spinoza, Baruch de 8, 39, 43, 50–52
Stekeler-Weithofer, Pirmin 95, 164
Steward, Helen 3
Sticker, Martin 159
Storr, Christian 29, 50
Strawson, Galen 5
Strawson, Peter 3f., 12, 206
Sullivan, Roger J. 18

Thomas Aquinas 152
Timm, Hermann 28
Tocqueville, Alexis 74, 88–90
Tonelli, Giorgio 220

Ulrich, Johann August Heinrich 17

van Cleeve, James 11
van Inwagen, Peter 3

Walker, Ralph C. S. 3
Wallner, Ingrid M. 45
Watkins, Eric 3, 5, 16
Williams, Bernard 146-148
Williams, Robert R. 159
Wittgenstein, Ludwig 136
Wood, Allen W. 3, 10
Wuerth, Julian 18

Zöller, Günter 73, 83, 85

www.ingramcontent.com/pod-product-compliance
Lightning Source LLC
Chambersburg PA
CBHW021938240426
43669CB00047B/544